MacDonald of the 42nd

MacDonald of the 42nd

BY

DONALD FEATHERSTONE

NEW ENGLISH LIBRARY
TIMES MIRROR

First published in Great Britain by Seeley Service & Co. Ltd.,

*

FIRST NEL PAPERBACK EDITION MAY 1972

*

NEL Books are published by
New English Library Limited from Barnard's Inn, Holborn, London, E.C.1.
Made and printed in Great Britain by Hunt Barnard Printing Ltd., Aylesbury, Bucks.

45001242 5

INTRODUCTION

During World War II an employee of the Port of Bristol Authority, bundling up yellowed papers for a salvage drive, came across a letter written by Hector John MacDonald, an elderly employee of the Port Authority. Stressing his claims for a better job by telling the story of his life, with faulty spelling and little punctuation, it was the tale of an eventful existence in Scotland, England, Russia, India, America, the Sandwich Islands, the Arctic, Mexico, Canada and finally back to Bristol. More than a story of a man's life—it was a saga of Victoriana!

It seemed evident that the letter's semi-illiterate highlights, given so curiously by Hector MacDonald, merely drew back the corner of a curtain concealing a colourful background of adventure, courage, fortitude and dogged endurance. Enquiries were made for further details of the old man's life, but proved strangely unfruitful. Regimental records of the Black Watch did not mention Hector John MacDonald, although there were many John MacDonalds. As Hector made no reference to when his five brothers enlisted in the Regiment, when they actually served or what their Christian names were, it was impossible to trace them. The Registrar-General's Office in Edinburgh could find no entry of his birth, but the registration of births was not made compulsory until some twenty years later.

Thinking the letter almost too good to be true, doubt crept in. Then, sixty-seven years after he died, his death certificate was discovered at Somerset House in London. No longer an anonymous private of a famous Highland Regiment, far larger than life, the grizzled old Highlander stood as a monument to all that he had written, the very epitome of all the illiterate, hard-drinking, rough and ready soldiers who fought in Queen Victoria's colonial wars. No one can tell, and there is no way of knowing, what the man actually did in these stirring times—only generals have their activities so meticulously noted. In writing of Hector MacDonald it is tempting to portray him as the leading character in these events, as the first in the charge and the last in the withdrawl, but to so surmise and conjecture would be turning fact into fiction. Every endeavour has been made to write with a minimum of supposition, only to use Hector MacDonald as an individual when it was felt reasonable and justifiable to portray him in such a role.

To have described his life from 1861 onwards would have necessitated so much guesswork as to transform a documentary manuscript into one approaching fiction. The fullest details are available of the activities of his regiment, the 42nd Royal Highlanders (the Black Watch), and the events recounted in this book involved that regiment, so that it is not unreasonable to assume that Private Hector John MacDonald played his part in those events. Therefore, the story of the Black Watch during the Crimea and the Indian Mutiny is the story of Hector MacDonald.

During the months of writing this book the author has acquired a great affection for the Black Watch. It is sincerely hoped that this sentiment is reflected in the writing and that Major A. V. M. Chapman, M.B.E., T.D., Curator of the Black Watch Museum, to whom the author is greatly indebted for much help and information, will feel that his Regiment has been faithfully dealt with.

Writing of Hector John MacDonald is not writing of only one man, but of them all. What happened to Hector MacDonald in the Crimea and during the Indian Mutiny was no whit different to what thousands of his comrades suffered and withstood. In an age when famous regiments are disbanded overnight, it is hoped that this book will be not only a memorial to the men who gave the regiments the traditions they so proudly hold, but also a tribute to the regiments themselves.

DONALD FEATHERSTONE

PROLOGUE

For the past twelve months a strange and unique sense of helplessness had gripped Hector MacDonald. Something had to be done—he must bring home more money for the bairns. He doubted if he could work any harder or for more hours. He came home exhausted each night and ached with tiredness all day. After all, he was sixty-six and had taken a lot out of himself over the years.

Standing on the newspaper-covered table top the flickering candle irregularly expanded and compressed the sparsely furnished room and cast shadows across his lined face and grizzled grey head. Rising stiffly to his feet he opened the door and gazed out into the black void beyond.

"Did ye call?"

"When are you coming up—what are you doing down there?"

"Go to sleep, my dear . . . I'm about to write a letter to Mr Harvey . . . asking for a better job."

Quietly, Hector MacDonald closed the door and sat down at the rickety table. Picking up the pen, he glared distrustfully at it as though doubting its ability adequately to record his story. Resolutely, he dipped it in the ink and laboriously scratched the first black letters on the paper's virgin whiteness.

3 Whippington Court
Horse Fair.
Bristol.
8th of October 1895.

To Mr. Harvey,

Sir,

I was born the 29 November 1829 in Edinburgh Scotland, my Father was born in Inverness and my Mother was born in Tober merry Argyleshire.

I listed in the 42nd Royal Highland Black Watch 24 November 1843 and part for 14 and 6 months. I had five brothers in the same regiment. I was sent to Parkhurst Barracks Isle of White, the Depot, I learned to be Bugler there I was then sent with a draft to the regiment in Bermuda West Indies. I went and learned cornet in the Band then I went to be a piper. I came home with the depot in 1851 to Aberdeen. Scotland while the regiment went to Halifax Nova Scotia. The regiment came home in 52 to Stirling Castle Scotland and our depot joined them. There we went from there to Chobsin Camp near London, that was before Aldershot. We went from there to Haslar Barracks Gosport we were there when the English and French fleet had there review at Spit Head on July 53 war was proclaimed while we were there. We left there for Angle Sea Barracks port Sea, while there we got the Order to hold ourselves in rediness for the seat of war we got the rout the 23 of may and sailed on the 24 for Scutaria in Turkey. The English Sardinian and German legion were under Sir Lord Raglan, the French under Marshal Pellesear and the turks under Omer pasha. We marched on for the Crimea our first Battle was Alma. the Highlanders was under Sir Colin Campbel we had a river to wade through before we got to the Heights the Russians had stakes planted in the ground on the top of the Hill as a mark for them when we got there to fire they lay about 300 yards back on the plain in Close Collum of Battle waiting for us to get up when they seen our feather hats appear they let of there Cannon and musketry at us but it flew over our Heads and done damage to those in rear. Sir Colin give us the order not to fire untill we could see the white of there eye when the russians seen us with aur feathers flying bare legs and kilt they did not know what to make of us they made a grand mistake for they took us for Horsemen and came to the resist Cavelery. We marched up to within about ten yards when Sir Colin halted us and gave us the order to present fire charge bayonets we ran right into them through down there arms knapsack blankets food and everything that would stop there race for we kept firing till we could see no more. It was a glorious day for us although many man of aurs bit the dust I got slitly hurt on the shoulder but it was all right in a week. It was laughable to see us next day English a Frenchman a turk a German and a Sardinian walking arm and arm to the Canteen to get a drink singing songs and not one know what the other was saying. Balaklava was aur next Battle. It was a very hard battle but I came through it all right then we had Inkerman. I got a bayonet wound in the side going up the side of the Hill but it was only a flesh wound. Our hardest work was in the trenches the guards was in the trenches at the Redan and the russions made a sortie on them at night so the Highlanders was called on to assist to drive them back. we went in and jumped over the brest work we captured nearly a whole regiment. There was one officer in front of me and I told him to surrender but instead he drew his sword and made a swinging lick at me it went through my knapsack and all that was in it and cut me for nine inches round the region of the heart I thought I was gone so I drove my bayonet through his throat and left him stickeing to the breastwork it was only a fracture of the ribs and flesh wound it soon healed up. We came home the latter end of 56. my brothers got 2 months forlough we went home and seen my father and sisters and brothers. My mother was dead since I was 7 years old but we did not stop at home we were called three weeks after we came home to join our regiment at Dover Castle. We sailed for Calcutta in the Spring 57. We marched up through Gandihar into Briley skirmishing all the time. We had about 500 miles to march to the relief of Lucknow, fighting all the way when we got there it was something Horrible to see Women and children butchered hacked and cut to pieces it made our men savage we showed no mercy when we came on them there used to be a shooting parade every morning. They would tie ten or twelve of these savages to the mouth of a gun and blow them away but I only seen one lot made away with. I took a fever in 58 and was invaleaded of to the mountains it was the marching and fighting and bad watter brought it on but I got over it and done dutty for six months till the order came to reduce the army all men that had 10 years good service could take a free discharge you see my time did not count till I was 18 year old

I took my discharge in the beginning of sixty. I had sixteen years good service but thirteen years and half was boys that don't count.

THE 42nd (ROYAL HIGHLAND) REGIMENT

THE BLACK WATCH

Am Freiceadan Dubh

Commanded by Lieutenant-Colonel **William Middleton, an officer to whose** distinguished merit no language can do justice.

"Wanted for this fine Regiment, a few dashing, high-spirited young men, whose hearts beat high to tread the path of glory. Young men of this description know the opportunity offered to them, which may never again occur, of enlisting into one of the finest Regiments in the Service. Highlanders! Join the Royal Highland Regiment, where the kind treatment the men receive is well known throughout Scotland!

"Each young hero, on being approved, shall receive a bounty of **FIVE GUINEAS** for volunteering for this fine Regiment, providing he is five feet six inches for a growing lad.

"This fine Regiment has just returned home from Corfu and other foreign parts where several of the men, by their increase of pay and prize-money, saved enough to purchase their discharge and provide themselves with a comfortable independence for life in their own beloved Scotland.

"Such, my fine fellows, are the advantages of a soldier's life, independent of the honour of serving Her Majesty the Queen, whose indescribable virtues render her an inestimable blessing to the country. The Regiment is at present quartered in your own town, where you have provisions remarkably cheap and luxurious living to the brave and ambitious mind. These gallant lads are at present eating their beef, bread and potatoes (which by the way are got for nothing) in peace and comfort.

"An early application by those of address and education will ensure preferment and immediate promotion. Your comforts in this Regiment surpass all clerks and mechanics, an hospitable table and a capacious bowl of punch are waiting!

"All you who are kicking your heels behind a solitary desk with too little wages, and a Pinch-gut Master—all you with too much Wife, or perplexed with obstinate and unfeeling parents, may apply to **Lieutenant James Farquharson at Edinburgh Castle!"**

Chapter 1

Displayed on many a wall in Edinburgh during 1836 this stirring proclamation attracted Alexander and Ian MacDonald, along with numerous other lads "perplexed with obstinate and unfeeling parents". The exciting noisy periods when they came home on leave in their doublets of scarlet cloth, with gold lace on the collars and heavy gold epaulettes, blue facings with more gold embroidery, the dashing plaid and kilt in the dark green tartan, topping the spotless white gaiters, made them excellent recruiting officers for brothers Charlie and Angus.

Hector and Jamie, the youngest of the six MacDonald boys, posed and postured in the four-tailed, twelve-inch-high black ostrich-feather bonnet with the famous red vulture's feather hackle on the left side. Hector could hardly wait until he was big enough and old enough to follow in their footsteps.

He learned how the Regiment got their tartans when, after the '45, all existing tartans were suppressed, so that the 42nd adopted a dark tartan. He knew why they were called "Am freiceadan dubh" or the Black Watch, black meaning "dark or sombre" and watch signifying "guard", to distinguish them from "Saughdeoran Dearg" or Red Soldiers of the English. The boy fondled the big bonnet, fingered the mottled surface of the St. Andrew's Cross, the garter and its motto, surmounted by the crown on the large badge.

He never tired of hearing the story of the red hackle which distinguished the Black Watch from all other Highland regiments. By heart, he knew how the 11th Light Dragoons, covering the 78th Foot at Guildermaslen on the 4th January, 1798, gave way and allowed the French to capture two pieces of artillery, which were turned upon the British. General Sir David Dundas had called out:

"Forty-second! For God's sake and for the honour of your country retake those guns!"

Major Dalrymple, the 42nd's Commanding Officer, led the charge forward and the guns were recaptured. General Sir David Dundas then called out:

"Forty-Second, the 11th Dragoons shall never wear the red plume on their helmets any more, and I hope the 42nd will carry it as long as they are the Black Watch!"

So, in June 1795, when the regiment was quartered at Royston near Cambridge, after firing three rounds to commemorate the birthday of King George the Third, a box containing red vulture feathers was opened and one distributed to each man.

Hector preferred the alternative ending to the story, in which the Highlanders plucked their white plumes from their bonnets at Guildermaslen and dipped them in the blood of the battlefield to make them as red as they were today!

In 1843, their mother dead and their father a morose tyrant, Jamie and Hector decided to join Alexander, Ian, Charlie and Angus in the 42nd. Leaving a roughly scrawled note, the boys crept out of the house in the early hours of a dark, foggy morning, to become soldiers, with no one to tender the *dheoch-an-doruis* or parting cup, no one to thrust out their snuff-mulls for the parting pinch or to give them money for their *leabhar-dhu* or black pocket-book; no one to wrap up bread and meat and place it in their sporran in the traditional Highland manner.

The boys had no trouble at all in being accepted for the Regiment; even without mentioning their four brothers, they felt that they would have been taken. They were given a perfunctory medical examination and their ages noted, but not without a sideways glance by the clerk. The fifteen shillings "bringing money" that the recruiter received for every man he produced, ensured that little trouble was raised on account of age, medical condition or general fitness for service as a soldier. Worried in case their father chased after them and secured their release by paying twenty shillings "smart money"[1] Jamie and Hector could hardly wait to be sworn-in, for once they were attested they could no longer be bought out. At last, the officer placed the bounty in their grimy hands—it was by far the largest sum they had ever seen in their lives, let alone handled.

There were six others joining the "Forty Twa' ", as the recruiter called the Regiment. They included a tramp enlisted in the police-court by special authority, and a convict just released from prison after a fifteen-month sentence. Two of the recruits were spotty-faced clerks who had found the petty cash an irresistible temptation and were joining the Army rather than go to jail. Preferably, only Highlanders were accepted for the Black Watch, but the prevailing economic conditions brought numerous recruits rejoicing in the names of O'Reilly,

O'Donnell and O'Brien; a dexterous stroke of the pen turned them into MacReilly, MacDonald and MacBrien, so that the formalities and conventions were not unduly abused.

In a shambling out-of-step travesty of a march, the ragged and bewildered bunch were jollied along to the Quartermaster's stores. Here, amid a choking smell of cloth and camphor, pigeon-holes ranged from floor to ceiling, all stuffed with bundles of clothing, piles of boots and feather-bonnets in round boxes. The regulations said that ". . . each sergeant, corporal, drummer and private man is . . . to have annually a scarlet coat, a waistcoat of white serge, a bonnet and four pairs of hose; six yards of plaid once every two years, and a purse every seven years. . . ." In addition, the recruits were laden with under-clothing, three shirts and three pairs of socks, a razor—Hector wondered what use he would find for his—mess-kit with knife, fork and spoon . . . they felt rich at the unexpected bounty. The Quartermaster's orderly supervised the recruits' fumbling attempts to dress themselves, and swiftly rolled up and confiscated their civilian clothing.

"Ye had naught in yer pockets, did yer?"

Briskly he disappeared with the bundles, before Hector could protest that a treasured clasp-knife was in his trousers pocket.

Grotesque figures in the stiff new clothing that hung upon their slim figures, arms laden with the remainder of their kit, piled so high that they had to stretch their heads to see where they were going, the boys trudged behind a disdainful trained soldier. After traversing what seemed to be miles of stone corridors, ascending and descending worn stairs made treacherous by the iron-studded new boots in which they noisily clumped along, the little party reached a large and solid wooden door. Their guide kicked it open and pushed them into a dark and lofty cavern that loomed before them. Curiously, the boys gazed around them, eyed the cribs crammed a few inches apart and noted the blankets hanging across the corners of the room, behind which they discovered the married men lived and brought up their families. The arrival of the recruits brought the barrackroom up to its full complement of 42 men, 4 women and 11 children.

After they had got over their amazement at seeing the two youngest members of the family suddenly arrive in their midst as fully-fledged recruits, Alex, Ian, Charlie and Angus MacDonald welcomed them uproariously. Haltingly, Hector told of their reason for joining. Alex nodded his head:

"Ay, at Mother's funeral I wondered how you were going to get on . . . what was going to happen to you."

Ian swept big arms round the shoulders of his younger brothers:

"Well, now we know! We've got to turn them into soldiers that the Forty Twa' will be proud of!"

Hector and Jamie were given beds close to those of their brothers, and they were shown the regulation manner of making them up. The straw-filled tick had to be rolled up and tied with a belt, then placed at the head of the springless iron framed cot: folded in four, the sheets and blankets were covered with a rug and placed on top of the tick, and resting on the bedclothes was a ticket showing the name, regimental number, company, rank and squad of the man occupying the bed. They were shown how to hang their kilt on two pegs at the head of the bed, their accoutrements on the right peg, the purse and gaiters on the left one; the knapsack had to go on the shelf at the head of the bed, the feather bonnet on the right, the canteen on the left, and the rifle was placed in a stand at the head of the bed. Obviously, there was a place for everything.

Tattoo was at eight o'clock, when all the men got into bed, after stirring up the fire. Both emotionally and physically tired, Hector slept like a log, but awoke in the morning to find himself on the floor, shivering and stiff with cold—he had fallen out of the narrow bed. The Quarter Bugle sounded at ten minutes to eight and the orderlies for the day brought the breakfast up from the cookhouse, and laid it on the tables that had been erected down the centre of the room in the narrow space between the ends of the cots. At eight o'clock the "Sit Down" bugle sounded and at once the door of the room was flung violently open to admit the Orderly Officer, followed by a Sergeant-Major. Prodded by their brothers, Hector and Jamie leaped to their feet and stood to attention in the unnaturally stiff manner of the recruit. Elegantly, the officer asked if there were "any complaints". There were none, so the officer turned upon his heel and left the room; behind him, the Sergeant-Major slammed the heavy door with the same violence he had used on entering.

After the breakfast things had been cleared away, the recruits watched bustling preparations for first parade. Suddenly, a heavy hand fell upon Hector's shoulder; turning he looked up into the face of a soldier in shirt-sleeves, behind him loomed two more soldiers.

"Have you got your bounty yet, laddie?"

Before the boy could gather his wits and answer, he was pushed aside as his four brothers moved between him and the questioning soldier. Alex looked the man straight in the eyes.

"There'll be nae fritterin' o' the lad's bounty, Duncan!"

Duncan made a gesture of protest:

"But, the laddies will be pleased to buy us a wee drappie, to be sure!"

"I said . . . the lads keep their money!"

Duncan shrugged his shoulders as he turned away:

"Och, awa wi' ye! They'll no want for friends as long as it lasts!"

Later, it was explained to the lads that the recruits' bounty was regarded by the old soldiers as the common and legitimate occasion for a carousal. Everyone who came into contact with the recruit after he had received the money imagined himself entitled to a share. That night, the recruits were "set up for auction"; one man brushing their shoes, another their coats and they were informed that ancient custom demanded that every recruit should stand treat to his room-mates. Whisky was quickly purchased and, when night fell, the barrack-room was cleared. The drinking began together with dancing, a bagpipe and two fifes providing the music. The wives of the married men took part in a stamping, hallooing and snapping of fingers. The pipes droned monotonously until the early hours of the morning. Men fought, imagining that each had drunk out of his turn; the lights were knocked over and the scuffle turned beds and chairs in all directions; finally the guard arrived and took off the worst offenders to the guardroom.

Alexander told them that they would be expected to see the Drill Sergeant "all right" and that the Recruiting Sergeant expected a supper from them. It was also customary to show hospitality to the Company Sergeants with a rum-punch or whisky evening! They were lucky that they had not been brought to the barracks by a Conducting Sergeant, otherwise he would have expected his traditional present of five shillings! The lads were also warned that their comrades would be incessantly trying to dun them for small loans, which they would later deny and even threaten violence if repayment was demanded!

"But don't ye worry . . . we'll look after you."

Alex looked around at his brothers; they nodded their heads in agreement, then he glanced at the excited, glowing faces of Jamie and Hector. Six brothers, and all in the 42nd!

Chapter 2

Whilst the Regiment remained at Stirling Castle, life was made easier than it might have been for the recruits, as the Mac-Donald brothers presented a united front that served to absorb many of the ruder shocks and aspects of the soldier's crude existence. Each day began in the same way when, at six o'clock in the morning, winter and summer, the sleep-drugged men shambled out from the foetid atmosphere of the ill-ventilated barrack-room, to perform their ablutions. Fighting and jostling, everyone crowded round the pump or conduit, trying to wash and shave in the icy water. What scanty clothing they wore was soon soaked in the struggle and, during winter, chilled to the bone by the bitter wind, feverish colds and chest ailments swept the barrack-room. The two "issue" buckets that would have slightly relieved the situation had long since been "borrowed" by another barrack-room, to replace their own buckets that had similarly vanished.

Each day two cookhouse orderlies were detailed to collect the men's food and bring it back to the barrack-room where it was served on a board and trestle table. The daily ration of food per man was one pound of bread and three-quarters of a pound of meat, consumed at the main meal at mid day. This was the last official food of the day and no more was issued for nineteen hours; if a man wanted to eat later in the day he had to buy food out of his own pay. The men took it in turns to be cooks; it was not a difficult task as the routine was always the same. Each company had two coppers provided, one for meat and one for potatoes. All that the cook had to do was to plunge the meat into the water and leave it to boil, first marking it with a piece of rag tied to it or an old button or a piece of wood, so that they could identify the piece belonging to their barrack-room. More often than not, the food was half-cooked because the first men to collect their lump of meat would gingerly handle it and upset the copper so that the rest of the meat received no more cooking. A broth made from the water in which the food was cooked served to eke out the boiled beef and the blackened potatoes.

There were no alternative means of cooking the food, such as roasting or baking.

Soldiers were invariably famished, but even the savage hunger aroused during the long periods when they were officially without food did not make the diet palatable. In the course of time, the soldier became hardened to the food, tastelessly he consumed whatever was slapped down in front of him, no longer feeling resentment when his share turned out to be all bone or gristle—someone had to have this portion of the rigidly weighed-out rations.

No effort was made to provide the soldier with amusement or recreation, so that his life was one of deadly monotony. In the infantry, the soldier had a great deal of leisure time and no wholesome means of occupying it. With promotion impossible to the illiterate, the soldier had no special reason for good behaviour so that habitual drunkenness became his besetting sin. If he had become inured to the coarse food so that he ceased to care as it was shovelled down, the soldier soon discovered that cheap alcohol provided a merciful oblivion to blot out the misery and squalor of his life, for a few hours at least. Each night, the men clustered round the two tallow dips allowed each barrack-room for illumination while cleaning their equipment. Some of the men who could read sat close to the wretched light, reading aloud to their comrades, although books were hard to come by—the only ones allowed to enter barracks were some twenty-eight volumes, all approved by a bench of Bishops, supplied by the War Office for the benefit of sick soldiers.

Thrown into a squad of partly-trained soldiers, Hector and Jamie could not get on at all with the drill. The screamed orders of the Drill Sergeant meant little to them, so that they had no idea of the movements that needed to be made in response to each order. Noting their difficulties, each night Alexander put the lads through drill movements in a space cleared between the cots, whilst the other three MacDonald brothers acted as guards to stop horse-play from the other men in the barrack-room. Both boys suffered agonies from the issue buckled shoes; made of hard unyielding leather, they were so well chosen to resist wear that they generally outlasted the soldier's endurance, even on a short march or a drill parade. The rigid quadrangular packs, when laden and adjusted, seemed to arrest the circulation and both Hector and Jamie hated them.

Although the standards of the Black Watch had been lowered

by the influx of men other than Highlanders, the Regiment was probably among the best of its day, both for the type of recruits and the finished soldiers who emerged. Initially, the Regiment had enlisted men from better walks of life than most soldiers of the day, some being cadets of good family, others sons and relatives of gentlemen farmers and land-owners. These men often felt themselves honour-bound to behave in a manner that would bring credit to the honourable houses from which they came, as well as to their country, which they invariably recalled with a single-hearted affection.

A country without commerce, Scotland offered no profession for its manhood but that of arms. In 1729, when the 42nd was formed, there was little difficulty in finding young men eager to engage in a corps to be stationed near their homes and to perform duties which were, for the most part, a mere pastime. At that period the Highlanders had a special incentive to enter a quasi-military service because of the laws, galling to a high-spirited and warlike race, that prohibited the carrying of arms. So that, in the early days of the Regiment, young Highlanders sought to serve, even as privates, in a service which gave them the cherished privilege of bearing weapons. As time passed and conditions changed, less men from respectable families and few wholly native Highlanders joined the Regiment. Nevertheless, in the 1840's there were still enough Highlanders in the Regiment to retain the old etiquette of military manners. Many of the officers were natives of the mountains, speaking their own language to men who, in their turn, addressed these officers with that easy but respectful familiarity and confidence which existed between the Highland people and their superiors. Pride of regiment reigned supreme and, in 1743 and 1779, when Highlanders enlisted into the Black Watch had been transferred to other regiments, lacking their native tongue and dress, they mutinied.

National characteristics such as dress, language, habits and manners give the regimental discipline of the Black Watch a distinctive and peculiar character. The messes were managed by N.C.Os or old soldiers, and were so arranged that in each room the men belonged to the same glen or district, or were connected by some similar kindred tie. Each barrack-room formed something of a large family circle, a fact which enabled the MacDonald brothers to stick together. There were fewer courts-martial and corporal punishments in the Black Watch than in almost any other regiment of the day, and on only one occasion did the young recruits have to stand stiffly on parade, fighting against faintness and nausea aroused by the sight of a comrade having the flesh stripped from his back by leather thongs wielded in numbered cadence. Even with all this, military life was still incredibly hard, based on punishment for the evil doer rather than a reward for the good soldier.

Insufficiently trained to take their place as full members of the Regiment, Hector and Jamie MacDonald were left behind, when, early in 1844, the Black Watch embarked for Malta. The brothers felt a deep and bitter sadness as they took their farewell and there was not a dry eye among them. The four going to the warmth of the Mediterranean had much that was new to occupy their minds; the two younger boys tried to find consolation in the novelty of their journey through the length of England to the depot at Parkhurst in the Isle of Wight. The boys had their first sight of the sea during the short sea voyage from Portsmouth; the ferry-boat struck them as being gigantic. At the depot, life was stern and monotonous, and implacable officers and N.C.Os maintained unquestioning discipline. Keeping together, Hector and Jamie tried to help each other out on all possible occasions and to present the same united MacDonald front as the six brothers had at Stirling. Whenever Hector passed the Band Room he stood and listened to the wail of the pipes or the brassy demanding notes of the bugles. Not only did he find the sounds fascinating, he was also aware of the extra pay he would get if he played an instrument, and he was less likely to be bullied or put on fatigues by the N.C.Os. One day, while he was listening, the Trumpet-Major came out of the Band Room; harshly, he asked the young soldier what he was doing loitering there.

"I was listening to the bugles, S'arnt-Major."

The Trumpet-Major, a man with sucked-in cheeks and moustaches carefully clipped away from his lips, ran meditative eyes over the boy's slim figure.

"Give me a look at your mouth, laddie."

Hector opened his mouth wide, showing fine white teeth. The Trumpet-Major thrust his thumbs in between Hector's lips.

"A good embouchure . . . come into the Band Room."

Inside, he handed the boy a bugle and ordered him to "Blow up the chord". In bewilderment, Hector stared at the instrument. The Trumpet-Major impatiently waved his hand at him.

"Blow into it! Make a noise!"

Rounding his lips on the mouthpiece, the boy swelled out his cheeks and blew until he was red in the face, but no sound emerged.

"Don't puff, you damn fool! Spit into it!"

At last, Hector produced a blurting sound that made the Trumpet-Major wince.

"For all that, you will probably make a good 'un. I'll talk to the Sergeant-Major about you and maybe he'll let you come to me."

A few days later, Hector was sent on a month's trial to the Band School, where he worked to succeed with desperate earnestness. To the amusement of his brother and the other occupants of the barrack-room he painfully rubbed alum on his lips to harden them, and spent cash he could ill spare on a tooth-brush. He was the only man in the whole barrack-room to have such a possession. Lying on his cot, he tootled the notes of chords in a boisterous treble until his comrades showered boots at him to silence the irritating noise. His efforts had their reward when he was eventually given the pay and grade of bugler, and became the proud possessor of a shining instrument of his own. Feeling richer than ever before in his young life, he was kept from indulging in the more vicious pastimes of his comrades through fear of losing the grade and possession of the bugle.

Chapter 3

The summer of 1853 was a wet one, and the month of July was the worst month of all; which made the first Great Camp of Manoeuvre on Chobham Ridges in Surrey a very uncomfortable affair for all of the 8,000 men taking part.[2] In company with troops from all over England, the Black Watch unenthusiastically converged on the bare, gorse-grown common. Bovinely, the men did as they were told, darkly muttering: "daft fules . . . aboot time tae gae hame . . ."; while the officers considered the whole enterprise . . . "a damned waste of time". Everyone suffered great discomfort in clothes that clung damply to them, and the soaked tents let the rain through at night in a constant shower.

It was obvious that no one seemed to know what they were doing and that their commanders appeared to have little idea of military tactics. Whole units got lost and were found advancing with grim determination on other regiments of their own side! Now and then, the men found themselves actually enjoying some of the activities. They showed considerable dexterity in making little huts, camp kitchens and sentry-boxes out of earth and brushwood. With the mud of Chobham still encrusting their bedraggled finery, the 42nd marched to Haslar Barracks at Gosport, thankful that the shambles they had just left was only a game, and not real war.

Now twenty-four years of age, Hector was a big, strong fellow, well known in the Regiment as a fine piper and a good soldier in those foreign parts in which the Regiment had served. He had liked Bermuda, in spite of the yellow fever; which all the MacDonalds had escaped. Generally speaking, conditions there had been better than in England or in Scotland, with abundant supplies of potatoes and other vegetables and the water was sweet and plentiful. Found to be more destructive to the troops than the heat of the day, the damp, chill tropical nights forced them to adopt clothing changes, doing away with their plaids, kilts and bonnets and wearing instead duck pantaloons and round hats, sacrifices ill-taken by both other ranks and officers. No species of dress was worse calculated for a tropical climate than this new garb; when wetted by the frequent torrents of rain, the pantaloons clung to the legs and thighs to be no sooner dried after one shower than wetted again by the next. Instead of the feather bonnet, they wore a cheap and trashy hat of coarse felt; its shape destroyed by the first rainfall, this headgear stuck close to the head and afforded no protection against the sun. Being of thick woollen stuff and covered with feathers, the bonnet formed a complete protection against the effects of the tropical sun; it also made a warm and unconventional night-cap! If the wet kilt and hose were taken off and wrung out, they might be immediately worn again with perfect safety; although the mosquitos were a great trouble to wearers of the kilt. All in all, it was felt that neither the duck pantaloons nor the round hat were suited to the country; and all were highly delighted to get back into the kilt when they returned to the British Isles.

Since the beginning of the year 1854, the whole country had seemed to be bent on war with Russia. The nation seemed obsessed with the idea of going to the aid of Turkey, who had been at war with the Czar since the previous October. Barrack-rooms everywhere hummed with rumours and counter-rumours; the men were incensed by the Russian naval massacre of the Turkish fleet as it lay at anchor in the southern Black Sea port of Sinope; an action which caused an irresistible tide of hatred for Russia to rise up on all sides. Long before any actual declaration of hostilities, the newspapers were printing hostile articles directed against the Czar of Russia. Existing in every soldier, be he private or general, was a craving for active service; war with all its chances of military distinction was an opportunity to be seized eagerly with both hands. After all, battle was the sole touchstone by which a soldier could be judged, and to be prevented from taking part in such a festival could be construed as a disgrace. Many non-commissioned officers over and above regimental establishments made up their minds to ask for reduction to the ranks, so that they would be able to go when their regiments moved off to battle.

A copy of the *Dublin Mail* for the 6th February, 1854, fell into Charlie MacDonald's hands. He read aloud a paragraph on the front page, ". . . the following are to embark under orders for Constantinople between the first and thirtieth of March next"—then followed a long list of regiments of the British Army: "4th; 7th; 9th; 14th; 17th; 21st; 27th; 28th; 35th; 38th;

39th; 42nd; 50th; 62nd; 63rd; 79th; 82nd; 88th; 89th; 90th; 93rd and 95th." The 42nd stood out brightly, and quivering fingers pointed out the number to all near enough to see. With professional approval, the men noted that the 79th, the Cameron Highlanders and the 93rd, the Argyll and Sutherland Highlanders, were listed—that meant that a Highland Brigade would be formed! In the Officers' Mess, *The Illustrated London News* of the 11th March was no less eagerly quoted, for it said, in black and white, that the 42nd were under orders to embark. This was a fact not even known to Colonel Cameron, the Commanding Officer! Everyone was aflame with impatience. When the Scots Fusilier Guards left London on the 2nd March, after being given a personal farewell by the Queen in the forecourt of Buckingham Palace, the 42nd had the frustrating experience of providing the band that played the Guards to the dockside. Other units had sailed or were flocking into Portsmouth but the 42nd, now at Anglesea Barracks, chafed impatiently, fearing that they would miss all the fun.

To add insult to injury they were employed in preparing a huge gun position in Portsmouth, where greater stir and excitement both ashore and afloat could not have prevailed had the Russians been invading the port, instead of it being necessary to convey fighting men to find them! An enormous heavy battery was being thrown up on the side of a well-known platform promenade; this had originally been used to parade the twenty-one little six-pounders used to salute important people. The new battery mounted a dozen sixty-eight-pounder guns on traversing platforms, pointing over a brick and earthwork parapet about nine feet in height and commanding the entrance to the harbour.

Officers and men raged at the senselessness of sending out their Division in bits and pieces; except for themselves and one other Highland regiment, the Duke of Cambridge's First Division had long since sailed! If ever it got into action as a whole, the Division was to consist of the three battalions of the Foot Guards, together with the three Highland regiments.

Daily, with fife and drum, recruiting parties were parading the garrison and suburbs, endeavouring to bring the units up to strength before they sailed. The 42nd needed no such assistance—the attraction of the kilt kept their ranks filled. Vans, omnibuses and other vehicles containing volunteers in parties of fifty, rolled along the main thoroughfares from the railway terminus as each train arrived. They were warmly greeted by the excited population and all of them seemed in excellent spirits.

On the afternoon of the 20th May, the 42nd paraded in the Governor's Field to be inspected and addressed by Major-General Simpson, the Garrison Commander-in-Chief. Before they marched from Barracks, Colonel Cameron, the Commanding Officer, told the Regiment that they were going out to defend the interests of their sovereign and country, and to succour the oppressed and he hoped they would not flinch in the performance of their duty or allow the honour and renown of the Regiment to suffer any diminution. Marching to the Governor's Field in the highest spirits, the ranks took up one of the airs played by the band, singing:

"Cheer, boys, cheer! Russia's all before us!"

Major-General Simpson was an impressive figure in cocked hat with flowing plumes; his bull-like voice echoed round the parade-ground:

> "Highlanders! You are embarking for the purposes of meeting the enemies of your country. Soldiers have nothing to do with the cause of quarrels, their duty is to fight. But in this instance you have a most noble cause to fight for; I mean, the protection of the weak by the strong. This is the cause you will fight for, and nobly will you and the rest of the army do your duty.
>
> "You will be led by Lord Raglan, a man who was on the right hand of the Duke of Wellington, a man who knows how to lead you to glory as well as you know how to fight to attain it. One thing I desire to impress upon you and that is to be good comrades to our gallant allies, the French. I say 'gallant' most truly, for they were once our foes; now you are to fight side by side with them, and I would rather fight along with them than with any other soldiers in the world, because they will never desert you.
>
> "Your conduct, Highlanders, under my command has been like that of every British Regiment, and I never saw a British Regiment that would not fight. I will answer for it that you will! There is one thing that I would urge on you—we soldiers are well provided for by our country, but protect the weak against the strong.
>
> "Colonel Cameron, I wish you and these Highlanders every success as well as the army generally. If I am not with you,

my heart is with you and it's that impulse which may be felt now by every British soldier who has to fight in the good cause of the Queen and glorious England!"

The assembled troops gave him three times three cheers, taking off their bonnets and waving them in the air on the barrels of their muskets. About to fall into marching order, the noisy cheering crowd insisted on one round more. Both the 42nd and the people gave it, then another and another; carried away by the enthusiasm of the moment, the men waved their muskets wildly and tossed their bonnets in the air. The baggage of the Regiment had been placed on board earlier that day, so there was nothing to be done but to march to the Dockyard where the steamer was to be boarded. The *Hydaspes* had arrived at Spithead about nine p.m. on Friday, 19th May, coming into Portsmouth Harbour early on Saturday morning to be placed alongside the harbour by Mr Richards, her pilot. The crew had embarked the horses and received the regimental baggage on board.

Formed in line, the muster-roll was called, then the 42nd marched in threes to the Docks, led by the Regimental Band playing '*Oh Susannah, don't you wait for me*'; '*Auld Lang Syne*'; '*Scots wha hae wi' Wallace bled*' and '*Oh where and oh where is my Highland Laddie gone*?' On the London Road, about a mile from the Dock gates, they were met by the bands of other regiments in the garrison, and the route was lined by large crowds, cheering and shouting. Keeping up with difficulty, a number of weeping women and children walked by the side of the Regiment. Drawn by lot, only twenty wives, two per company, were allowed to accompany their husbands on active service. Those unfortunates who were left behind without money or allowances for themselves or their children, cried and screamed distraughtly at what might well be the last sight of their husbands. The wife of one private, being prevented by the regulations from accompanying her husband, dressed herself in full uniform and, with musket in hand, marched with the Regiment into the Dockyard. She was detected on getting aboard, but made such a fuss that the Commanding Officer laughingly granted her permission to go with her man.

The crowd was very large at the Dockyard gates. They cheered, shouted, waved handkerchiefs and hats and stretched out their hands to grasp those of the soldiers as they marched by, crying out:

"Never say die, lads!"
"Give 'em cold steel!"
"God bless yer!"
"Keep your pecker up, Old England depends on you!"

The officers were singled out for this personal farewell along the whole line of the march; many a toil-worn hand put out from the crowd being grasped "in the most cordial manner". The cheering was kept up all along the road, men stood up in omnibuses and thrust their heads out of cabs to contribute to the general acclamation. There was a general rush upon the stocks of all vendors of oranges, and the public thrust them upon the troops; others encouraged the men to take deep draughts of beer. With difficulty and in some disorganisation, so that strict military formation was momentarily lost, the troops forced their way through the cheering crowds.

The embarkation of the 42nd began soon after 4 p.m. on the afternoon of Saturday the 20th May, 1854, when thirty-two officers, forty-five sergeants, twenty drummers and pipers and 850 men were loaded on to the *Hydaspes*. On reaching the side of the Docks at which the ship lay, the men formed themselves into line. They were stripped of their ammunition, told off into messes and marched, in single file, on board.

The actual departure was in curious contrast to the tumult of the previous day. The *Hydaspes* left harbour at six o'clock on Sunday morning, with no bands, no fluttering handkerchiefs and no tears. Seamen and dockers careered madly about, cursing and swearing; stores were rushed to the quay at the last minute; goods forgotten and still on land were rescued by fatigue parties tumbling ashore to find them by flickering lantern-light. Some of the soldiers were singing in a maudlin, drunken manner, others, in spite of the bustle and confusion, lay asleep on the damp decks. Officers cheerfully puffed at their cigars and talked of the glories to come. Finally, the *Hydaspes* let go her moorings and steamed out of harbour, without anchoring at Spithead as was usual.

Soon it was blowing quite freshly, and it was not long before the soldiers were lying all over the decks, huddled in postures of acute misery, weakly wishing they could die. Hector and his brothers were no exception; and for some days they endured what was, up to then, the most wretched period of their lives. The troopship was horribly uncomfortable; they were shut below decks for hours at a time, with barely room to stand; let alone lie down. The food was of the coarsest quality and, in their miserable plight, completely uneatable. However, within a few days, most of the troops were back to normal and enjoying the unusual aspects of the sea voyage. They called at Gibraltar for coal, where everyone marvelled at the impressive strength of the fortress. Continuing up the Mediterranean to Malta, it became unpleasantly hot, but not hot enough to prevent them lining the rails as the vessel slowly moved into the crowded Grand Harbour on 1st June, 1854. They had a first sight of their French allies, who clustered on the quays, spontaneously cheering, the sight of the red-coats seemingly causing emotional outbursts in their Gallic hearts.

Valetta was dirty and shockingly overcrowded, and alive with troops—English and French infantry and artillery jostled each other in the narrow streets, whilst the native Maltese stared in wonder. The 42nd marched to a camp set up on the Hornwork outside Port Bombe, where they camped for a few days, then they were marched to the Docks and packed aboard ship, the shortage of fresh water requiring a lessening of the numbers of troops on the island. As they sailed out, they marvelled again at the Maltese boys who dived right under the ship and came up on the other side with a coin from the bottom, thrown by a generous soldier. In the heat, such antics looked very inviting to the heavily garbed men.

The more knowledgeable men talked of Constantinople, but one of the officers' batmen was heard to utter a queer name that was to become frighteningly familiar to them:

"Scutari . . . that's where we're gae'ing."

Chapter 4

It was a monotonous voyage, there was nothing to do or see until the *Hydaspes* passed through the Dardanelles and entered the Sea of Marmara. Closer to the shore, it was possible to detect warlike signs, lines of white tents and the dots of scarlet uniforms. Slowly, on the 7th June, the vessel sailed into Scutari harbour. Beneath them, the sparkling carpet of water was changing, becoming muddy and carpeted with refuse and dead animals; an unpleasant stench arose from it. Noisily the *Hydaspes* dropped anchor at a rotting old jetty, where the sea slopped under its stinking carpet of refuse. As the vessel tied up, Hector saw a bloated dead horse being dragged shorewards and eaten by squabbling dogs.

For two days that seemed a lifetime, they waited in frustration and despair at the old jetty until orders came for them to land on the morning of the 9th. Everyone was tired of gazing at the rising mass of glittering domes and minarets of Constantinople on the European shore; the novelty of diseased beggars, Turkish soldiers and Greek pedlars soon palled. From daybreak onwards they crowded on the quay, calling up to the soldiers hanging over the ship's rails above them. When the Regiment landed and formed up on the jetty, they had literally to fight their way through this ragged, evil-smelling, screaming mob. It was a relieved 42nd who marched into the tented camp of the Highland Brigade outside the town, where they were formed into a single brigade with the 79th Regiment and the 93rd Regiment.

A few days later the brigade received their movement orders, and on the 13th June the 42nd found themselves back on the rickety old jetty and marching single-file up the same gangplank that they had so lightheartedly descended four days previously. The crowd of noisy sighseers and beggars did not seem to have altered in the slightest, and the same repulsive, scabby faces leered from out of the same rags. The troops cursed and complained at these aimless movements and the Commanding Officer confided to fellow-officers that he had no

MOT—2

idea of their destination—only the thought of fighting to come made life bearable.

Scuffing their white-gaitered feet against the rotting timbers, Hector, Jamie and Charlie stood together on the jetty. Occasionally they had to break off their conversation to turn and push aside a too-persistent beggar or pedlar.

"What are we waitin' for?"

"Dinna ye ken? The officers have got to go aboard before the rank an' file."

A bustle and flurry was taking place at the ship's side and a party of Highlanders were detailed to stand guard over a steadily enlarging pile of war-stores being unloaded from the ship. There were tents, poles, shovels, palliasse-covers and all the carefully stowed war-stores that had been put aboard at Portsmouth. Ian pushed his way through the heaving crowd; Hector called to him:

"What are they taking the stores off for?"

Ian shrugged his shoulders:

"What d'ye think? Do you wish to carry it all over Roossia?"

"But . . . I ken it gets mighty cold in Roossia!"

Helplessly, Ian spread his hands and marched off. Then came the order to fall in. Slowly, the soldiers were marched on to the boat again, fending off the crowding hangers-on. Men resumed their old positions at the rail as though they had never been away. The 42nd returned the compliment as shipload after shipload of cheering troops glided towards the Black Sea but, tiring of the pastime, they returned to grumbling at their own inactivity. The picturesque vista presented by Constantinople lay wasted before them—no one had eyes for the minarets and domed roofs of the mosques that glittered in the sunlight against a background of cypress-covered slopes, or the storks silently gliding across the blue sky above the masts of the ships. Frail and intricately carved caiques glided over the dirty water with timeless grace, their passengers lying on carpets and cushions.

The *Hydaspes* shuddered and creaked as seamen rhythmically worked the capstan bars to the tune of a squeaky fiddle. Encrusted with scum and weeds, the huge anchor rose dripping from the sea and the men cheered heartily. After further infuriating delays they were moving, leaving behind them the splendours of the Bosphorus, past Therapia, where the huge Hotel d'Angleterre stood out on the shore. The two-day journey was boring and uneventful until, on 15th June, the 42nd disembarked at Varna and, with the rest of the 1st Division, went into camp near the town. Like most of the towns in this part of the world, Varna looked pleasant and white from the sea but rapidly changed its character on closer acquaintance. It was a dirty and evil-smelling place; the worn-down paving of the main street slippery under the marching feet, with large pot holes abounding. Outside the town the rolling Balkan countryside was vividly green and dotted with trees and masses of shrubs rising invitingly from the very shoreline.

In camp the atmosphere was one of tension and excitement, encouraging a spirit of war that was fully savoured by every officer and man, all of whom hoped fervently that soon they would be marching to do battle with the Russians somewhere near the Danube. Mountains of stores, shot and shell, boxes and bags lay everywhere, unable to be moved because of lack of transport. Troops moved about in martial fashion, regimental colours flapped, band instruments flashed rays of light in the bright sun, drums and fifes stuttered and squealed as red lines of infantry wheeled and turned in solid blocks. Even the clouds of white dust in which they moved could not dim the brilliant uniforms that coloured the scene on all sides; green-jacketed Riflemen marching jerkily to silver bugles, whilst the exuberant Irishmen of the 88th Regiment let out wild Irish screeches. Limbered batteries jingled as they jogged past while cavalry horses pranced and reared. It was all so stimulating and exciting that no one was so dull of soul as to fail to be aroused. Sickness was light and the troops were high-spirited, in spite of the sun and flies and dust that plagued them.

On the 1st July the 1st Division marched ten miles west to a new camping area at Aladyn. For some reason the men found it a hard march, and 180 of the Guards dropped to the rear, although only eighteen or twenty out of 2,500 of the Highlanders did not come in with the main body. If the soldiers found it hard, the women accompanying the Army found it much worse. They had no transport allotted to them and could only get a ride on a baggage-waggon on sufferance—or by winking at the driver.

The new camp was on the spur of a hill about two miles from a narrow river which joined two lakes. Although the river ran through a swampy bottom, it was the only source of water supply for the Division, who had to send mules with leather bottles to the river whilst the men had to walk to and fro with their little canteens and cooking pots. It was a pleasant-looking area of rich meadows that stretched for miles on all sides, bordered by dense woods invaluable as a source of cooking fuel. They had only been there two days when they were beset by a storm of hail and rain which continued intermittently for a day and a night. As the tents were pitched in a fine garden loam, the floors soon became a swamp. To let off the water the men dug trenches around their tents; they did this naked, leaving their clothes under their far from waterproof shelter. Unfortunately, Hector was detailed for a picket during the storm when the party had to march off, all wet through to a spot in the woods about one and a half miles distant. Here, without tents, they spent twenty-four hours as an outlying picket, performing the duty of protecting the British left flank from any possible threat from the retreating Russians. Soaked to the skin and chilled to the bone, the picket returned to a scene of devastation and misery that continued until the sun came out and dried everyone off.

After nearly a month in the area, the swamp between the lakes began to have its effect, sowing the seeds of disease so that cases of cholera began to appear. On the 11th July, two Highlanders came upon the corpse of a Frenchman lying in the bushes by the river. Thinking he had died of a fit, they bore his body to the French camp. The doctors looked at the blotched face of the twisted corpse and realised that cholera was amongst them. Thirteen soldiers died during the night and cholera was confirmed in the French camp. It was next officially confirmed that the disease was in the camp of the Light Division and that sixteen men of the Rifle Brigade had died. So virulent was it that one man, seized at seven o'clock was a corpse by twelve. Frighteningly aware of the horror in their midst, men became undisciplined and moved about the camp aimlessly. Nightly, drunkenness and disorder disturbed the lines—in fact, drink was the only Christian vice in which they had much chance of indulging as gluttony was out of the question and there were no women nearer than Bucharest.

Insidiously, and with a relentless momentum, the disease increased and at every hour of the day corpses were stitched in blankets and hurriedly borne to holes on the outskirts of the camp. There was no ceremony or funeral party, and the tired padres, often unable to conceal their own fears, rambled hurriedly through the funeral service. Terrified victims were bundled off in bumpy wooden country carts to the Varna hospital, fearful because everyone knew it as a charnel-house from which it was said that no man ever returned. Everyone had heard of the burial pits at Varna where disfigured corpses were dropped pellmell by the drunken pensioners of the Ambulance Corps. Men had blown out their brains rather than be sent to the Varna hospital. Poor food, an inevitable part of active service, caused outbreaks of diarrhoea and dysentery, and every slight spasm, every abdominal discomfort was taken to be the herald of cholera, so that the debilitated and frightened men were an easy prey to disease.

Old soldiers considered the outbreak to have been caused by the British and the French being left too long in the same encampments. The experience of their Algerian campaigns told the French that they should be changing their encampments every ten days or so. In spite of orders, the British soldiers persisted in throwing offal, heads and entrails of fowls, bones and skins, into the bush and brushwood around their camp. causing clouds of flies to hover in the hot sun. The 1st Division had taken over an area recently vacated by the Light Division, who had been particularly guilty in the matter, and the thickets in the rear of their camp smelled to high heaven, becoming so offensive that the 1st Division made a new camp a short distance from the affected area.

During the four-hour drill periods held every morning under the relentless sun men slumped heavily to the dusty ground, unable to remain on their feet through sickness and lack of food —only a cup of coffee had passed their lips that day. Because of their poor and scanty rations, the famished troops ate unripe local apricots, causing outbreaks of diarrhoea. The officers did not suffer in anything like the same proportion as the men, perhaps because they had tents to themselves while the other ranks slept fifteen to a single tent.

Considering that large, open encampments might check the disease, orders were given to split up the British camps. On the 28th July, the 1st Division marched five miles from Aladyn to Gevrekler, a flat place on top of a hill with nothing remarkable about it except the absence of inhabitants and of cultivation. Considered to be the cream of British infantry, the men of the Guards and Highlanders were so weak that they had to make two marches to cover the short distance, and their packs were carried for them by other troops less affected. At a distance, the column looked a splendid sight, but closer inspection revealed wild and ragged bearded man, whose tattered and torn uniforms covered bent frames marching with dragging feet. At the tail of the column shambled a weirdly assorted concourse of English servants in top hats, of Greeks, Turks and Bulgarians, officers' horses and carts, camp pedlars and bullock-waggons.

The gaps in the ranks caused by sickness threw more labours upon those still on their feet, who found it all they could do to carry out the bare essentials necessary to live in a reasonably decent condition. They had to cut their own firewood with blunt bill-hooks, pitch tents, make ditches around them, cook, wash their clothes, turn out cleanly and smartly for parades and continually carry out fatigue duties for Commissaries, Engineers and Staff Officers besides normal regimental duties. The strictest orders were issued from Brigade Headquarters concerning hygiene and camp cleanliness.[3]

By the 8th August, the battle strength of the 1st Division had been diminished by about 800 men, not far from a sixth of their total numbers. The Guards Brigade of the 1st Division had suffered more heavily than the Highlanders, losing one hundred out of the 160 men who went down with the disease. Perhaps this was due to the high sense of personal discipline found within the Scottish regiments, or perhaps Highlanders held their liquor better than most—in Bulgaria, drunkenness could be death. The days were not very cold, but the nights were cold out of all proportion and the sudden changes of temperature, combined with the fact that the men lay on the ground and lacked most comforts necessary to cure sickness, accelerated the onset of the disease. A large hospital marquee was put up in the lines, soon to be packed with cases of cholera, enteric fever, typhoid, dysentery and diarrhoea. Everyone kept studiously off the subject of who had died or who was dying of cholera, but all were aware that the majority of men who were carried into the sun-bleached canvas walls of the hospital would not emerge other than as a corpse on a blanketed stretcher.

Each evening, the MacDonald brothers conducted their personal roll-call and heaved sighs of relief when they found that they were all still in good health, although consumed with a mighty apprehension. Alex recalled how they had escaped the plague and epidemics in their native Edinburgh and they hoped that the guardian angel that hovered over the heads of the MacDonalds would continue his patrolling.

On the 17th August the 1st Division prepared to march to a camp three days away on the south side of Varna Bay. The officers commanding the Guards persuaded Lord Raglan to let them have their packs carried and Lord Raglan, having agreed to that, was compelled to order all the other regiments to have theirs carried likewise. This order was received with great indignation by the 42nd, who felt perfectly fit to carry their packs and did not wish to be separated from their property. So, at the appointed time, the Regiment appeared on parade with their packs on their shoulders. This dreadful fact was immediately reported to the Assistant-Adjutant-General, Colonel Gordon, who galloped up to the 42nd, and ordered the fuming Lieutenant-Colonel Cameron to take off his men's packs. Cameron protested, saying that he had received the order to be on the appointed ground at a certain hour and also to have the men's knapsacks packed upon mules, but he realised that if he attempted to comply with the latter order, he would be too late for the time at which he was ordered to be on the ground from whence the column was to march. Therefore, he decided to let the soldiers carry their packs, not being aware of the importance attached to the scheme of employing mules. Notwithstanding, the men had to discard their packs and were then delayed two hours in the sun whilst stowing them on mules and ponies—each mule could only carry six packs so this required about one hundred mules for a battalion in order that this unsoldierlike plan could be carried out.

They marched for three days in easy stages; even so, there were more stragglers and men lying by the roadside than anyone in the 42nd could remember. The route was marked by the shallow graves of another division who had recently passed the same way. Heaps of loose earth, sometimes with a protruding hand or foot, showed where local inhabitants had stolen from the dead the blankets in which they were buried.

In the Highland Brigade there was a great feeling of indignation against the Guards, who were blamed for their separation from their packs. The men considered themselves very unlucky to be in the same Division with the Guards who, always on the right by virtue of their seniority, did not take detachment-duty, which fell on the left Brigade. On the march they were usually right in front; this meant that those who came last had to sweep up the baggage and the sick and the ammunition, and had a great deal of dirty work to do. The men considered that, in all fairness, the Guards should take their turn at the dirty work.

After marching for three days, the Division camped in a high and beautiful spot close to the sea, where walnuts, wild pears and cherry trees abounded. The men picked the unripe fruit and caused themselves to become sick. There was a great many troops in the area and large numbers of horses, so that water was hard to come by. Nothing could be bought and everyone had to exist entirely on rations—breakfast was dry ration bread, made of rye and sand, with milkless tea. Although diminished, sickness continued to take lives; there were a good many deaths among the officers and many went home sick. Both officers and men were sick of the inactivity.

During the night of the 28th August orders came to embark, and on the 29th the 42nd marched to Varna and boarded the *Emeu* steam-transport, commanded by Captain Small. Considerable amazement was felt when they were told that nothing was to be carried on shore except ammunition and three days' provisions; everyone supposed it was intended that they should throw up entrenchments until the ships could return and bring the remainder of the baggage, horses and mules. In the event, thousands of horses and mules were left on the hillside to take their chance, and were never collected.

The vast armada assembled in Balchick Bay, a few miles north of Varna, filling the roads in a bright and colourful panorama under the bright sun. Packed like sardines, the red-coated troops crowded the decks as the transports gently swung on their anchors for several days. On board the various ships, regimental bands played marches as though in competition with each other in an effort to take the men's minds from the increasing toll of sickness and their personal searches for real or imaginary deadly physical pains.

On the 7th September, 1854, the fleet up-anchored and passed out into the open sea, filling the still waters of the Black Sea from horizon to horizon in an imposing spectacle. That night, there was a bright full moon and the troops packing the decks could see the ships around them as plainly as by day. Early on the morning of the 9th September signalling flags fluttered colourfully from the flagship and were repeated on all other vessels. With a great splash, anchors dropped into the calm sea on all sides and the mighty armada lay at anchor about sixty miles west of Cape Tarkan and 110 miles from Sebastopol. No one knew why they had delayed and in spite of boats passing from ship to ship, no signal to move came from the flagship. The only signs of activity occurred now and then when from one or other of the motionless vessels a blanket-covered corpse plummeted into the calm sun-sparkling sea. Cholera was still present aboard the *Emeu*, six men died on the 9th September and one man fell overboard in his sleep.

Inevitably, with little else to occupy their attention, every man in the fleet played his ample part in circulating the wildest of rumours. They were going to Odessa. Sebastopol had announced that it intended to surrender as soon as they arrived and the war would be over. There were Russians watching every move they made, in addition to Russian spies within their ranks, and a hot reception was being prepared for them wherever they landed. No rumour was too wild or extravagant to receive consideration. What was definite however, was that they were to land without tents, each officer and man with no more than he could carry except three days' rations of cold pork and biscuit and a canteen of water. Once ashore they were to make good their position against all comers.

On Monday, 11th September, they got under way, after having waited a whole day for the French transports, which were lagging behind. Bodies continued to be dropped overboard from the various transports, indicating that men were continually dying of cholera or other diseases. On Wednesday, 13th September they were still very little farther on their way, having been anchoring and keeping the fleet together, but that morning they started down the coast from near Eupatoria. When they began to move rippling cheers echoed around the fleet and, aboard the *Emeu*, sailors told the Highlanders that they were aiming for a point near Sebastopol and that the flagship was flying a signal, "Make every preparation for landing troops". They were sailing so close in to shore without any interference from coastal batteries that every man could see with his own eyes the enviable paraphernalia of peace—houses, cattle, cornfields and moving carts paraded before their eyes. At twilight, the fleet dropped anchor in Calamita Bay; in the gathering gloom the long reaches of the shore seemed to stretch away to infinity. Now there was an exciting air of bustle and urgency about the fleet and, like little minnows in a pond, boats darted from ship to ship.

The next day dawned magnificently and the sun shone brightly on the little waves, sparkling as they broke on the bright yellow sands. Laden with kit, the Highlanders mustered on deck tightly wedged together. They could see people gathering on the shore and once a small group of Russian cavalry, probably Cossacks, stood on a small headland silhouetted against the blue sky. Although they were within range of the new Minié rifle[4] with which they were armed, no orders were given to try and pick off any of the mute witnesses and they were allowed to sit, small and motionless with their lance pennons fluttering in the light breeze.

The fleet sat in silent anticipation, then a cluster of black balls ran up the masthead of the flagship. At once, the ships' boats that had been bobbing alongside gathered before the fleet in a spectacular regatta with glistening oars raised. Then, with oars dipping and flashing, the regatta split apart and the boats raced to the ship they were ordered to serve. Bringing additional theatrical drama to the situation, bugles and drums began to rend the air from all parts of the fleet while the French were frantically tootling fanfares and rolling fanfarades that first amused then irritated the British soldiers. Seemingly more practised at the operation, the French troops climbed smartly down into their boats so that they were moving towards the shore before the British boats had been filled. Sailors aided each heavily-laden infantryman as he came creeping down the ladder, taking his musket from him and packing his knapsack under the seat. Treating the men like large and not very intelligent pets, the sailors patted them on the back, saying "Do not be afeerd on the water, sojer!" Reaching the shore, the sailors stood in the bows and handed each man and his equipment down the plank to half-naked sailors standing waist-deep in the surf. When the boats ground into the shingle the sailors swung them ashore with cries of "Come on girls!" as the wide kilts flew out when they skipped through the shallow water.

Not among the first away, the 42nd stood at the rails gazing downwards, jeering at the officers of other infantry regiments, taking themselves very serious in tightly buttoned, gilded and epauletted regimentals. At last their turn came, and the Highlanders clambered laboriously down into the boats. Each soldier carried his blanket and greatcoat strapped into a knapsack, together with a pair of boots, socks, a shirt and a forage-cap. Over one shoulder was slung a wooden canteen of water and over the other a haversack containing four and a half pounds of cooked salt meat and a bulky package of the same amount of biscuit—rations for three days. In addition, each man carried a portion of the mess cooking apparatus, a musket and bayonet, a cartridge box and fifty rounds of ball cartridge.

On their way to the beach they could see the part on which they were going to land narrowed to a thin strand of shingle fronting a lake of calm unruffled waters, and beyond this a lonely crumbling fort with a half-ruined white tower. It all looked very quiet and peaceful. Longing to feel dry land under their feet again, the men were in high spirits and exchanged oaths and quips with the sailors. Not every man laughed and joked, many faces were putty-coloured or ghostly white, lined and drawn with pain and weakness as their owners struggled to cope with the weight of their equipment. Nothing could be done to help them, no transport had been taken ashore, not even ambulance waggons, neither was there any tentage or shelter landed. Watching comrades struggling under their burdens to reach the hill beyond the beach, men shook their heads and hurried over to help them as they collapsed in agony or exhaustion. Within an hour of landing, several men were buried beneath the sands over which they had so painfully struggled a short time before.

It was not long before the beach, from one end to the other, was a colourful mass of red-coats, brass-mounted shakos and feather bonnets, with bayonets and other weapons glistening in the bright sunlight. Shrill words of command struggled to be heard above shouts and laughter as the excited troops once again stamped their feet on solid ground.

By one o'clock, the Light Division, led by the 2nd Battalion the Rifle Brigade, had moved off the beach and over the hill, across country towards a village which was also being approached by the French left flank. Clouds of skirmishers covered the advance. Finally the Duke of Cambridge, on horseback, led off the 1st Division. Most of his staff marched on foot as their horses had not yet been landed. Many officers would never see their horses again because the cavalry mounts, fully equipped, had been thrown into the sea and left to swim ashore, and many had been lost.[5] Delighted at having a horse to hold and pat during the voyage inshore, the sailors made no bones about expressing their unhappiness and disapproval of this mode of getting them ashore.

The sun had disappeared behind threatening clouds and a light rain began to fall. The heavily laden boats wallowed and splashed over waves tipped with white caps, often to be toppled over by the breakers at the shoreline. Throughout the afternoon the drizzle increased, thoroughly soaking the shelterless troops who moped miserably around, staring through the mist at the ships tossing and heaving at anchor. Disembarkation became so hazardous that it was cancelled until the following morning.

The British troops found their first night upon the Crimea to be a severe trial. A storm broke at nightfall bringing wind that blew in cold gusts and violent rainstorms that fell throughout the night. Tentless, without a waterproof sheet among them, thousands of men crouched in greatcoats and blankets on a bubbling morass or wandered, moaning and shivering, through the storm. The 42nd had been halted for the night in an inland ploughed area, lacking wood and water. Some of them marched back to the beach and collected driftwood with which they unsuccessfully tried to light fires. Everyone was full of envy and anger at the sight of the lines of little white bivouacs in which the French troops snugly slept under the damply flapping red, white and blue tricolour flag of France.

Daylight broke grey, chill and misty. The surf still roared on the bleak sands, although the sea was calmer and soon boatloads of soldiers, drenched to the skin, were hurtling ashore. From every regiment, parties of men bearing corpses struggled down to the shore and laid their burdens in a long line, awaiting burial. The morning stayed grey until ten o'clock when the dim light slowly turned golden, the sky became blue and the sun beat down, scorching everything to dryness within the hour. At first everyone rejoiced at this heartening warmth which seemed to strike comfort down to their very chilled bones, but soon it caused everyone to go hunting for drinking water because the little lakes had turned out to be salt. Plentiful supplies of wood had been thrown up on the shore by the storm and cooking fires were burning brightly on all sides. With hot food and drink inside him, every man felt better and spirits rose with the incredible optimism of the untutored British soldier of that day and age.

For the next four days, the Allied army moved aimlessly inland. On the 19th September reveille was sounded at three o'clock in the morning, the clear sharp notes of dozens of bugles shattering the cold and silent darkness that cloaked the camps. First in darkness and then in the grey early morning light, everyone bustled around in apparent confusion as the men, swarming like ants, dug graves, carried stretchers or dragged back to the boats the equipment and supplies they could not carry. Much was thrown away or left where it stood. Dotted over a large area, the fitful and flickering red glow of camp fires gave the scene an artificially wild and romantic atmosphere. Bullied, pushed and shouted into position, the British soldiers were not given sufficient time to cook their rations and they had to carry their meat raw until the opportunity arose to boil it. Nor were they given time to line up at the single well to fill their water canteens, in spite of these preliminaries taking nearly six hours.

The quickly-rising bright sun indicated that the day was going to be hot and clear and by nine o'clock, when they were ready to march, the sun was blazing down from a cloudless sky. At first glance, it was a flashing, scintillating panorama, but closer inspection revealed that uniforms already bore stains and tears that could not entirely be hidden by the pipe-clayed strapping. Words of command rang through the air; the French, who had been impatiently tootling and drumming on the right for hours, strained to move forward. Bands struck up gay tunes, sending spirits soaring, and the sun-baked earth quivered to marching feet as the armies flooded forward across the plain.

Nearest the shoreline were the Turks, then the French, whose red legs and flashing white gaiters twinkled in the sunlight; the British had the inland flank, forming a huge solid oblong more than a mile long. Led by the drummers and bands, regiments marched in column, spaced to wheel into line, their cased colours jutting up out of the mass of men. The Highland Brigade were on the left of the 1st Division who were on the very left flank of the British Army, marching in the second line behind the Light Division. Cavalry were out in front and behind them. As they had not yet been brought ashore from the ships, no field ambulances followed the marching troops—there was nothing but a few purlioned country-carts, camels and odd beasts of burden straying and struggling along behind the host.

The countryside was beautiful and undulating, in places covered with fern and lavender and a strange unrecognisable herb which, when crushed under thousands of heavy boots, gave up a curious, strong, and bitter smell.[6] Everyone was in high spirits, singing and calling cheerfully when they were not singing obscene verses to the tuneful marches played by the regimental bands. This façade, put up by an invalid army, could not survive long under such a sun and soon the burdened men, worn out by waiting and stifling in their padded jackets, lost their gaiety and energy and began to stumble and falter in their stride. The slight sea breeze that had tempered the heat began to drop and the sun grew hotter, causing throats to become dry with thirst. Within an hour not a band was playing as, halting repeatedly, the British Army trudged along in a desperate silence, strewing behind them a trail of exhausted stricken men and discarded equipment. Constantly, parties had to be sent back to pick up stragglers who were wearily trailing hundreds of yards behind the marching columns.

Before the march began, the doctors had declared that the men, in their sickly condition, were unfit to carry more than a blanket, a greatcoat, ammunition, canteen and three days' rations. Even with this light load, soldiers stumbled along, heads held low and faces darkening, finding it as much as they could do to carry on. Sometimes, their blue-rimmed mouths filled with vomit and they tottered a few paces from the ranks before slumping to the ground—cholera was still pursuing its grim course. Completely unable to march for more than thirty minutes without a rest, men collapsed in their tracks when the order was given to fall out. When the fall-in was called, progressively fewer men staggered to their feet. Many were near to delirium and some sank to their knees begging for water—but the plain was waterless. Greatcoats, shakos and even ration-bags were discarded by exhausted, wild-eyed soldiers, until the regiments in the rear found it difficult to pick their way through the crumpled bodies and accoutrements that littered the ground. Bodies lay clustered like a vast field of poppies so that a path had to be laboriously picked through them. Some were dead, others were convulsed with cholera, groaning with dysentery or rigid from fever and heat-stroke. To an unenlightened observer it would have seemed more like an army struggling in retreat rather than one advancing towards the first engagement of a campaign.

The thick carpet of grass, fern, thyme and lavender over which they marched muffled the sound of boots so that the army progressed in a silence that was foreboding. Only the mumble of gun-limber wheels, the creaking of the country carts and the jingling of the cavalry rose above the subdued monotone of moans and curses that hung on the still air. Above them, against the background of a cloudless bright blue sky, larks sang and fluttered happily in a ceaselessly cruel mockery.

After what seemed a lifetime of marching (actually it was only two o'clock) the struggling army came up to the crest of another ridge and saw below them the River Bulganak sparkling in a peaceful valley. Falling gently down from the sloped plateau to the level of the stream, the ground rose again from its south bank in a series of terraces. The sight of water aroused an outburst of energy in the troops so that they broke ranks and, out of control, shambled down the slopes to plunge their burning heads into the cool water, gulping, choking and spluttering as they allowed it to run down their throats. Even the rages of thirst were not allowed to loosen the discipline of the Highland Regiments—Sir Colin Campbell halted them before they reached the stream so that the first mad rush had subsided before they were permitted to descend to the now trampled and muddy banks.

Sitting up, gasping and momentarily revived, all eyes were drawn to some Russian cavalry moving along the highest ridge. After some delay, four squadrons of the cavalry advance-guard clattered and jingled past the infantry and over the shallow brook, on their way to reconnoitre the far bank of the river. Soon they came trotting back, having encountered the enemy in numbers too great to engage. The resting infantry jeered and shouted at them, full of resentment because they had had to struggle on the dreadful march while the cavalry complacently rode. Every foot soldier felt this was further evidence that when there was any real fighting to be done the infantry would have to do it. Lying next to Hector, a bearded Highlander glared at the horsemen, calling out:

"Silly gawking peacocking bastards."[7]

Stiffly and reluctantly, the army struggled to its feet and shambled forward in an almost orderless mob up the ridges of the Bulganak. Involuntarily the entire host halted on reaching the top ridge, sobered at the sight of the vast black mass of the Russian Army slowly moving away before them until they retired out of sight beyond the heights. Although they had only marched eight miles, it was clear to the allied commanders that they had come far enough for that day, and welcome orders were given to bivouac for the night. Although they had touched nothing for ten hours, most of the men were too tired to eat, even if they had been able to cook their meat on the scanty fires they had made from the only available fuel, weeds and long grass. It was a long, cold and damp night for the troops wrapped in greatcoats and blankets on the bare dewy earth. Too cold to sleep, most of them shivered the night away. Beyond the river hundreds of Russian camp-fires, stretching as far as the eye could see on the steep ridges, burned and blinked unceasingly throughout the night.

Chapter 5

Reluctantly, the cold left the earth and the rolling landscape changed from brown to green. Unheralded by drum or bugle, the chilled soldiers morosely rose to their feet, stamping stiffly and flapping their arms in the manner of cab-drivers. It was seven o'clock; on their right the French had been briskly preparing to march for the past two hours. Paralysed with cold and weariness, Hector MacDonald found himself incapable of performing even the simplest task until his brother Alex, reverting to his role of Sergeant, told him sharply to get a grip on himself. Ruefully, Hector looked down at his bedraggled finery, mud-stained, torn and crumpled; pieces of grass clung to the damp cloth. He brushed his kilt with his hands and pulled the heavy cloth into some semblance of shape and tidiness. Moodily, he crouched on his heels, together with Charlie and Jamie, eating salt pork and hard biscuits. As they ate, they looked from under lowered lids at the scenes of disorder about them. Charlie called to a humped figure lying motionless under a stained greatcoat.

"Duncan! Waken, man! The Sergeant will see you!"

Twice, he called but the sleeping man did not move. Rising to his feet, Charlie put his toe under the man and gently pushed to no effect so he bent down and pulled the blanket from the man's face. Sightless eyes stared up at him.

"It's the cholera—Duncan wasn't to live through the night."

Hector looked thoughfully at his brothers:

"A month since there wasn't a stronger man in the regiment than Duncan and now he's just a bundle of skin and bones—and dead."

Jamie nodded:

"Aye, Duncan was a goodly man once and would not let his life be taken lightly from him."

It was already hot at nine o'clock when the 42nd were called on parade. They were inspected, cursed, reprimanded and booked for punishment just as though they had spent the previous night back at Dover Castle, furbishing their equipment. Then, for a long time they stood at rest. Hector pondered on the unaccountable way these parades and marches were managed and delayed. Bearing orders, a horseman clattered up and in a few minutes the Regiment drew themselves up, struggled into readiness and then swung off. The relief felt at moving was soon changed to irritation as the whole army became involved in a complicated wheeling movement involving extra marching distance. Next they halted, set off again and then halted again; a whispered rumour spread through the ranks that they were trying to restore contact with the French Army on their right. After an hour of this, the whole army halted; the rest was welcomed because it had become really hot and already everyone was tired. It seemed that they had come up level with the French but now had to halt so that the French could come forward to conform to the agreed order of march. After a while they were called to order and the march resumed. Their route lay over a grassy plain bleached nearly white by the hot summer sun and patched here and there with dusty brown earth; these patches were repeated on the faces of the hills to the south, where a belt of bright green vegetation and a few colourful villages could be seen. They had taken two hours to march only three miles, but everyone felt as tired as though they had done ten over the gently rising ground, which needed so much effort to place one heavily shod foot in front of the other.

Suddenly, a buzz of talk rippled from the front of the column, so that weary heads lifted to look slowly from one side to the other and to peer over the shoulders of the men in front. To their front, the wall-like formation of rising hills climbed in a series from the ridge over which they were marching; through narrowed eyes the soldiers could see some dark patches in regular oblong formations on the upper levels of the hills. Excitedly, men turned and told their neighbours that there were the enemy they had come 2,000 miles to fight; men stepped out of the ranks to see and were quickly roared back into position by officers and N.C.Os.

It was noon and the sun was at its highest, bearing down strongly on the mass of heavily-laden soldiers halted at the foot of the slope that rose to the steep hills on which the Russians were massed. In front of them, the ground fell away before beginning its rise and the silver streak of water sparkled as a river wound its way down to the sea. Noise departed from the world in a strange, timeless and dramatic silence that hushed and washed from the air the sigh of the wind and the cry of the birds.[8] As though fearing to break the silence, 60,000 men stood motionless; even a cough sounded as loud as a pistol-shot and men started in fright as a nervous neigh from a horse broke the silence, or turned angrily to discover the offender when a musket clanged against a mess-tin. Not understanding the silence, Sir Colin Campbell did not like it, the irascible down-to-earth veteran saw it as an intrusion that did not fit into his pattern of war. Subconsciously, he demolished it by speaking in a normal voice that could be heard by the entire Brigade:

"This will be a good time for the men to get loose half their cartridges!"

Unnerved by the unearthly hush, the Highlanders accepted the order with relief, dispelling their nervousness by making more noise than was necessary, tearing open packets of cartridges and clattering their equipment with a vigour that restored their sense of comradeship. Men found comfort in grinning at each other and winking their eyes. Hector smiled at Jamie and then leaned forward to look down the file seeking Ian—their gaze met and they smiled at each other. The noise and bustle was contagious, causing the whole Army to take a deep breath and to feel their feet firmly on the ground amid an undercurrent of military noises. Having bitter memories of the previous day's waterless hardships and remembering how veteran soldiers had told him that fighting was a thirsty affair, Hector was trying to conserve the water in his bottle, although he felt very dry. Covertly, he looked at the men about him, noting that their faces bore expressions of deep interest as though they were about to investigate a matter that had long fascinated them. Some fidgeted as though balanced on a slippery surface while others, resolved and quiet, were deeply engrossed with the business to hand.

Startlingly, bugles rent the air to repeat and echo their shrill premonitory refrain in rippling cadence along the stationary ranks of the Army. In the distance, the distinctive bugle calls and drum rolls of their French allies replied, arousing derision from the British soldiers. At exactly 1 o'clock the Army was ordered to move forward and the 42nd stepped out rhythmically, their dark kilts swaying in time to a step suddenly lightened by the sense of urgency that swept over them. With the 93rd marching to their extreme front, the 79th behind, the 42nd were at the rear of the three battalions of the Highland Brigade on the flank of the whole British Army; save for a few skirmishers of the Rifle Brigade there was only open space to their left. Underfoot, the grass and scrub crunched fragrantly, mingling with the clinking of equipment and the soft rustle of the swinging kilts.

Hector licked his dry lips, reluctantly his legs moved forward; he had a hollow gnawing feeling in the pit of his stomach. For a panic-striken moment he feared that he was suffering from cholera, then he realised that it was only nervousness. Momentarily possessed by a crazy feeling that he was the only one in the whole army who felt this way, he looked about him to note how his comrades kept their eyes sternly forward; he gained comfort from their resolution. Wryly, he reflected that escape was impossible; he was being borne along on an undeniable tide with the Regiment enclosing him on all four sides. From his file he could see nothing save the men moving all around him; iron laws of tradition and discipline imprisoned him in a moving box. His range of vision limited to a Highlander immediately in front of him, Hector noticed that he had a torn muddy patch on his red shoulder and a feathered bonnet that swayed aside with each step to reveal an angry boil on his neck. Hector found a strange comfort in this singular consciousness of what was going on in his own restricted field of vision. The sun bore fiercely down on the heavily clad and laden men; here and there in the moving files steps faltered uncertainly as ragged nerves and apprehensive thoughts were jangled by shouted orders to "ease to the right!" . . . then they had to reverse the process, now they had to "ease your files back to the left!" . . . evidently they were crowding too much upon the French. Men discarded knapsacks with shaky fingers or threw off heavy feathered bonnets to be kicked and trampled into shapeless masses by the remorseless feet marching behind them. Eyes had continually to be lowered so as to avoid tripping over prostrate bodies of the shakoed infantry of the Light Division, marching to their immediate front, men who had fainted or were ill and had dropped to the ground.

Suddenly, the rhythmic jangling of equipment and the rustle of feet was over-ridden by the sharper note of a single musket shot, immediately followed by similar spatterings to their front and left. Heads cocked so as not to miss a sound as the Highlanders realised that the Rifle Brigade skirmishers in front and on the flanks had made contact with the enemy. Over the heads of the file in front of him, Hector could see a large dark hill on which minute figures moved. Then he saw a flash and a billow of smoke quickly followed by a dull roar. Other guns repeated the refrain until the air seemed to be full of a thousand heavy doors being slammed by giant hands. Most of the enemy fire fell on the north bank of the river in front of the leading British file, and although none of the shot reached the 42nd their soft flesh cringed at the first roar, anticipating a bloody lane torn through their closely packed ranks.

Evidently taking the Russian shells as the signal for which he had been waiting, the British Commander deployed his leading division into line; the divisions marching in the rear remaining in open column of company's. In the van, the Light and 2nd Division found deployment difficult, although it was a manoeuvre that each company had practised on the parade ground more times than they could remember. But this time it was an evolution involving 10,000 men, many of them under fire for the first time. For once, the Highlanders did not laugh or make derisive remarks at the confusion of the English soldiers, wondering whether they might do no better in their own attempts to cover a front of more than a mile in length. Overlapping and broken in places, the line unfortunately masked their own incorrectly positioned artillery. Working under no such difficulties, the Russian gunners fired their well-positioned guns upon the advancing allied infantry.[9]

Advancing into the area the Light Division had vacated, the 1st Division came under artillery fire, heads bent forward and shoulders hunched as a shell screamed overhead to land in the soft ground behind them, flinging a shower of red earth skywards, to be followed by another and yet another. Not all buried themselves in the ground—some tore their way through soft and yielding flesh and bone. They were ordered to deploy so that, from their rearmost and extreme left position, the 42nd now found themselves in line with the 2nd Foot Guards on their immediate right and the 93rd Foot on their left. The whole divisional line extended for more than a mile, while the long shoulder-to-shoulder ranks of the British Army covered an area of nearly six miles.

Now that they were actually under fire, a feeling of resigned calm took possession of Hector MacDonald; mouth held half-open and head shrunk into shoulders to compress his body into the smallest possible target, he was borne forward by the men around him. Now and then he brushed a tunic-sleeve across his brow, sweat streamed down his face so that it resembled the visage of the grubby urchin he had once been in Edinburgh.

Bullets began to whistle overhead as they came within range of Russian skirmishers in the vineyards on the river bank. Fired at the advancing Light Division, most of the balls that reached the 1st Division were spent. The frequent picking-up of their dressing became irritating, although it took their minds off the dangers around them. Then, inexplicably, they were halted and the whispered word passed through the ranks that they were . . . "waiting till the Froggies come up". Everyone felt an unreasoning exasperation at the foreigners who kept them stationary under fire; seething with rage, Hector longed to acquire a sudden power that would enable him to make a sweeping gesture with his arms and bring everyone up into line. Angrily, he looked around to see how his comrades felt. Practically every face mirrored rage mingled with intentness; from some men came low snarling noises, others mouthed oaths or perhaps prayers in an almost unintelligible chanting monotone that blended into a loud humming that hung on the air. Stamping his feet and swearing in a loud voice, the Highlander on Hector's right suddenly ground out from between clenched teeth: "Och! What do they think they're doing? Why don't they send us in . . . they think we're scairt?"

Hector gazed down the ranks—no one looked heroic nor was anyone poised in a heroic attitude or making threatening or menacing gestures. For one long frightening moment, Hector wondered whether they would play their part like men, then his doubts left him and he was certain that every man in the 42nd at least would do his duty.

Almost insidiously, striking indiscriminately along the line, death was stalking amongst them with horrifying stealth and cunning. It seemed to be quite a simple matter to avoid being hit by the roundshot that you could see curving towards you from the big guns up on the hill. After the puff of smoke, the roundshot got larger, blacker and rounder as it came swiftly towards you, striking the ground to your front and, like an advancing wave, bounding in great curving bounces, getting larger and larger as it got nearer and nearer. If you kept your eyes on it and it came straight at you, it was possible to step smartly aside at the last moment and let the huge bounding black devil pass harmlessly by. Of course, such an unauthorised movement brought an immediate screaming rebuke from an officer or an N.C.O. with promise of a punishment after the battle. Hector thought it was better to risk a punishment than to lose an arm or leg or even your head! The Highlanders did not have as much time to get out of the way as the men to their front, in the second line they were unable to see the cannon-balls until they came bowling through the ranks of the Light Division. With horrifying suddenness, the air was filled with a horrible squelching noise or a muffled cry or a piercing scream. Startled, a man's head would sharply turn to see his neighbour struggling convulsively on the ground by his side, limbs oddly askew and with hot blood pumping out on to the green grass. To move a wounded man was to disobey orders, so most casualties were left lying where they had fallen; occasionally, his comrades would take pity on him and move the writhing man clumsily out of the way to await the help that would not come for hours.

The Light Division to their front suddenly lay down, tumbling grotesquely to the ground as though dead. The Highlanders stared in amazement until the same orders reached them and then, with cries and laughter, they flung themselves thankfully to earth. His nose a few inches above the fragrant turf, Hector looked sideways at the man lying next to him, who surprisingly winked his eye at him.

Pounding hooves shook the earth and with a jingling and crashing a battery of guns clattered up, unlimbered and belched into action. At the thoughts of the Russians getting back some of their own medicine everyone cheered lustily. But after a few rounds which fell short, the out-ranged British field-guns limbered up and clattered away, speeded with groans and jeers of derision from the long-suffering infantrymen.[10] The noise of battle grew louder until they had no chance of making themselves heard over the tumult unless they shouted. Men began to raise their voices shrilly and unsteadily in grim humour, giving nicknames to the most persistent enemy guns, usually the names of the wives of the more unpopular officers or sergeants.

"Watch it lads, here's another scolding fra' big fat Emma!"

A chorus of shouts greeted the black ball that bounded menacingly towards them; unnecessarily, men warned each other and their mounted officers of its approach. On other occasions, the roundshot would suddenly be upon them without warning and after a rush of air there was a sickening thud as a man was hit and had his life crushed from him. The Highlanders bore it with singular inherited courage, each man desperately trying to conceal his fear from his comrades lying about him. For an hour and a half they lay upon the open slope, feeling as naked as the day on which they were born.

Grimly resigned, drily humorous and stoical, occasionally men came stiffly to their feet to drag still quivering bodies to the rear of the Regiment, to return immediately and lie down again in their place.

Sir Colin Campbell heartened his Brigade by riding up and down the lines talking to the men; he seemed unperturbed by the noise and the danger to which he was exposing himself, but his horse was very frightened, capering and shuffling along the serried ranks of prone men. Gradually, a lull fell over the field—those who had watches noticed that it was half-past two. Only artillery fire had been exchanged, except for some brisk musketry over on the extreme left of the British front, where the Rifle Brigade skirmished with the Russians on the north bank of the river. Reluctantly, this spattering died down and all battle activity seemed to cease. Men lifted themselves up on their arms to see what was happening, eyes following a blue-clad staff officer in a big cocked hat who rode quietly across the front of the Light Division to stop at the group of mounted divisional officers. After some brisk talking and gesticulations, they dispersed to their regiments and a tumult of shouted orders assailed the air. Like puppets drawn up on their strings, 10,000 British soldiers, redcoats gleaming and brasses shining, rose stiffly to their feet to have their ranks dressed by roaring N.C.Os and warrant-officers, with all the ceremonial precision of the barrack square. Like an anthill stirred with a stick, these movements aroused the Russians; with crashing roars their guns opened fire. Bowling, bounding roundshot punched bloody holes in the splendid, impeccably aligned ranks of the Light Division who, formed two-deep, took their time reaching a formation that satisfied their officers. At last, set in motion by the notes of a bugle that rang brassily above the noise of the guns, the whole array, in perfect step and dressing, marched down the slope to the river.

Impatiently, the Highlanders waited for the staff officer to trot round the Light Division and give the same orders to the Duke of Cambridge, their Divisional Commander. Seeking the staff officer turning his horse around the end of the files, all eyes traversed back and forth along the lines of moving soldiers. But he did not come and the Highland Brigade were left, forlorn and furious, lying in the position they had occupied for nearly two hours. Overcome by disappointment, Hector felt as though he was going to suffocate and in a flurry of indignation he began to scramble to his feet; he was roared back into position by a sergeant. The shout turned Hector's rage into a sort of relief and he experienced the joy of a man who had at last found time to look about him. He felt an overwhelming interest in the thought that he was going to see fierce fighting close at hand without taking part in it himself. Without taking his eyes from his front, he reached for his canteen and took a long swallow of the warm, brackish water.

The sides of this hill dropped steeply from its crest, flattening out to comparatively gentle slopes for the last half-mile, down to the little cliffs above the river bank. Scarring these slopes was the dark earth of a long emplacement, from behind it a number of the heaviest Russian guns were firing at them. On the 42nd's immediate right, on the far side of the road that ran down to the river, a small white village* suddenly and dramatically caught fire. Huge red flames and billows of black and white smoke belched straight upwards into the still sky. The burning houses seemed to Hector to be even more representative of war than the guns that had been firing upon them for so long—ah, now, he felt . . . this is really it.

The prone Highlanders watched the infantry lines moving crabwise to the left as they maintained dressing and spacing, the pressure easing as men spread out to fill up the gap when a roundshot punched a hole in the lines. An increasing weight of roundshot, canister, grape shot and musketry was poured upon the Light Division—but still their impeccably-dressed lines marched meticulously onwards, shoulder-to-shoulder. Walls, gardens, rows of vines and deep furrows forced breaks in their ranks, to be reformed as soon as the obstacle was passed. Eyes veering first right and then left to take up the dressing, each man, as they neared the river bank, closed up to the man next to him, picking up the step just as though they were on a parade ground.

The British artillery had got into action and their shot caused clouds of smoke and spurts of dust to rise in the Russian lines. The Highlanders could hear the guns firing to their right and behind them. The men pointed out to each other that the river did not seem to be very deep, in places it came up only to the ankles, although others were waist deep and it was breast high in the very deepest places, so that muskets had to be held up in upstretched arms. Like black hulks, bodies floated face-down in the water.

Reaching the far bank, the exhausted, heavily-laden infantry

*Boulíouk.

were finding the ten- or fifteen-foot climb to be beyond them. The watching Highlanders saw that most of the infantry were not trying to climb the bank, but were crouching and huddling beneath its lip where the artillery could not reach them. More and more of them crowded together in confusion; officers tried to get them to go forward while mounted generals calling out unheeded orders cavorted and weaved about. On the far left, where the ground sloped away so that the bank did not exist, the British infantry were being halted. The farthest battalion lay down facing out to the flank whilst the next regiment to them formed square, with their front facing up the hillside.[11] At this apparently senseless manoeuvre the Highlanders moaned with fury and frustration, no one could see any Russian cavalry that might cause alarm. Hector was watching a staff officer who had scrambled his horse up on to the top of the steep bank to sit shouting orders and waving his arms, the plumes on his cocked hat tossing rhythmically in time to his agitated movements. Deeply interested, Hector waited to see how long it would be before he was hit and tumbled from the horse, but he seemed to bear a charmed life.[12] Above him, the dense, dark Russian masses seemed to be poised menacingly as though about to descend and engulf the disordered infantry on the bank. In a way, Hector could sympathise with the Light Division, reluctant to advance up the glacis that rolled upwards from the bank for about four hundred yards to a big redoubt, wreathed in the smoke of its own guns. Troops ascending to attack the redoubt would have to face point-blank fire from the guns commanding the slopes.

Slowly, order began to emerge from chaos as British infantry started to scramble up the bank and move forward on the slope leading to the redoubt. Now, they were in groups and bunches, far-removed from the mathematically-ordered lines that had gone into the river a few minutes earlier. The men advancing up the slope were taking heavy casualties from the guns in the redoubt, the shot tearing through their ranks as the men crowded closer and closer together. By now the air was full of black and grey smoke, so that it was impossible to see more than shadowy figures darting in and out of the gloom.[13] Amid the noise and tumult that engulfed them, with shot ricocheting and bounding through their ranks, the Highlanders realised that they would see little more until they were ordered to closer quarters. Not knowing what was going on, and in a fever of despondency and frustration, they had a horrible fear that they had been forgotten. Then, when all hope of being thrown into the battle had gone, the Highlanders were suddenly ordered to their feet and shouted into position. Moving stiffly, slapping grass and dust from uniforms and shifting equipment into more comfortable positions, they formed their ranks. With muskets tightly gripped in sweating hands and eyes keenly scanning the smoke-obscured battlefield ahead, they strained to go forward. Sir Colin Campbell rode up to their front, standing in his stirrups he shouted above the noise of battle:

"Now, men, you are going into action. Remember this, whoever is wounded—I don't care what his rank is—whoever is wounded must lie where he falls until the bandsmen come to attend to him. No soldiers must go carrying off wounded men. If any soldier does such a thing, his name shall be struck up in his parish church. Don't be in a hurry about firing. Your officers will tell you when it is time to open fire. Be steady. Keep silence. Fire low." His voice faltered slightly: "Now men, the army will watch us—make me proud of the Highland Brigade!"[14]

He raised his arm and pointed towards the river "Forward, the Forty-Second!" Pulling round his horse's head he led them forward. The sun was beating fiercely down so that it was hotter than ever. Weakened by illness, parched with thirst or affected by the hot sun, men faltered uncertainly as they took their first baby-like steps. Bonnets and equipment began to add to the litter already strewn on the slope by the Light Division. Glad to be up and not lying wondering what was going on, Hector stepped over the twitching body of a man from the front rank who had fallen in front of him, then moved to one side as the ranks opened to avoid a Light Division man, lying on his back staring at the sky. The soles of his boots had been so worn that there was a hole in one of them. Glancing down at the ashen face, Hector felt a desire to stop and stare at the body, to find out why life had left it, to see what had squashed out its spark. Misery and distress flooded over him but, at the same time, he was conscious of an overwhelming relief that it was some other unfortunate and not to himself that disaster had struck. Such thoughts inevitably led him to very graphic ideas of what he was going to do within the next few minutes, although he found it impossible to keep his mind on any one aspect of his situation as it was fully occupied with the constant problems of maintaining dressing, alignment and step and heeding roaring officers and N.C.Os.

The whole 1st Division advanced in beautiful order—the Guards Brigade moved perfectly because they knew no other way of marching, the Highland Brigade because they did not intend to let the Guards show them up. Maintaining near-perfect formation, halting for the purpose of dressing afresh after negotiating obstacles, they came to the river where the same standards were maintained as the whole formation marched in step, shoulder-to-shoulder, into the water. Here and there it was possible to march through without even breaking step, at other places it was necessary to wade and even swim. Some men were shot in the water, to sink silently out of sight or to float downstream.

Emerging on the far bank, the 42nd found that they were foremost in a direct echelon of regiments falling back to the left. Coming up with one of the infantry regiments that had halted on the far bank of the river, the Highlanders scoffed at them. The infantry shouted back:

"You are madmen—you'll all be killed!"[15]

One man cried out:

"Let the Scotchmen go on—they'll do the work!"*

Ordered to incline to the left to give themselves room in which to work, the 42nd moved forward, each man touching shoulders with his neighbour, the front ranks holding bayonet-fixed muskets aggressively at the ready, the rear ranks with arms sloped at the precisely correct angle. Sir Colin Campbell rode alone in front of them.[16] It was a spectacle claimed later to have been seldom seen before on the battlefield and unlikely to be seen again.

The slope that climbed up from the far bank of the river was steep and broken, strewn with rocks and scored with gullies, so that the 42nd were breathing heavily when they reached the ridge. Before them lay a broad and deep hollow, on their right was the redoubt just abandoned by its garrison, who were scurrying back through the hollow. Beyond the retreating men a huge grey column of Russian infantry moved ponderously towards the 42nd. As soon as he saw the enemy, Sir Colin Campbell halted the 42nd, knowing that a successful line formation must have perfect alignment so that each man has a full field of fire. He had no intention of permitting one of his regiments to engage the enemy with an uneven formation. At the halt, the 42nd went through the maddeningly protracted business of ceremoniously dressing their ranks into imposing

*Kinglake, Vol. 2: Chapter XVI, Page 445.

lines of men in scarlet jackets and dark green kilts, made gigantic by the tall bonnets with the red hackle.

Showing supreme confidence, Sir Colin ordered a manoeuvre only possible with well-trained troops possessing the highest standards of steadiness and discipline—the 42nd were to advance forward into the hollow, at the same time firing their muskets at the enemy column. Distorted by smoke and dust, the Highlanders in their strange garb were a fearsome sight as they swung down into the depression, preceded by a wall of flame from their muskets. Firing and loading to orders, as they strode forward with kilts swinging through the acrid smoke that wreathed the battlefield, Hector found that he was easily able to maintain his share of the volleys. He could see the enemy very clearly—tall, stout men in very long drab grey coats, some wearing black leather helmets with brass mountings, others with white linen forage caps. Their large, flat white faces were expressionless and immobile.

Startlingly, Hector was halted in his tracks by a violent blow on the point of his left shoulder just as though someone had fended him violently off with the butt end of a musket. His feet instinctively continued to plod so that he kept pace with the men around him. He gazed fearfully at the place expecting to see a large hole in the red tunic and a growing dark stain as his life-blood welled from the wound. Amazed and almost disappointed, he was unable to detect even the smallest mark on the red cloth! Nevertheless, his shoulder ached and throbbed alarmingly and it was painful to move his arm. Hector never found out what caused the huge black, blue and orange bruise that he later discovered over the whole left side of his body as far down as his waist.

Sir Colin Campbell had his horse shot under him—he did not fall, but loosened his feet from the stirrups and, jumping clear, landed lightly on his feet. He was immediately re-horsed by one of his staff officers.[17]

There was no hand-to-hand fighting. It was a situation where the side which could not endure the fire of the other would break and retreat before a melée could take place. In the event, Russian discipline and quality fell short of that of the 42nd, so that they suddenly broke and were gone from sight in the smoke, leaving behind them an unearthly sorrowful wail that made Hector's blood curdle.[18] In self defence he let out a wild Highland screech, taken up by the men around him. Only then did Sir Colin Campbell raise his hat in the air, giving permission to shout. The Highlanders cheered so loudly that it was said to have been heard two miles away, over the reluctantly diminishing noise of battle.[19]

Grounding the butt of his musket on the soft turf, Hector pushed up his feathered bonnet and thoughfully mopped his brow. Now began a slow mental reversal until he could regard himself from without as though he had been merely a dazed and puzzled onlooker. He felt full of self-satisfaction . . . it was over at last . . . he had passed the supreme trial. Hector turned to the man on his right towards whom he felt friendliness and inestimable good will. Mopping his face with his coat-sleeve, the man laughed:

"Yon Roossians maun ken little o' the Forty Twa'!"

Hector nodded hearty agreement. Then the Regiment was called to order, ranks were dressed and, finally, they were allowed to "stand-easy". Almost at once, Alex MacDonald appeared in front of Hector.

"I canna find Jamie . . . he's not with the Regiment!"

Chapter 6

Except for occasional bursts of cheering and odd shots as though men were reluctant to let the fighting finish, the noises of battle had ceased. But no silence followed. Above the battlefield rose a moaning like a million bees buzzing, made up of groans, curses, choking sobs, death-rattles and the swishing sound made by disabled men painfully and laboriously dragging themselves through the grass.

For the rest of the day and into early evening, the five MacDonald brothers searched the battlefield for Jamie. They picked their way through a vast jumble-sale of death—a litter of broken drums, abandoned muskets, shakos, helmets, forage caps, bitten cartridge-cases, split haversacks with their sparse rations trampled into a bloody slush, cast-off shoes and gaiters, treasured letters defiled with blood and dirt. The wounded, dead and dying of both sides littered the slopes in shapeless mounds, lying in the usual mingling of battle casualties so that scarlet-coated British infantrymen and green-jacketed riflemen lay beside Russian infantry in grey, while young officers and veteran sergeants shared the same blood-soaked patch of earth. The area around the redoubt was carpeted with the bodies of men and horses; with clothing, cartridge-boxes, canteens, muskets, bayonets, cannonballs and barrels of gunpowder. Caissons and limbers stood where their horses had been killed, leaving them lying on the pole. In the redoubt itself, the casualties lay thickly strewn and many men who were only wounded had been suffocated to death by the weight of the shattered bodies lying upon them.

Together with many other men similarly seeking comrades, the MacDonalds moved slowly across the slopes. Bandsmen, handfuls of buglers and drummer boys acting as medical orderlies, worked without the slightest medical knowledge or equipment and with only the roughest capacity for sympathy. Apart from a drink of water, there was nothing they could do to relieve the pain of the wounded. Wondering how long it would be before they were picked up, most men lay quietly in fortitude—it was merciful that they did not know it would be at least two days.

Bowed down by an overpowering lassitude and depression, Hector found the task almost beyond him. The pain and aching from his rapidly stiffening shoulder added to his mood. He was horrified at the ghostly similarity to actual battle he could see on all sides, as though the action had suddenly stopped, freezing the combatants in postures of mutual belligerence. Some had met their death where they dropped for shelter behind small hummocks or rocks. Sightless, glassy eyes peering down musket barrels gripped by hands convulsed in death. Twisting leaves and grass in their agonies, some had buried their faces in the loose soil and filled their mouths with earth. The low monotonous mumbling, rising and falling, filled Hector's ears so that he shook his head to rid himself of the sound. On all sides he could hear voices that spoke to no one yet addressed everyone, that said nothing yet said everything.

"Water, water, please! For Gawd's sake, bring me water!"

"Ah . . . aaaagh . . . me leg . . . it's hurtin' me!"

"Help me! Can't anyone hear me? Take this man off me! He's dead! Take him off me!"

Instrument cases slung across their shoulders and still wearing full-dress uniforms, surgeons went from man to man.

"Here, Sir! For pity's sake, come here, Sir!"

"Thank'ee, Sir. I can walk if yer'll help me!"

"Sir, that Russkie over there is mighty bad . . . he's bin spittin' blood over me fer this past hour!"

"Have we licked 'em sir? We have? Good! I'm not hurt bad but I don't seem to be able to move my legs, sir."

It was now after five o'clock, the shadows were beginning to lengthen over the open grassland and the high hills were turning black against a sultry purple sunset. Hector and Charlie, their faces blackened by burnt powder and with nigger-minstrel-like circles around their mouths from biting cartridges, had wandered out to the left to the smouldering remains of the village that had burned during the action. Rows of wounded men lay against the charred and smoking buildings. Inside the shattered houses, the surgeons were at work on the bare ground or on doors wrenched from barns and cottages, cutting, sawing and probing. After the sun went down and in the darkness that followed, the surgeons did their best to carry on without light, for there were few lamps. In the flickering light of fires, on the cold and open ground, they crouched over suffering bodies whose screams, cries and whimpers of pain made the air full of agony. Hector and Charlie searched among the hundreds lying in the open, finding many others of the 42nd whom they knew but not their brother, and no one seemed to remember seeing him. Peering into every face, they lifted bloody blankets and greatcoats from torn bodies, gently replacing them when they saw that the heavily breathing man was not he whom they sought.

They went inside a house. The dark night sky was visible through the bare timbers of the roof and the partially wrecked end-wall. The stench that lay heavily on the still air sickened them as they looked around at wounded men lying on the ground wrapped in blankets saturated in blood and ordure. A surgeon called to them:

"Come on, come on, lads! Don't stand looking! Give them a drink! Some of them have had nothing since this morning!"

Filling wooden buckets with water from a barrel the brothers picked their way through the prone bodies, gingerly lifting heavy heads to press a cracked cup to parched lips. Appreciating even the smallest kindness, the helpless men thanked them in halting whispers. A host of helpless soldiers lay on blankets, greatcoats, straw or just the bare ground, bloody rags bound around their hands, arms and legs. There were men with limbs sheared clean off by the plunging round-shot; others with indescribably horrible wounds in the face and head. Mutilated, torn and gouged, many were mere boys, others wrinkled-faced veterans of old campaigns finding themselves in such a situation not for the first time. All lay patiently waiting their turn, making little or no fuss save for suppressed groans or a scream of pain as they were lifted from the ground. Examinations were brief and perfunctory—if they had torn intestines or some similar mortal wound, there was no hope for them and treatment was a waste of precious time, so they were passed over. Amputation without anaesthetic was the only treatment for a badly smashed limb, most surgeons realising, with humility, that they were really competent human butchers or carpenters who, by sheer speed of operation, saved lives by minimising the deadly effects of shock.

Hector could only prevent himself retching or fainting by diligently over-attending to the task of giving water to the wounded. Seeking an orderly, a bearded surgeon called to him:

"Here, you! Come and give me a hand!"

"Me, Sir?"

"Yes, you, come on, make it lively! This man needs attention now—not in your good time!"

Apprehensively, Hector moved to the improvised operating table and gazed down at the man who had just been laid upon it. The pain-wracked face of his brother looked up at him:

"Jamie!"

"D'ye know this man?"

"He's our brother, Sir!"

"Well then, you'll want to help him, won't you?"

Fearfully, Hector's eyes travelled down his brother's body to where his leg ended just below the knee in a bloody tatter of flesh and white bone.

"A roundshot did this," said the surgeon. Methodically he wiped his hands and then his knife on a bloody apron. He looked sideways at Hector:

"Come on, lad. Pull yourself together, ye want to help your brother, don't you? Now, both of you, hold him down while I amputate, no use trying to save that leg, it must come off."

He pulled a flask from his pocket:

"Here, fill the poor devil with rum."

Weakly, Jamie gulped the rum, coughing and retching when the flask was removed from his slack mouth. Averting their eyes Hector and Charlie pinioned their feebly-struggling brother as the surgeon's saw grated its way through Jamie's leg. Jamie shrieked. Shocked, Hector released his grasp.

"Damn you, man! Don't drop him! I hope to God you never have to have any surgery!"

Through chattering teeth, Hector muttered:

"By God, so do I! I'd rather be killed dead!"

Tenderly, they moved Jamie from the table and another pain-wracked body took his place on the bloody boards. They laid their brother on a dirty blanket spread out on the ground, his head on a pair of boots and covered him with a greatcoat stiff with blood. Finding it difficult to leave, they stood helplessly gazing down at him. A bloodcurdling shriek from the man on the table hurried them from the house.

Outside, they stared wordlessly at each other and then turned away to find themselves in front of a heap of feet and legs and arms, beyond were rows of blanket-covered dead bodies. They could hear the sound of pick and shovel as fatigue-men dug shallow graves. A loud, harsh voice shouted:

"No, no! You bleedin' fools! We don't want too many single

graves! Single graves are only for the orficers; other-ranks have one big mass-grave . . . dig a bloody big pit over here!"

They never saw Jamie again. No. 2984 Private James MacDonald was buried in an unknown grave in the Crimea.

Chapter 7

The Army spent the next two days picking up the wounded and burying the dead. The 42nd did their share of the harrowing work, carrying wounded comrades for four agonising miles to the river-mouth, where they were lifted into a boat and taken through the tumbling surf to a ship lying offshore. On the hill, in the vineyards and on the riverbank lay more than a thousand wounded Russians, unattended as British first considerations were naturally for their own men. On the third day after the battle, about 750 Russian survivors were carried down to the river and laid out in rows under the shade of a grove of trees. Even the hardest of the rough and sentimental British soldiers was touched by the tortured plight of their late foes. Oddly embarrassed by tending the men they had been trying to kill a few days before, the soldiers tried to talk to the suffering men, gave them water and food and picked grapes for them, placing them between crusted lips. At first Hector tried hard to conjure up hatred for the men who had brought such suffering to his brother Jamie, but soon he found himself desperately sorry for these quivering, ragged bundles of humanity who were so grateful for even the smallest mercies.[20]

Set to collecting Russian firelocks, knapsacks, bayonets, cartridge-boxes and other equipment that littered the battlefield, the men made a game of adding their load to the huge pile gathering near Lord Raglan's tent until the heap was twenty yards long by ten yards broad.[21] Seeking food or loot, men tore open knapsacks, but few held more than lumps of black bread and hard biscuit, although one lucky man discovered a picnic basket containing six cold chickens and two bottles of champagne. Shawls, parasols and bonnets, together with pearl-handled opera-glasses were found on a specially erected wooden platform, indicating that Russian aristocrats had regarded the battle as a picnic or event worth watching.

The 42nd were elated to hear that the Russians they had routed were the famous 16th Division, formed of the Vladimir, Sousdal, Kanzan and Ouglitz Regiments, the *élite* of the Czar's troops. The old two-sweep British line formation, famous in the Napoleonic Wars, had sent twelve Russian battalions packing! Cordially Lord Raglan, the Commander-in-Chief, shook the hand of Sir Colin Campbell, their Brigade Commander, who was so proud of the men under his command that he asked for the honour of wearing a Highland bonnet throughout the campaign.[22]

On the morning of the 22nd September, a brigade parade was ordered on the battlefield of the Alma. Sir Colin Campbell rode into the square formed by the regiments of the brigade wearing the bonnet that had been made for him. He was greeted with such volumes of spontaneous cheering, repeated continuously and echoing over the bare hills, that British and French troops came across to see what was going on.

Hector was not excused any duties on account of his wound because he had not reported sick. But the movement he had to give it, although painful at first, soon made the shoulder much looser and after three or four days he forgot it. Constantly, their brother Jamie was in their minds; they prayed that he was alive, and not one of the dead dragged by the heels and dropped into a long trench, to be covered with a thin layer of earth. At the first opportunity, the brothers walked to the half-burned village of Boulioúk, but were told that Jamie had been moved out to a boat which would take him back to hospital.

Fortunately, they were not to know that the wounded had been roughly borne down to the beach for six miles on men's shoulders or in rough canvas slings. Unattended since their ordeal on the crude operating table, the wounded were left for hours on the sand, waiting their turn for the boats that carried them out to the tossing transport. Exposed for days to the elements on the shelterless decks, closely packed amid a sickening stench of putrefaction, many men died on the voyage. The survivors were taken ashore to the military hospital that had been established in the old Turkish Army barracks at Scutari. At this time, few men went into the building and came out alive, dying not necessarily of their wounds but more often of diseases contracted when in the hospital. Had they known all this the MacDonald brothers would have rushed down to the sea and torn Jamie away from such inhuman conditions.

Eager to move now that their first battle was over, everyone wondered why the enemy was being given the opportunity of organising his defences. There was nothing that anyone could do—it was an age when commanders were held in awe and respect and everyone unquestioningly accepted their sometimes bewildering tactics; the vast majority of officers and men trusted implicitly in the decisions of their generals. The bewhiskered, cocked-hatted generals were followed by rounds of cheering whenever they cantered by amid a concourse of gaily attired staff officers.

On the warm and sunny morning of Saturday, 23rd September, 1854, the Allied armies marched down from the heights above the Alma. The hilly, barren, thistle-covered ground bore so great a resemblance to Scotland that the Highlanders felt homesick. At about three o'clock in the afternoon they came into the lovely valley of the River Katcha where the scent of thyme and lavender filled the air. The soldiers nodded appreciatively at the walled villas and cottages that played hide-and-seek amid patches of shrubs on the ridges. Coming on cultivated areas, the men picked bunches of grapes and filled their pockets with apricots and pears. Now and then they passed large country houses that had been looted by the Cossacks, where beds had been ripped open, books torn apart and furniture reduced to shreds and splinters of timber; bottles, ornaments, clothing, shoes and items of all descriptions had been trampled into a mass of jumble.

In this valley they passed the most cheerful bivouac since landing, and morale was high. Although many of the men were suffering from eating unripe fruit, health was improving. The next day was a Sunday, and church-parades were held before they moved off at noon. After marching about six miles up the far side of the Belbec valley, they arrived on a hill-top to see the town of Sebastopol spread out below them, cut into two by a long stretch of sparkling blue water where many ships lay at anchor. The men crowded forward to gaze down on the dazzling white buildings, the bisecting streets, and the beautiful green copper domes. A star-shaped fort of obvious strength could be seen not far below where they stood, and on the steep cliffs were numerous gun emplacements. The armies bivouacked for the night in this area and during the night were disturbed by Cossacks firing into the camp.

Under arms at five-thirty in the morning of Monday, 25th September, the Allied armies, led by the British, marched off at half-past eight in a south-east direction, towards Mackenzie's Farm.[23] It was an unpleasant march through the thick brushwood of a dense oak forest, causing the troops to be unavoidably thrown into disorder so that Guards marched with Highlanders, and Highlanders with infantry of the line. Stumbling along, hot, bad-tempered and parched with thirst, the soldiers pushed the tangled branches aside, cursing and swearing as they sprung back to smartly sting their faces. Many men were so tired that they sank down and were left behind in the coppices, to be picked up by Cossack patrols. Descending by the Mackenzie Farm road, the advance troops fell in with the baggage of a Russian column, marching out of Sebastopol. There was an outburst of musketry as the two columns passed close to each other. Few realised that, had the Allies marched out two hours earlier, another battle would have taken place.[24]

Crossing the River Chernaya at Traktir, the march continued with Sebastopol on their right. Late that night they encamped on the Fedukine Hills; with the baggage miles behind. It was a miserably cold and hungry night.

Chapter 8

On the morning of the 26th September, 1854, having marched completely round Sebastopol, the army gained possession of the harbour of Balaclava, which became their new base, and the heights above it. Close to the camp of the 1st Division was the small village of Kadikoi, where occurred something the like of which Hector never saw again in his army career. Coming upon the village unexpectedly, apparently in a spirit of fun as they were not drunk and were quite obedient to their officers, the soldiers completely gutted the place within half an hour. Furniture was thrown from windows, shattering as it hit the ground below; drawers were pulled out and boxes smashed open, their contents thrown piecemeal into the streets below. There was no dramatic looting nor did there appear to be any acts carried out in the spirit of revenge; throughout the men laughed uproariously, as though carrying out a great prank.

The Guards and the Highlanders of the 1st Division, with the exception of the 93rd Highlanders who were left behind at Kadikoi, moved up to a camping area before Sebastopol on Monday 3rd October. The officers had been provided with tents but the men still had to lie on the ground without cover, except for those fortunate enough to have found bundles of hay or straw. Each morning the men woke up soaked to the skin as most nights were accompanied by a very heavy dew, but the sun soon got up and became quite powerful. The men remarked that it was a charming climate if you had a house in which to live. No one had taken their clothes off since the 14th of September when they landed

At the first opportunity, Hector and his brothers wandered off and had a good look down into Sebastopol from the heights surrounding the town. It did not seem to be very large, but the defences, still under construction, looked quite formidable.[25] On the south side of Sebastopol harbour, where the town lay, the Allied armies were unable to prevent the Russians entering and leaving from the north and the east as there were just not enough men to surround the whole town. The camp of the 1st

Division was just out of range of the Russian guns, although their batteries frequently fired both roundshot and shell at the outlying picquets. Invariably, their aim was poor and few men were injured.

A few tents came up and were distributed, but most of the men had to lie on the bare ground at night, covered by a greatcoat and a blanket. Cholera continued to carry off officers and men, but in the Highland Brigade it seemed to have burned itself out. Food was poor and scarce, consisting solely of salt pork and biscuits and tea without milk. By the 6th October, there were just about enough tents to cover the men so that everyone could spend a more comfortable night before turning out an hour before daylight to stand-to under arms.

With little else to occupy their minds but the traditional British soldiers' habit of complaining, the Highland regiments found the conduct and attitude of the Guards Brigade, with whom they formed the 1st Division, to be continually provoking. It was a marriage of convenience and not a very happy one at that. On one occasion, when Hector was on sentry duty, his relief (a guardsman) was very late in arriving. Noticing this, the Brigade-Major of the Highland Brigade mentioned the fact to the Brigade-Major of the Guards. The complaint was overheard by a general, who spoke most insolently to the Highland officer. Throughout the tirade, Hector stood stiffly to attention, eyes staring unseeingly to his front, whilst inwardly he boiled with rage. Later, it was rumoured that Sir Colin Campbell, on behalf of his Brigade-Major, had spoken to the Guards general, only to be told that ". . . he would be damned if he would say anything in the way of an apology".

Before daylight on the morning of the 6th October there was a lively skirmish with a patrol of Cossacks just in front of the camp. Bullets came whizzing and screaming through the lines of tents, musket flashes in the pale light of the morning moon illuminated the scene in a picturesque manner. Everyone welcomed the little excitement and hoped for more, feeling that fighting with all its dangers was vastly preferable to the boredom and routine of their daily life. No one could get anything to drink so, in spite of bitter complaining on this score, the men were in good health. The officers knew that the men would make up for it as soon as they got into winter quarters, when old habits would prevail.

Everyone was very irked by the fact that the army had not replied with a single shot or shell to the many hundreds fired at them by the Russians. The men were told that it was intended to have 199 heavy guns in position and that they were to open fire with a grand crash, smashing ships and defence works into one great ruin, preparatory to a general and final assault. Every night the 42nd, together with all the other regiments, supplied working parties who dug approaches and made batteries. The Russians always directed a heavy fire upon these parties, but the 42nd seemed to be remarkably fortunate and lost very few men. Unfortunately, the unceasing roar of guns prevented those who were not working parties from sleeping. Nevertheless, with the weak soldiers weeded out by disease and overwork, everyone seemed to be in very good health. Uniforms were filthy and in rags, but small arms were kept bright and clean, and everyone longed to use them. Writing of the men whom he commanded, the Brigade-Major (Lieutenant-Colonel Anthony Sterling*) said:

> "The poor rank and file are wonderful; with nothing to gain, and all to lose, they submit to the hardest manual labour, and confront the highest perils without a murmur, and even cheerfully; and as they cannot get drink beyond the daily gill of rum, there is no crime."

On the 14th October, Sir Colin Campbell left the Brigade to take command of the troops at Balaclava, consisting of the 93rd Highlanders at Kadikoi, a weak battalion of invalids picked from all the army stationed in Balaclava, two battalions of Marines, some Marine Artillery and several thousand Turks. With this oddly assorted command, Sir Colin Campbell was expected to defend and hold the port of Balaclava. The 42nd and the 79th remained in their bivouac area in front of Sebastopol.

All the English guns were in position by the morning of the 17th October. With one great ear-splitting crash they opened fire, to pound away, causing continuous echoes and reverberations. This battering against Sebastopol continued without intermission but did not seem to have the desired effect. The Russian town was a great arsenal filled with guns and stores and no sooner was a gun dismounted than the Russians were able to bring up another and replace it. From their position on the heights, the Highlanders grimly noted the small effect of the artillery fire, realising that when the ammunition came to an

*_The Story of the Highland Brigade in the Crimea_ by Anthony Sterling (1897).

end they would probably be launched against the place and asked to storm it, with great loss of life. Rumours abounded; it was said that some Russian officers who had deserted had told of the suffering of the inhabitants, the burning of their hospital and town and the killing of Korniloff, the town Governor, on the second day of the bombardment.[26] It was said that galley-slaves worked at the guns and that women were forced to assist in digging entrenchments. The British approaches got nearer and it seemed that something would soon have to happen. If Menschikoff, the Russian commander, knew his business, he would certainly venture out and attack the small besieging force.

Apparently Menschikoff had the same thoughts, for at seven o'clock on the morning of the 25th October an enemy force, consisting of eighteen or nineteen battalions of infantry with thirty to forty guns and a large body of cavalry, attacked the defensive redoubts occupied by Turkish infantry and artillery. Beaten from their defences, the Turks fled across the plain and the Russians pushed on their cavalry and guns, detaching a large body of cavalry to attack the 93rd Highlanders, drawn up in double rank, who were the last line of defence before the harbour at Balaclava. Had the 93rd, who were under the immediate command of Sir Colin Campbell, been broken there was nothing to hinder the cavalry from galloping through the flying Turks and destroying all the stores in Balaclava. Finding that roundshot and shell were causing casualties amongst his Highlanders, Sir Colin retired them a few paces behind the crest of the hill on which they were positioned. As soon as the cavalry began to charge, he advanced the Highlanders to the crest again and opened fire so steadily that the cavalry were driven off. They swept off to their left, trying to get round the right flank of the Highlanders and cut in on the fleeing Turks. But Sir Colin wheeled up the Grenadier Company to its right, and peppered them again, sending them flying back in near-rout.[27]

The rest of the Russian cavalry were driven off by the English Heavy Cavalry Brigade, who charged a Russian mass five times their own number and beat them in splendid style. Then the Light Cavalry Brigade were, due to a mistake in the copying of an order, ordered to charge a battery of guns at the end of a long valley. Later, it was learned that the cavalry commander, Lord Lucan, and Lord Cardigan, the commander of the Light Brigade, objected, but on the insistence of Captain

Nolan, the staff officer who brought the order, the Light Brigade charged. They galloped right into the battery and killed the gunners, but were unable to take the guns away; finding themselves under a heavy cross-fire of artillery and surrounded by superior numbers of cavalry, they cut their way back with frightful losses.[28] There the affair ended for the day, and was later known as the Battle of Balaclava.

The 93rd remained in the position they had held until dark, and then retired into Battery No. 4, 500 yards to their rear. The 42nd and the 79th Regiments were marched up to the position at nightfall, to be posted on the heights to the right of the 93rd. No one was very happy about the position in which they had been placed, conscious that if it was decided to defend Balaclava, they would have to stand and die—in fact, that was exactly what Sir Colin Campbell had told the 93rd, and everyone knew he meant what he said.

It was a most responsible position for such a small force, consisting of 1,200 Marines, three Highland regiments and a body of French on their left, with a number of dispirited Turks who were worse than useless. Conscious of their small numbers, Sir Colin's force expected to be attacked at any time, and were therefore continually under arms and on the lookout. Hector and his comrades found life to be one perpetual picquet, which was very wearing under the conditions. To add to their discomforts, it began to freeze each night.

Morning broke on the 5th November with rain and fog, through which the light of day struggled to assert itself. The conditions were ideal for the stealthy approach of an attacking force, so that Sir Colin Campbell's men protecting Balaclava were doubly alert. Suddenly, at about 6 a.m., a spatter of musketry fire was heard from their right, in the direction of Inkerman. The muffled sound of firing increased in intensity until it became evident that a large scale Russian attack was taking place on the English right wing. With hardly any let-up, the sound of musketry and cannon fire continued to roar throughout the morning until eleven o'clock. Throughout this period the force guarding the Balaclava lines were on the alert; the Russians had sent in several feint attacks on other parts of the English and French lines.

Catching the English completely by surprise, the grey-coated Russians had emerged from the mist along the narrow defile from the Inkerman bridge, where the old coast road climbed the heights and which the English had protected by a few half-manned field works. A success on this English right wing would have given the Russians an immense advantage—occupying the heights on both sides of the ravine they could have brought their offensive army into immediate contact with the garrison of Sebastopol, employed their superior numbers of cavalry against the Allies and forced them to abandon the siege of the eastern part of the town. They sent out some 35,000 infantry and 134 guns against an English force which never totalled more than 13,000 men. Companies and battalions were sent piecemeal into the battle, which became a wild hand-to-hand conflict amongst the brush-clad slopes of the area. After initial gains through surprise, the Russians were finally beaten back into Sebastopol when French reinforcements arrived half-way through the morning. Their losses were very heavy, said to be about 12,000 men, whilst the English lost 2,622 men and the French 1,726.[29]

Denied even the dangerous distractions of battle, the Highland Brigade soldiered on, lacking any pretensions to comfort or even decency. Eating dirt, sleeping in dirt and living dirtily, they were now presented with the roughest and rudest side of war. In a perpetual state of tiredness through being on the watch by night and day, half the men were constantly behind the parapets while the other half lay in inches of mud under the scant protection of tattered tents, fully accoutred and with their loaded muskets by their side. Nevertheless, even under these conditions men retained characteristic traits and a sense of rough humour, tinged with the macabre. The 42nd and the 79th Highlanders were posted on some hills a mile to the right of Sir Colin Campbell's headquarters. They were ordered to dig breastworks in their front to cover the men from enemy fire and enabling them to fight with the advantage of cover. At the end of the day, when their work was inspected they were taken to task because the ditch was too shallow and the parapet not high enough. Spreading their hands wide, the men blandly replied:

"If we made it so, we could not get over it to attack the Russians, could we sir?"*

A continual watch was kept with spy glasses from Battery No. 4, from the camp of the 42nd and from the Marine Heights. Every movement of the enemy was observed, noted down and daily reports sent up to headquarters. During the dark gloomy

**The Story of the Highland Brigade in the Crimea* by Anthony Sterling p. 117.

nights, up to their ankles in mud, the sentries watched the enemy's fires that flickered in the darkness to their front. There was enough to eat now, although the food was coarse, but there was a growing need for firewood, both for warmth and for cooking.

In such conditions of cold, wet and discomfort, Hector MacDonald was surprised to find himself feeling so healthy and fit. One day Ian came up to Hector and, after regarding him for a few seconds, said:

"Have you any idea what you look like?"

Hector shook his head:

"No . . . I haven't seen a looking glass since we landed in this damned country."

With a flourish, Ian produced from his pocket a sliver of mirror:

"I found this in a ruined house . . . have a look at yourself."

Taking the piece of looking glass, Hector gazed deeply into it. Staring back at him was a brown and healthy face framed by a long and untidy beard. His eyes did not look as he remembered them—a more discerning man might have said that they had narrowed through cynicism and hardened through hardship.

Constantly grumbling and complaining, the men did their duty and put up with the conditions. Anthony Sterling, the Highland Brigade-Major, wrote of them:

> "If ever men did a fair turn of work, these soldiers have done one, the real wonder is that any of them are alive. The Government at home are giving them a new suit of clothing and many extras gratis. This is wise; a small unexpected gratification acts powerfully on these poor fellows."*

Not everyone was prepared to put up with the conditions' however; occasionally the men would be infuriated to hear that a certain officer had applied for a Medical Board—in other words, he was going home. The privates could not go home, they never went home except when really sick or when their regiment went home. So why should the officers who chose to pay their passage get leave or a home posting? The men reasoned that it was only fair that the officers should stick the mud, accepting the discomforts and hardships as much as the physical danger which provided the only spice to life.

*Ibid, p. 129.

Chapter 9

It had long been obvious to everyone, down to the youngest drummer boy, that the arrangements for taking the British Army into this war had been completely chaotic. Without baggage or transport, the army was deposited on the shores of the Crimea for a stay that would almost certainly include a Russian winter. Under the pretext of conveying more soldiers in the ships, thousands of animals had been left behind at Varna to die from neglect. Once ashore, the army had been sacrificed in a foolish and reckless manner through lack of materials to keep them efficient. On the other hand, the French had noticeably come complete and ready for war and had been improving their organisation ever since. In mid-December, there were nearly 4,000 sick lying in the mud before Sebastopol, waiting to be brought down to Balaclava on ambulance mules kindly provided by the French. The whole affair seemed almost unbelievable to Hector when he considered that the army belonged not only to the richest country in the world but to the country richest in horses and ships.

Even simple needs like firewood had been neglected. Although there had been only a little snow and sleet, Christmas was near and fires would have been most agreeable, but firewood had to be reserved for cooking.

In mid-December, rain began to pour down without mercy upon the unprepared British Army. Unable to move by day or by night because of heavy enemy fire, the wretched men in front of Sebastopol remained in their waterlogged trenches. In the lines before Balaclava, the Highland Brigade were rather better off by being out of range and without so many men on duty in the trenches. Nevertheless, with nothing to amuse them nor to take their minds off the hardships around them, their life was very monotonous.

On the 21st December, the shortest day of the year, there came an almost miraculous break in both weather and monotony. The rain stopped and bright sunshine with a warm easterly wind dried up the ground so that everyone felt happier.

A parade was called and the men were told that they were to make an armed reconnaissance, or as the French cavalry who accompanied them called it, a *promenade-militaire*. The 42nd, a wing of the Rifle Brigade and some French Zouaves went along the mountains on the right while the French cavalry patrolled the plains, passing shattered villages and houses dotted among poplar-trees. On the hills above they could see Russian troops and Cossacks, scarcely out of cannon-shot, but kept off by the skirmish-line. On reaching the farthest point to which they were ordered, they halted and stood staring at the enemy. Then, while the French cavalry in the plain had a slight skirmish with some Cossacks, a group of young British cavalry officers, who had accompanied the party of their own free will, decided to ride out in front of the skirmishers and look for spoils in some Russian huts. All they found were some lances, a water jug and some dirty combs and brushes. Grey-coated Russian infantrymen crept quietly down among the poplars and opened fire, sending one of them crashing to the ground as his horse was shot. They all turned and galloped back as fast as they could, with the dismounted man bringing up the rear on foot. Everyone laughed heartily and then, without seeing any further action, the force turned and retired to the entrenchments.

Constantly standing ankle-deep in water in the trenches before Sebastopol, and with no overhead shelter, the troops were going sick in increasing numbers. A private soldier of the Light Division told Hector that on the previous night, with the thermometer at 20°F, he had been twelve hours in the trenches. Coming off duty at daylight and without time to get breakfast, he had been sent back seven miles, leading the ration-horses. At Balaclava, where Hector had talked to him, the horses were loaded up with his company's rations and now he had to lead them back. It would be dark before he reached the Light Division camp and, after a night on the cold ground, he would have to take his turn of trench-duty in the morning. Without realising that only men of the hardiest constitution could stand it, and that all the weak were already dead or dying, Hector marvelled at how well the man looked.

There was no fuel, all the roots and brushwood had been exhausted and the entitlement of charcoal could not be drawn because the regiments in the trenches were unable to spare the men to bring it the six or seven miles from Balaclava. Unable to dry their stockings or boots, the men in the trenches had frost-bitten toes, swollen feet and chilblains; if a man took his boots off they froze and he could not get them on again. Some men carried on with their duty, some preferred to go into the trenches without boots or cut away the heels to get them on. One company had gone into the trenches a mere fourteen men strong—all the rest were dead, sick and broken; another company of forty-five men carried nineteen of their number out next morning, nine of whom died. None of the fine warm clothes said to have been sent out had yet reached the men and it was not uncommon to see kilted Highlanders crying with the pain of their frozen knees.

Lieutenant-Colonel Anthony Sterling wrote of these men:

> "The fine part of this war is the British private: those who have gone through this business should have ample provision for life at the national cost—a quart of turtle and a bottle of champagne per man. It will be a clear gain for the country. They will really get a shilling or thereabouts per diem, when incapacitated by age or wounds, and the Crimean medal. What we have a right to admire in war is a display of very admirable qualities called out by it in poor, uneducated, but brave men, who have nothing to gain except, perhaps, the approbation of the company they belong to, and of their own convictional conscience, or that thing which we cannot shake off, which is so variable in its quality that the same might belong to an angel or a demon at different moments. You know how I have praised these poor peasants all along; yet they have wonderful vices—drunkenness, lying, thieving. Still they are—humanity; enduring and daring all things for a principle, many of them I verily do believe."

On the 14th November, 1854, a hurricane added to the unhappy plight of the besieging army. The weather had been rainy and windy for two or three days previously, so that the ground was a swamp of deep mud. It was about seven o'clock in the morning and the Highlanders were lining up for their morning dose of cocoa and rum. Suddenly, as though a giant hand had stirred the air, violent gusts of howling wind and countless spears of heavy rain burst upon them. Almost at once, all the tents fell down; in some the poles were broken and in others the pegs had drawn. A crazy mixture of articles became grotesquely airborne—Highland bonnets, shoes, chairs, bits of wood and innumerable sheets of paper. Some of the men flung themselves on to their fallen tents and grappled with the clinging wet canvas in their efforts to prevent the canvas from being completely blown away.

Later, they heard that the army before Sebastopol had suffered far more than they had, their tents being more vulnerable because the rocky ground did not securely hold the poles or pegs. For some days previously the shipping had not been able to get into Balaclava harbour so that the vessels were anchored in deep water with cliffs close upon them. Many were lost, as were immense amounts of stores and about 400 seamen.

Now followed incessant storms of rain and wind. The mud and marl soil on which the Highland Brigade were encamped covered every man from head to foot, the glutinous mixture made their kilts heavy and plastered them to the body, so that every movement of the legs was painful as the mud abrasively lacerated the insides of the men's thighs.

In such conditions it was not surprising that sickness from exposure increased daily. Towards the end of November, Charlie MacDonald began to perform his duties with obvious difficulty showing clear signs of illness. Continually racked by a barking dry cough, he alarmed his brothers by being burned-up with a fever that made him loosen his clothing when other men huddled down into theirs to escape the rain and biting wind. For more than a week, Charlie stubbornly struggled to carry on until, on the morning of the 6th December, he was unable to rise from his blankets when the men were roused for the pre-dawn stand-to. His cough was weaker, being replaced by the frequent need to clear his mouth of frothy, sometimes blood-streaked sputum. Removed to the Regimental Hospital at Balaclava, No. 3139 Private Charles MacDonald died of broncho-pneumonia on the 7th December, 1854.

During the night 6th/7th December, the Russians in their front decamped, taking with them all their guns and stores and leaving some Cossack picquets to burn their huts. Nothing now remained of the Russians on the left bank of the Chernaya except a few Cossacks in Kamar. Perhaps they considered the English position too strong and too well-defended to be attacked or perhaps they were concentrating their force for a general attack on the front—whatever their reasons, they had gone.

It seemed savagely ironical to the MacDonalds that conditions should ease at almost exactly the same moment as their brother Charlie had died. To add to their bitterness, the weather cleared and the 7th December was as fine a day as one could wish to see. Rumours were coming in on all sides that the force were to be moved nearer Sebastopol so that all their labours in defences and making huts would be for other people's use.

Christmas came and went like any other day, bringing with it two sharp frosts but some fine bright sunshine. On the last day of the year, the snow began to fall and soon covered everything with a white blanket, while the sky told of more to come. There was a grave lack of transport to carry up supplies to the soldiers before Sebastopol. On the 4th January, with the thermometer at freezing point and the snow eighteen inches deep, the men of the Highland Brigade were pressed into service as baggage mules. Bags of biscuits weighing 112 pounds had to be carried on sticks between two men through snow and mud for four miles, with a relief of two more men. Thankfully, this exhausting business only lasted for a day or two—the increasingly bad weather made the biscuits so wet that the fatigue was called off.

Chapter 10

At this stage of the war, it was perhaps a good thing that only Lord Raglan and his higher officers knew that the army, constantly being weakened through sickness, numbered no more than 16,000. After a nightmare period in the dreaded hospital at Scutari, many who did not die would never be fit to join again, and of those who did rejoin, many would relapse as soon as the causes that made them sick began to act again.

Each morning, when daylight came, thousands of men had nothing to cook with so that raw meat, biscuit and rum was all they could get. The cavalry as a fighting force had vanished and it was likely there would not be a horse left standing by spring. Having no trench or night duty, the troopers themselves were not too badly off, and being at Balaclava they could make themselves pretty comfortable. By mid-January it was rumoured that Balaclava was full of stores sent out from England for the men, but as they could not be carried up to the soldiers who needed them, they were of no value and many would be thrown away. Those men who managed to get hold of fur clothing soon found that it became matted with mud, filled with vermin and a perfect nuisance. For some reason the ammunition boots sent out from England, although strong and beautifully made, were too small, so that the largest size sent ought to have been the smallest and very few men could get them on their feet.

The valley of Balaclava was entirely stripped, there was not a tree or a bush or an inhabitant remaining. Almost all the cottages, which had looked so white and smiling among the vineyards when they arrived, were down, and even the vine roots had been dug up for use as firewood.

Many of the sick men of the 42nd who had been suffering from fever were found on examination to have ulceration of the intestines. Hardly anything but salt meat was issued and many of the men could eat it no longer. The French army were said to have fresh meat every other day, together with dried preserved vegetables that came in small hard cakes; these were soaked in warm water until the vegetable swelled and became themselves again and could be cooked in the normal manner.

The days were beautiful and the sun shone warmly after sharp frosts at night. But the mud was indescribably horrible—frozen hard on top in the morning, by 10 o'clock it was melted into a gluey slush and everyone had to wade about for the rest of the day.

Some rare amusement was caused when the story got about at the end of January that a man had been sent out from England to build a light railway from Balaclava. The first thing he had said was that he wanted labour and horses—500 men and countless horses! It caused the best laughter for days as the men knew that if they had had labour they could have made a good road, and if they had had horses they could have sent up their stores without the railway. Anyway, everyone knew that there were not going to be any locomotives, only 1½-ton waggons which had to be drawn along a tram road by miserable undersized ponies. Some navvies arrived with spades and sledge hammers and began to make the foundation for the railway, although everyone felt that a good Macadamised road would have been far more sensible. One of the navvies transgressed in some way that put him into the power of the Provost-Marshal, who ordered him to be flogged. It was said that he roared like a bull but afterwards had the heart to say that he had been flogged for the honour of his country! These men, on far higher rates of pay than the soldiers, grumbled constantly at salt provisions, so different from the beef steaks and porter they were used to at home.[30]

In early February, frost set in again so that it was nearly as cold as before, but there was not so much snow. Quantities of boxes full of clothing arrived for the use of the Highland Brigade, together with all sorts of odds and ends such as the men had never been used to. There were oat-cakes and currant buns to eat, and bottles of whisky, and everyone was so overloaded with warm articles of clothing that it became a problem to know what to do with them if they ever had to move. But warmly clothed, and providing they could keep dry, the men's sufferings were very greatly reduced.

Rumours, the soldiers' very life blood, circulated constantly, as they had done in every campaign since Hannibal and Alexander. One that strongly concerned the Highlanders reported that Lord Raglan was to be recalled to England and that Sir Colin Campbell was to become Commander-in-Chief. Although they knew that Sir Colin would make an excellent Commander, not a Highlander wished to see him go. As for Campbell himself, he heard the rumours and reflected how much happier he would be to command a Highland Division built up from the present Highland Brigade.

Everyone was grumbling at the numbers of guards and duties that they had to do, conscious that although the laid-down establishment of the regiment was over 800, they would do well to bring 500 into the field. There were so many absentees from the Highland Brigade that, at this stage, there was reckoned to be nearly one battalion out of the three absent at a time. First-class fighting men were taken to be clerks, orderlies and officers' servants—the Commissary of the Highland Brigade had seven and all the officers had one each, whilst the mounted officers on the Staff had two soldier servants. Thirty more men were accounted for by the band and pioneers, whilst regimental hospital orderlies and others employed by the Quartermaster brought up the absentees in each regiment to about sixty men. Then there were those commandeered by Miss Florence Nightingale, who kept all the Highlanders when they were discharged from hospital and made nurses of them. It was believed that at one stage she had about 300 men of the Highland Brigade thus employed. The men felt very strongly about this, believing that there ought to be men enlisted as nurses and that soldiers should be left to fight.[31]

It was decided on the 19th February that a French force of about 18,000 men, together with about 1,800 British soldiers should make an armed reconnaissance in the hope of surprising the Russian troops at Chorguna, a small village on a line with Battery No. 4 and Canrobert's Hill, only three miles farther off. At first it was proposed to start off at one o'clock in the morning, then this was changed to half-past two. All arrangements were made during the evening, but at eleven o'clock, from a moonless sky, the rain began to fall. At midnight the wind changed to the north and it blew hard with a drifting snow, and it was impossible to see ten yards. The British force consisted of the 42nd, the 71st, the 79th and the 93rd with guns and about 300 cavalry. The three first-named regiments were to march so as to join the 93rd, the guns and the cavalry under Canrobert's Hill, and then all were to pass on, leaving that hill on their left. The whole force started out in the middle of the night so as to be in position above Chorunga at half-past five in the morning. Soon after daylight on the following day, a despatch rider from Lord Raglan reached the British camp with an order cancelling the expedition, as the weather was so bad that the French force would not start. The messenger had got lost during the night and had been exhaustedly riding round in circles until daylight.

This meant that the small British force were out alone, supposing themselves to be supported by 18,000 French troops. Luckily, when they reached Chorguna they found very few Russians so that nothing was done and no larger force was present to overpower them. But everyone was very cold and exhausted and glad to get back; and although the march was made in very severe and difficult circumstances and in bad weather, they suffered no casualties.

Early in March, the Highland Brigade were ordered to carry up shot to the artillery engaged in the siege of Sebastopol. The small railway line that had been built ran right into the Ordnance Wharf at Balaclava; the 32-pounded shot, in sandbags, was placed in waggons and drawn by railway horses to Kadikoi. Here the Highlanders paraded and, approaching the waggons in single file, each picked up a sandbag and shouldered the heavy iron shot. Then began the weary uphill trudge to the batteries. Although the railway saved the fatigue men a good deal of time as well as labour, everyone was worked very hard and, on top of their manual labour, they had to do duty in the trenches on alternate nights. Luckily the weather had become fine, without rain or extreme cold.

About the middle of March, a female nurse turned up in the camp and attached herself to the hospital of the 42nd. She was one of Miss Nightingale's ladies, but she had quarrelled with her patron and refused to acknowledge her authority. It was said that an official letter on the subject had been written to Lord Raglan, and the men were highly amused at the thought of a field general court-martial composed entirely of nurses![32]

Great indignation was aroused in the ranks of the Highland Brigade when they heard of a newspaper report circulating in England which attributed the superior health of the Highland Brigade to that of the Guards to the fact that the Guards had been overworked in the trenches while the Highland Brigade was doing nothing at Balaclava. Sick to death of the continual preference for the Guards over the Line Regiments and conscious that between the Guards and the Line there was a difference of just two inches and a penny, the men were highly incensed. They knew that in the first place the Guards had completely broken down in Bulgaria so that they could not carry their packs and, as a result, the Highland Brigade were not allowed to carry theirs. This was a piece of folly which every man knew was at the bottom of much of the early inconvenience suffered afterwards in the Crimea. If the men had not been allowed to go without their packs on the march to Varna then no one would have thought of landing them in the Crimea without packs. During the worst part of the bad weather, the Highlanders had worked quite as hard as any of the other men at the siege. They had dug three and a half miles of trenches, had slept every night on their arms with half of their numbers in the trenches throughout the dreadful weather. In addition, they had carried shot, shell, bread and charcoal, to the depot at Lord Raglan's headquarters for the rest of the army, and had then to carry their own rations.

One morning, while he was going about his duties, Hector MacDonald was approached by two old ladies accompanied by a young child. They showed him a spoon and asked him if he would buy it so that they could buy food; apparently it was the last possession that they had to sell. Calling some of the men over, Hector soon gathered together some food and even a few sweetmeats for the child. He felt depressed for the rest of the day. On the one hand he would try and convince himself that if the unfortunate women had stayed quietly in their houses they would not have been molested, on the other hand he knew his comrades, when in drink, did many things of which they were afterwards ashamed.

Early in May, a plan was made for a force to land at Kamish, nine or ten miles south of Kertsch, to take the Russian batteries in reverse and to push on to Yenikale. The force, under General Brown, was to consist of 3,000 British troops and 7,000 French with some artillery and cavalry. Included in the British force were the 42nd, the 21st, the 93rd and a wing of the Rifles. On the 3rd May, the force went aboard the transports but, to everyone's astonishment, they returned to Balaclava on the 6th May, having been recalled by telegraphic messages from Paris and London just as they were about to land. The bitter complaints and annoyance were directed towards the French General Canrobert who had recalled the expedition, but later it was understood that the French Emperor had recommended as a general maxim to Canrobert that he should not separate his forces, and Canrobert had misunderstandingly thought that he meant the expedition to be recalled.

A couple of weeks later, the expedition again set off. It was reported that Sir Colin Campbell was sadly put out at the Highland Brigade being lent to Brown for the Kertsch Expedition, and that Campbell had said quietly to Brown "I am giving you good troops."

Brown, known as a tough soldier with a harsh tongue, had shot back:

"I would have soon had my own!"[33]

Brown was Campbell's superior officer, and the Highland Brigade commander had asked to go to Kertsch and serve under Brown but Lord Raglan had made the excuse that he could not leave the Balaclava position in the charge of an inexperienced officer.

On the 1st June another 3,000 troops were embarked to join the fresh expedition, 1,000 of them were British. The expedition was a complete success, meeting with no opposition and with no casualties, except for a soldier of the 42nd killed by the accidental discharge of a French soldier's musket, as he used the butt to batter down a door in search of loot. It was supposed that the non-resistance of the Russians arose from their not expecting that the allies could spare any troops from the siege for such an enterprise. Russell, *The Times* correspondent, smuggled himself aboard one of the ships on the Kertsch Expedition, but Sir George Brown refused to let him land.[34]

On the 20th May, three days before the Kertsch Expedition left, the 42nd made a promenade from their heights with a battalion of Turkish riflemen and three companies of Marines. They encountered only a few Cossacks, and everyone enjoyed the leisurely excursion, carried out in ideal weather and over country as beautiful as anything that the men could remember. The whole plain was a mass of flowers—campanulars, larkspurs and many dog-roses.

New allies began to arrive. In the early part of May, the first body of Piedmontese soldiers arrived, 5,000 strong, under General Della Marmora. On account of the weather which had suddenly changed to heavy and continuous rain, they were not landed at once. Then came the Sardinian contingent, a splendid-looking body of about 10,000 men with their own ambulances, forage-carts, commissariat officers and other military equipment. Reserving their judgement, the British troops noted their neat and compact cavalry mounted on good, strong horses and their well-disciplined infantry. Dressed in green, with hats decorated by large bunches of green feathers and worn at a jaunty angle, the Sardinian rifle regiments marched off at a terrific pace, almost at a trot, that aroused lusty cheers and humorous remarks from the watching British soldiers.

Miss Nightingale came to Balaclava in May. An immediate result of her arrival was the increased numbers of orderlies taken out of the ranks to be employed in the hospitals.[35] For some reason it always seemed to be the finest men who were taken for this duty and, as it was forbidden to relieve them, they were compelled to remain until they became sick, when their regiment was ordered to send others to replace them. Big grenadiers from the Brigade of Guards were appropriated by Miss Nightingale to be used as permanent nurses. These men, the biggest in the army, were permanently on board the six steamers that went backwards and forwards between Balaclava and Scutari. Occasionally they caught the fever and on the ship's return to Balaclava had to be replaced. Then there were the numerous soldiers employed in the hospitals at Balaclava, Scutari, Abydos and Smyrna, and the attendants in the regimental hospitals. The system was much hated as it meant that those men remaining with their units had to do extra duties and additional spells in the trenches.

Even the most unintelligent soldier in the ranks believed that a unit should be formed specially for the purpose of looking after the sick and wounded. The men in every regiment who could least bear the fatigue of marching or the exposure to cold and wet should be weeded out and formed into a regiment of nurses under medical officers and military officers of low medical category. The general opinion of the Highland Brigade was that philanthropy was a plaything to the ladies and that they were making ducks and drakes with splendid soldiers.

Returning from Kertsch, the Highland Brigade formed their Division, the 1st, in readiness to take part in a large scale Anglo-French attack on Sebastopol. Eventually the Division was held in reserve in rear of the twenty-one-gun battery on Frenchman's Hill. The attack was a costly failure, marked by errors that doomed it from the start. The French advanced the time of attack by two hours without informing Lord Raglan, then a French general mistook a mortar-shell for the signal-rocket and sent his column forward thirty minutes too early, and the British artillery ceased firing as soon as the storming columns left the trenches, thus allowing the Russian defenders to pour uninterrupted fire into the attackers. From their position the

Highlanders could see the French attack on the Malakoff Tower and the ground thickly strewn with corpses when they retired. Later they learned that the French had lost 6,000 men, including two generals.

The 42nd were among the 2,000 men of the 1st Division who took over the trenches from the survivors of this abortive attack. They spent twenty-four hours there before being put in the Quarries. The Highlanders were thoughtful and silent when told by the men who had returned that the inferno of fire prevented anyone from getting farther than the abattis on the glacis of the enemy works. Reminded that he had three brothers serving with him, Hector felt chills run up his spine as he saw exhausted men, besmeared with dirt, powder and blood, enquire anxiously for comrades "Have you seen Tom Crisp . . . did Sergeant Jones get back . . . I saw Billy Smart lying in the ditch with his leg shot off . . . never mind, we'll warm them up next time!"[36]

The 1st Division remained stationed in the trenches in and about the Quarries, to assist in carrying on the siege. Heavily laden with packs, ammunition and rations, the 42nd marched down the middle ravine where the English and the French trenches joined each other. Before moving off, they had all been told of their different posts in the various *boyaux-de-tranchée*, advance trenches, batteries and saps into which they percolated after moving along the trench leading from the ravine to Gordon's Battery on Frenchman's Hill. To prevent a sortie, the front line of sentries, lying flat on the ground, were placed in position after dark outside the advanced trench. During daytime the enemy fired hails of musketry whenever they saw a head and plagued the troops by continually firing small mortars, called coehorns,[37] pointed nearly perpendicularly so that their bombs dropped vertically down into the trenches. The Russians had also devised a method of firing grape into the air so that it dropped down in an iron hail. In the shadeless, dry and dusty trenches, life by day was a hot and exhausting hell. Being on the northern slope of a gentle declivity, the trenches were exposed to the full heat of the southern sun, shooting its rays into the soldiers' backs so that the men were regularly baked. At night it was more pleasant, and if he could find a corner Hector would lie and gaze at the bright stars directly overhead, whilst his ears were assailed by ceaseless discordant noises. There was the whistling of the shells as they passed overhead, then the report as they burst and the buzz of their cascading fragments. Every now and then the ground shook as a great mortar was discharged from one of the Allied siege batteries. Repeatedly, men had to press themselves against the dusty walls of the narrow trenches as wounded or dead men were carried by on stretchers by their comrades.

A turn in the trenches took place every second or third day, commencing with a parade at five o'clock in the afternoon and then the men were marched down and posted before setting to work on fatigues such as rebuilding battered earthworks. It was a monotony broken only by the exciting promise of an assault by storm. The 1st Division lost about forty men per week during their normal trench duty, besides a variable number by sickness.

As though fate were adding a piquancy to the dangerous situation, sometimes their own shells burst as they issued from the guns, causing considerable damage to the men who were exposed to the rear, although covered towards the enemy.

One day, during a truce, the Highlanders left their trenches to aid in burying the dead. It was horrible work and Hector was appalled at the shocking wounds and the way in which the corpses had putrefied in the sun. Russian soldiers carried them halfway towards the British trenches where they were taken up by their British comrades and carried back to where the graves had been dug. Hardened as he was to the sight of battle, Hector was still unable to see a field of battle, with the dead still lying about, without horror. Never could he become accustomed to the sight of bodies torn by frightful wounds, with legs and arms shot off; some twisted into strange attitudes, exposed by the derangement of their clothing and swelled up by the sun or blackened by blood. Whenever he had to aid in collecting together bodies for burial in a great ditch he would find himself continually repeating "Here, but for the grace of God, lie I."

One night a body of Russian infantry advanced so stealthily that they were able to leap unopposed into the advanced British trench. The resistance of the English Guards who garrisoned the place was not as good as might have been expected, owing to their being surprised, and the Russians began to pull down the gabions and fill up the parallel. Inspired by their success, they advanced to another parallel, but here they were met by deadly and more sustained volleys from the 42nd, who had been alerted. The Russians fell back in confusion, leaving many dead and wounded on the ground behind them and, followed by the Highlanders who jumped over the breastwork. Hector, after lunging out and bringing to the ground a tall Russian soldier, found himself facing an officer with sword in hand. He's a good-looking devil, thought Hector as they faced each other with bared weapons poised threateningly. Sharply, Hector called out for him to surrender but the officer shook his head and slashed out viciously with his sword. Unable to dodge because of the wall of the trench at his back, Hector half turned and received the weapon through his knapsack. It must have been razor sharp, for it slashed through the pack and its contents and took a large and neat slice of flesh from Hector's ribs, rather like carving the breast of a turkey. For a moment, Hector thought that he was done for but, gathering himself in spite of the searing pain in the area of his ribs, he lunged forward at the officer so that the pointed tip of his long bayonet took the man in the throat under his chin and transfixed him to the earth wall of the trench. Painfully, Hector made his way back through the parallels until he was able to find someone to attend to him. Luckily, he only had two ribs fractured and a very extensive flesh wound; stitched up, it healed cleanly and without trouble in a very short time.

On the 29th June, the whole Allied army were shocked to hear of the death of Lord Raglan. It was known that he had died from illness and it was said that it was the dreaded cholera. Rumours flew on all sides as to his successor. A strong favourite was Sir Colin Campbell, but the command of the army, in the usual uninspiring fashion, dropped into hands of the next senior officer, a General Sir James Simpson. Suffering from gout, it was thought that he would have been very glad not to have had such a charge laid upon him.

Lord Raglan's remains were conveyed to England with every respect. Each regiment sent guards of honour to line the road to Kazatch Bay and Hector MacDonald, on parade with the guard from the 42nd, found it very impressive and moving. The coffin, covered by a British flag on which lay Raglan's cocked-hat and sword, rested on a gun-carriage. The pall bearers, Marshal Pelissier, General Sir James Simpson, General Della Marmora and Omar Pasha, rode on each side. Then followed Raglan's charger with boots reversed in the stirrups; next a large body of staff and other officers of the four armies. British and Sardinian lancers rode in advance, the red and white pennons of the first, and dark blue of the last, dancing in the breeze. The British cavalry looked lusty and rode excellent horses and the Sardinians made a gallant show; their officers had an abundance of silver lace about them, and seemed to ride with pride. The French Horse Artillery, in fur caps and red-braided jackets, were followed by the light and active Chasseurs d'Afrique, in sky-blue jackets and red trousers. Next came Imperial Cuirassiers in their glittering steel helmets and cuirasses, and manes hanging down their backs; but the finest men who passed along seemed to be the British Horse Artillery. Turkish Cavalry in their fezzes and with carbines on their thighs assisted on the occasion, also the Tenth Hussars and the broad-backed Heavy Dragoons, their metal helmets judiciously covered with white cotton against the blazing sun. Last of all, some of the Land Transport, in red jackets with black braid, brought up the rear.

One or two officers who had returned from England were wearing the Crimea medal awarded by the Queen. Typically, the soldiers scorned the decoration, scathingly talking about half a crown's worth of metal and a penny worth of ugly ribbon from a grateful nation.

On Friday the 24th August, the Highland Brigade got a sudden order to march that night down to the Kamara area to support the Piedmontese and Turks against an expected Russian attack. It was rumoured that they were to be attacked in the morning by 60,000 to 80,000 men, including Grenadiers who had just arrived from Poland. Marching at one o'clock on Saturday morning, the Highland Brigade took up a position about Kamara Church before daylight and stood eagerly awaiting the sun and the enemy. After a chilly night, the welcome sun arrived but no enemy showed up, and after waiting for some hours, they marched back to their camp on the plateau, packed up their belongings and tents and moved down again to encamp around Kamara Church. Told to be ready every morning for an attack, the men were pleased to be relieved of the trenches and to spend their days with nothing to do, although, they had to sleep accoutred in order to be ready for the Grenadiers whenever they chose to come. The Highlanders were not at all sure that the enemy would ever attack, as the position was very strong. On the 7th September, they were withdrawn to take part in the great assault on Sebastopol that commenced on Saturday the 8th September.

Chapter 11

The Highland Brigade marched on the morning of the 8th with the instructions to form the second reserve of the 2nd and Light Divisions, who were to assault the Redan. In company with the other regiments of the Brigade, the 42nd deposited their knapsacks and feathered bonnets in their old camp on the plateau and filed into the first parallel of the trenches, just as the French began their attack on the Malakoff. Following the reserves of the assaulting troops, the Highlanders filed along the trenches until they reached the position assigned to them in the third parallel. The entire move forward was made under a very heavy Russian fire which cost the 42nd about seventy casualties. From their new position, the Highlanders could see the French rushing up the salient, apparently unresisted, to swarm up the earthworks and gabions of the formidable Malakoff and disappear from view. Then, after a few moments in which everyone imagined the gallant Zouaves fighting grimly for their lives, a French tricolour was planted on the ramparts and everyone knew that the place was theirs.[38]

A wild outburst of cheering and jubilation arose from everyone in the Allied trenches, having the unfortunate effect of so inspiring the storming party that they could no longer be restrained and before there was time to get the ladders to the front or the Sappers could advance to cut away the abattis, the storming party were over the parapet and rushing forward in a struggling line towards the salient. Advancing with the greatest spirit, the British soldiers rushed forward over 200 yards of rough broken ground and began to cross the abattis under the enemy fire. Men fell on all sides, being tumbled over like ninepins to lie in huddled red heaps that grotesquely coloured the shattered terrain. The survivors reached the twenty-foot-deep ditch that bordered the Redan, and there most of them were stranded because the parties laboriously carrying the heavy scaling ladders had not yet arrived, or had been killed crossing the rough open ground. Now followed a terrible half-hour, when the men in the ditch strove to climb the steep face upwards towards the strong defences of the Redan, whilst others struggled on the parapet above to get down into the ditch. Throughout, a galling and heavy fire both from front and flanks was poured upon them. Men huddled behind rubble and began to return the enemy fire while others, struggling up in inefficient disorder, were unable to press into the works as the men in advance refused to go on, in spite of the frenzied encouragement of their officers.

The attackers were rapidly becoming disorganised and such was the state of their morale that they were unable to persuade themselves to advance, nor would they retreat. They looked frantically around over their shoulders for aid which did not appear to be coming. Behind them, the British trenches were crammed with men—in the first trench was General Codrington in command of the remainder of his Division; behind him was General Markham with his men and behind them Sir Colin Campbell with the Highlanders. Sir Colin had no orders to interfere with the assault, which was under the command of Codrington and Markham. So long as their men remained in the trenches neither the Highlanders nor anyone else could go forward.

Vainly attempting to induce their men to advance, three officers of the 41st Regiment rushed forward together and were shot down as one man by the cross fire of the Russians from behind their strong defences. This proved to be the turning-point of the men's indecision—visibly wavering, they suddenly turned and fled back towards their own lines. The whole living mass on the salient began to reel and sway and men standing up or moving forward were knocked down and trampled upon by the frantic fugitives fleeing over them. All the time, grape shot whistled through the air and the Russians, exultant with success, stood on the tops of their parapets and fired volleys into the backs of the fugitives.

The survivors of the assaulting columns flung themselves desperately down into the crowded trenches, knocking men over as they plummeted among them. Packed together and disorganised, the men in the trenches were filled with shame, rage and fear to such an extent that it was obviously hopeless to attempt to renew the attack with the same troops.[39]

At about 4 o'clock the Highland Brigade and the rest of their Division were ordered to occupy the front line trenches, and the beaten troops were sent back. Sentries had just been posted and the trenches fully occupied when Sir Colin Campbell was summoned to see General Simpson, Lord Raglan's successor, who gave him orders to assault the Redan on the following morning. On being given his orders, Sir Colin Campbell told General Simpson that his men had marched twelve miles and had gone straight into the trenches where they would spend the night, and that they had no rations whatsoever. Helplessly, General Simpson shrugged his shoulders:

"Oh, but the young people about me (apparently he meant his aides-de-camp) are so anxious it should be done!"

Grimly determined to succeed where the English regiments had failed on the previous day, the Highland Brigade prepared itself for the grim struggle that lay before them. The MacDonald brothers agreed to stick together and to give each other all possible assistance in the descent and ascent of the deadly ditch in front of the Redan.

At half-past twelve in the morning of the 9th September, Sergeant Alexander MacDonald stared out from the trench at the threatening black mass of the Redan that loomed against the night sky to their front. Somehow it seemed to be different; there was a silent lifelessness about the position which struck him as odd. He turned to his brother Hector, standing in the trench by his side, with other men of the guard.

"Do you know what? I believe the Russians have gone!"

"Gone? Why should they go . . . they turned us back yesterday!"

"No . . . I think they've gone . . . who is coming out with me to see?"

The ground was marked by pools of blood and the smell was already noisome; swarms of flies were settling on dead and dying; broken muskets, torn clothes, caps, shakos, swords, bayonets, bags of bread, canteens and haversacks were scattered all over the place, mingled with heaps of shot, grape, bits of shell, cartridges, case and cannister, loose powder, papers and cooking tins.

The ditch around the Redan made Hector feel sick. It was piled up with English dead, some of them scorched and blackened from the explosions and others lacerated beyond recognition. Placing a ladder against the steep parapet, the Highlanders climbed stealthily upwards, their flesh cringing at the expected impact of musket balls. Reaching the parapet they looked down into a deserted position. The ground was covered with broken gabions and on all sides dismounted guns, shattered platforms and broken carriages abounded. Nearly every square yard of the place was torn up by roundshot and exploded shell. How any human beings could have existed in such a pandemonium of explosive horrors puzzled the soldiers who looked down in wonder at the place. Standing on the parapet, you looked down on a deck as you would standing on a frigate's hammock nettings, so that assaulting the Redan must have been very much like boarding a frigate from boats.

Nothing was heard but the heavy breathing and groans of the wounded and dying, who, with the dead, were the sole occupants of the massive work.

With the Malakoff captured, Sebastopol became untenable and so, during the night of the 8th and 9th, the Russians began their evacuation. The crashing explosions of their magazines and the blazing of the town, which they set on fire, lit up the night sky in a grim if beautiful spectacle. The Russians made a magnificent retreat, carrying off their whole garrison intact over the bridge, which they removed at daylight, leaving the Allies in quiet possession of the ruins of the town, a vast amount of stores and a large number of ships they had sunk in the harbour. Before leaving the Redan, the Russians dressed the British wounded and, humanely, they did not blow up the main magazine.

As soon as dawn broke on the 9th, the French began to steal from their trenches to the burning town, undeterred by the flames and explosions, by the fire of a lurking enemy or even by the fire of their own guns, which were discharging cannon shot and grape into the suburbs at regular intervals. Before five o'clock in the morning, before the last Russian battalions had marched out of the city, there were numbers of men coming back with loot, and Russian relics were being offered for sale in the camp. Sailors from the batteries were not behindhand in looking for loot and could be seen, staggering under tables, chairs and old pictures, making their way back to the trenches. Several men lost their lives by explosions whilst seeking plunder.

Throughout Sunday, the 9th, there was a lurid glare in the sky and an immense canopy of thick heavy smoke overhung the town. Shells and explosives from burning dumps still exploded with crashing roars, but there was a strange absence of the hitherto ceaseless pattering of musketry, the angry surge of roundshot or the twanging hum of falling pieces of steel. In their place could be heard the creaking of wheels as ambulance waggons rolled along filled with wounded and dying freight.

Piles of dead lay on the ground awaiting burial.

As soon as it was evident that the Russians had evacuated Sebastopol, everyone sought to visit the Malakoff and the Redan, still littered with dead and dying men. A line of English cavalry was posted across the front from the extreme left of the British position to the French right, and stationed in all the ravines and roads to the town and the trenches with orders to keep back all persons except generals and officers and men on duty, and to stop all British soldiers returning with plunder from the town and to take it from them. As it did not stop the French or Turks or Sardinians, this order gave rise to a good deal of grumbling, particularly when a man, after hauling a heavy chair for several miles, was deprived of it by his own sentries. French and English soldiers, together with sailors, many of them drunk, staggered all over the place laden with a strange miscellany of loot—weapons, mirrors, crucifixes, books, clothes, animals such as pigs and parrots, pieces of furniture *et cetera.* All this served to announce the fact that a major city had fallen and, like other captured towns, was being pillaged, in spite of provost-marshals.

Chapter 12

September 20th was the first anniverary of the Battle of the Alma. It also marked the distribution of medals to the soldiers of the Crimea and Sir Colin Campbell read out an order of the day. When he finished, bonnets were hoisted upon bayonets and waved vigorously as round after round of cheering split the air. Hector MacDonald felt more proud than ever before of being a Highlander of the 42nd Regiment of Foot—the Royal Highland Regiment—the Black Watch.

With the dispirited Russian Army massed on the Belbeck, the war was more or less over, although they showed no signs of evacuating the Crimea. They could be seen building huts and preparing for winter, and regularly fired red-hot shot into the ruins of Sebastopol to annoy fatigue parties of British soldiers who were working amid the ruins. So suddenly had the war ended that no plans had been made, nor did anyone appear to have any idea of what to do with the British Army. By the 2nd October orders had still not been received to settle down for the winter and rumour had it that Omar Pasha's Turks were to go to Asia and that the Highland Division were to man the outposts for another winter. Everyone prayed that they would be hutted before the bad weather, realising that to do this in the short time that remained would take all of their energies. The days immediately following the evacuation of Sebastopol had been very bad, with a great deal of cold and rain. A few huts arrived, but these were immediately sent to Kertsch for the 71st. The bitter memories of those who had survived the winter told them that it was quite time to make preparations for the forthcoming bad weather, and only the most optimistic could reckon on more than six weeks of good weather from now on.

It seemed that the frantic longing of the Victorian soldier for active service appeared to have been assuaged and the majority now yearned for peace and quietness, praying that nothing further would be attempted that autumn. The inevitable reaction that followed the end of the fighting made life painfully monotonous. For days on end, the 42nd were employed in cutting fascines to make a road from Balaclava to the camp on the plateau. In common with most other regiments, their replacements were very young and inexperienced, and it would take six months hard training to bring them up to the required standards of the Regiment.

The weather in October 1855 turned out to be very much more changeable than in the previous year; nevertheless, the men continued to be healthy in spite of their drinking vast quantites of all the liquor, both good and bad, on which they could lay their hands. On 8th October some excitement was caused by an order detailing how much, or rather how little, the men were to carry in case of their being called upon to move in light marching order. Of course, this immediately caused a host of rumours that further action was imminent. An expedition of 7,000 French and English soldiers had already embarked for Kinbourn with the object of blocking up the entrance to Nicoalieff but, to their annoyance, the Highlanders had been left out of it. However, there were those who felt that it was a lucky omission as the fort to be attacked was on a tongue of land frozen up in winter. This meant that the garrison would not be able to be reached and the expedition would therefore be exposed to the attack of the Russians, who were better equipped for winter campaigning.

Impelled by visions of the forthcoming winter, everyone was feverishly working to get the huts erected before the bad weather commenced. In the Kamara area, large parties of officers and men prepared the ground, levelling it and making roads, while another party sorted out the huts, classified the pieces and laid them out in bundles for issuing. Country carts, called *arabas*, had been hired together with their Tartar drivers these men, although paid and given rations, were always wandering away and had literally to be caught and kept under guard. Every morning the carts with fatigue parties of a thousand men left the camp for Balaclava, where they were loaded; they then commuted backwards and forwards throughout the day. Each man of the fatigue-parties was given a piece of hut to carry on his shoulders for half the distance to the camp, where they were met by another thousand who brought the loads into Kamara. Working steadily, it was hoped to have all the men hutted by the end of October. Everyone prayed that the rains would keep off, for their present system of transportation would then have to end and the pieces of hut would have to go by the railway up to the front, and then be brought back down the Woronzow Road, a tremendous roundabout journey.

On the 13th October, a sudden order was received to embark the Division and two batteries for Eupatoria, to act on the enemy's lines of communication. The order caused consternation because it made it impossible to have the huts ready for the winter, which would mean a repetition of the cold, mud and misery of last year. On the 15th October, the expedition was postponed because of lack of shipping to carry the 3,700 animals necessary for the baggage and ammunition.

During the middle of the month, the Highland Regiments were raised to heights of indignation and fury by a leading article in *The Times* of the 4th October which implied that Sir Colin Campbell and his Highlanders had been "laid up in lavender all the winter". Everyone who could write rushed to put pen to paper in an indignant rebuttal and there is no doubt that *The Times* must have been inundated with these hastily scrawled and furious letters. One such letter has survived. Written by Lieutenant-Colonel Anthony Sterling, Sir Colin Campbell's Brigade-Major, it is given in Appendix II.

The huts were completed before the bad weather arrived and the Highlanders moved into them in early November. At the same time, winter kits were distributed to the British soldiers. Each man received an excellent tweed coat, lined throughout with rabbit or cat skin, a larger and still warmer sheepskin coat, two pairs of thick worsted drawers, two jerseys, one pair of worsted gloves, one worsted cholera belt, one pair of long waterproof boots, one waterproof sheet, one pair worsted stockings, one pair of socks of the same quality and one sealskin cap which turned down and completely covered the neck and ears.

Although inestimably more comfortable than in the previous year, the winter seemed to drag on interminably and everyone felt it was the most boring period of their lives. It seemed as though the winter would never end and, at the end of February, after some very heavy snow storms and just as everybody began to think that the fine weather was about to arrive, first it rained and then it began to snow again. In March the weather was fine but very cold with a bright sun and a north wind. It froze hard every night and the Division remained suspended at Kamara with nothing to do but shiver at the cold. March dragged on with the frost continuing as intensely as ever, with the night-time temperature at 14°F. and a bright and impertinent sun by day with a cutting north wind direct from the Steppes.

For more than two-thirds of the twenty-four hours of each day, the men were crowded into their huts. The fug that arose from their charcoal stoves and their sweaty bodies more than made up for the thin, split timbers of which the huts were built.

Armistice negotiations were dragging on, like the winter. The French and the Russians seemed determined to end the war, whilst the British were disappointed in the terms of peace. Rumour had it that, if the armistice broke down, an attack was to be made by way of Eupatoria, leaving a force to hold Sebastopol and the Balaclava area. Everyone knew that the Engineers were tracing lines for fortifications all around Balaclava, both east and west, and the wise ones nodded their heads and said that this was to allow us to embark behind them and to enable the rearguard to defend itself for two days while the embarkation took place.

Race meetings and games were held on the plateau, but the stubbornly continuing winter weather brought a wind so cutting that only the most hardy would face it. Towards the end of March the weather improved, but on the 27th, when everyone believed that spring had commenced, there was a snow storm and a hard frost. For days there was frost, sleet, rain and cold weather, and even at the end of the first week in April a heavy snow storm made drifts around the huts and flurries of snow blew in through the now yawning cracks in the woodwork. Every morning the ice had to be broken before the men could wash and shave.

On the 19th April a great review of British and French soldiers was held for the benefit of a large party of visiting Russian officers. The story spread around that they were surprised at the state of the men and horses and that they had accused the Allies of only parading picked men. It was reported that one Russian had said he could see porter and beef steaks in every man on parade! The Highlanders were highly delighted to be told that the French General Pelissier had publicly stated that he considered the Highlanders to be the finest soldiers in the world. The men were very heartened by the review and had little doubt that the Russian officers would write to their Emperor to let him know that he would be very wise to make peace. The warrant officers and sergeants of the 42nd privately told each other that the Army was not all that it really looked, as both men and officers were undrilled and very rusty after the long winter.

The weather turned rainy, which was a good thing as everything was very parched and the flowers could not poke their heads up easily through the hard crust of the earth. Word spread around that the French General Vinoy had got his orders to embark his Division and was to be off in a few days, and that the Artillery had a letter fiom their own Department warning them to be ready.

Life, although horribly boring and monotonous, was more tolerable now that the days were fine and the sun was shining, although the night thermometer was often down to 23°F. and there was always a frost.

On the 9th May Sir Colin Campbell, who was going home to England, ordered a parade of all the regiments of the original Highland Brigade. Looking around him, Hector MacDonald wondered how many men were left of the old brigade and, without moving his head too much and thus incurring the displeasure of the Company Sergeant, he tried to count the men around him who had been with the 42nd since the beginning. Their Commander's address was a stirring one, and left hardly a dry eye.

> "Soldiers of the 42nd, 79th, and 93rd; old Highland Brigade! with whom I passed the early and perilous part of this war! I have now to take leave of you; in a few hours I shall be on board ship, never to see you again as a body—a long farewell! I am now old, and shall not be called to serve any more, and nothing will remain to me but the memory of my campaigns, and of the enduring, hardy, generous soldiers with whom I have been associated; whose name and whose glory will long be kept alive in the hearts of our countrymen. When you go home, as you gradually fulfil your term of service, each to his family and his cottage, you will tell the story of your immortal advance in that victorious echelon up the heights of Alma, and of the old Brigadier who led you, and who loved you so well; your children, and your children's children, will repeat the tale to other generations, when only a few lines of history will remain to record all the enthusiasm and discipline which have borne you so stoutly to the end of this war.
>
> Our native land will never forget the name of the Highland

Brigade; and in some future war that nation will call for another one to equal this, which it can never surpass. Though I shall be gone, the thought of you will go with me wherever I may be, and cheer my old age with a glorious recollection of dangers affronted and of hardships endured. A pipe will never sound near me without carrying me back to those bright days when I was at your head, and wore the bonnet which you gained for me, and the honourable decorations on my breast, many of which I owe to your conduct. Brave soldiers! kind comrades! farewell!"

Then, in early June, came the news for which everyone had been waiting—the 42nd were to go home! Now followed a frenzied flurry of packing and dismantling and discarding that culminated on June 15th, 1856, with the embarkation of the 42nd at Kamiesh for England. They landed at Portsmouth on the 24th July, two years and two months after their departure. The Regiment were disembarked almost at once and began to march to the railway station, where trains were waiting to take them to Aldershot. News of their homecoming had preceded them and the streets were lined by excited crowds who, weary of the maimed wrecks of humanity they had seen, now wanted to suitably welcome the men who had won the war. Some wives and relatives of the Highlanders had come specially down from their homeland to greet their loved ones. Completely unprepared for such a spontaneous and vigorous reception, the Highlanders were shaken from their stride as the crowds, in their excitement, pushed the Highlanders right out of the ranks, carried them on their shoulders through the streets, thrusting all kinds of food and drink into their hands. Wives, mothers and sweethearts greeted shaggy-bearded husbands, sons and sweethearts, and numerous bewildered children were thrust into the arms of sweating hairy men whom they did not recognise but were told were their fathers. It was a homecoming that almost blotted out the memories of what they had seen and done.

After a few days of re-kitting and polishing at Aldershot, the returned troops were reviewed by Queen Victoria, accompanied by the Prince Consort, the young Prince of Wales, the Duke of Cambridge and a host of other officers and dignitaries. The Queen said a few kind words to the assembled soldiers and thanked them for doing their duty. All were deeply touched by her "kind and motherly feeling". The 42nd then marched to the station and were taken to Dover where they went into garrison with the 41st, the 44th, the 79th and the 93rd Regiments. The wheel had turned full circle, and peacetime garrison life was upon them again.

Chapter 13

On the last day of June, 1857, the monotonous routine of garrison life at Dover was interrupted by news of the mutiny of the native regiments of the Honourable East India Company's Bengal Army in northern India. Groups of men gathered attentively around the owner of a newspaper, listening as he read of the outbreak at Meerut, forty miles from Delhi, and the uprisings in other stations where British officers, officials and their wives and children were murdered and subjected to the worst atrocities. The papers told how the Court of Directors of the East India Company had made a requisition to the Government for four full regiments of infantry, in addition to those already decided upon. Patiently, all listened to hear the names of the lucky units. They were the 19th Foot; the 38th Foot; the 1st Battalion of the 1st Foot. With relish, the readers rolled out the name of the last regiment, which was greeted with groans and disgust. It was the 79th Foot, from their own garrison!

Whilst they wished the 79th nothing but the best of luck, their choice aroused within the 42nd a smouldering, sullen resentment which was not dispersed until the 16th July. Another mail had arrived in England with news of further disasters, causing the Directors to apply to the Government for six more regiments of infantry and eight companies of the Royal Artillery. Subsequently, the Government named the six regiments which were to be sent out in compliance with this request—they were the 20th Foot; the 34th Foot; the 54th Foot; the 97th Foot; and the 2nd Battalion of the Rifle Brigade. Then followed a significant pause before the reader dramatically intoned "the 42nd Foot".

A great cheer arose and the men danced gleefully with their arms around each other's waists, feathered bonnets were thrown in the air in a wild burst of enthusiasm shared by all from the Commanding Officer downwards.

Like everyone else in the Regiment, Hector MacDonald was tired of home soldiering and, once more aflame with the thirst for active service so typical of the Victorian soldier, longed to be on his way.

"I want out to India . . . I hope we get out there in time to have some share in avenging the horrible atrocities committed on our women and children by those fiends."[40]

It was almost a year to the day since the Regiment had returned from the Crimea. The prospects of a release from twelve months of boring peace-time military routine looming near aroused feverish activity in every corner of the barracks as the Regiment prepared to depart. Rumours abounded; indeed, there existed considerable grounds for conjecture—there were four possible routes for the troops to take to India and everyone held strong views as to which was the best. The quickest was the overland route through France to Marseilles; steamer to Alexandria, railway or some other means to Suez and then again by boat to Calcutta. Opponents of this route pointed out that it required an immense amount of changing and shifting, with three lots of embarking and disembarking at Boulogne, Alexandria and at Calcutta. The 3,000 miles from Southampton to Alexandria could be covered by boat, then an overland passage through Egypt to Suez, then another boat to Calcutta. This was a much shorter route to India than via the Cape of Good Hope, being about 8,000 to 12,000 miles. The Cape route had its supporters, divided into those who would go by sailing ship and those who would go by steamer.

The first two alternatives were not really practicable for large numbers of troops, so it remained to be settled whether sailing ships or steamers were best fitted. When the authorities at the War Office commenced their arrangements for dispatching troops to India, they had to provide for a sea voyage of between 12,000 to 14,000 miles.[41]

In the event, 10,000 troops intended to be sent out as reinforcements, reliefs and recruits *before* the news of the disasters reached England, were dispatched as originally intended in ordinary sailing vessels; the 4,000 additional troops immediately applied for by the Company were dispatched, half in screw-steamers and half in sailing clippers; while the 6,000 supplied on a still later requisition were sent almost wholly in steamers. The month in which the 42nd sailed was perhaps the busiest, both as to the number of ships and the average freight carried in each; there were forty troop-laden ships carrying from 208 to 1,057 soldiers each; nearly half were steamers.

For some reason, the 42nd were split into batches and sailed for India in five hired transports. They were the steamers the *Australian* (carrying 420 men of different regiments) and the *Golden Fleece* (carrying 1,000 men of assorted regiments). The remainder were split up among three sailing clippers—the *Champion of the Seas* (996 men of different regiments); the *Whirlwind* (350 men of various regiments) and the *James Baines* (996 men of various regiments).* The *James Baines* and the *Champion of the Seas* were the largest and fastest sailing clippers in Britain, they belonged to the Black Ball Line of packets and more than a hundred men were employed at Liverpool to get them ready for the voyage. Their owners confidently expected them to finish the voyage in seventy days and so outstrip the steamers; it was written at the time[42] "in these . . . splendid ships, the troops were conveyed with a degree of comfort rarely if ever before attained in such service."

The old heavy smooth-bore muskets were withdrawn and replaced by the Enfield rifle—it was said that the Duke of Cambridge had personally ordered the substitution. The men viewed the new weapons with mixed feelings, admittedly they weighed only 8lb 14oz as against the 14lb of the old weapon, but change is always viewed with suspicion in hidebound institutions such as the Army. The Enfield rifle was a muzzle loader with an effective range of about 800 yards, far superior to the musket it replaced. Needing a close fit of cartridge and ball, the cartridges were encased in grease paper so that they could be quickly rammed down the thirty-nine-inch barrel. The ends of the cartridges had to be bitten off so that the powder could be poured down the barrel; the remainder, containing the wad and bullet, was then forced home with the ram-rod. To enable it to be driven down the muzzle without undue effort, the cartridge and ball had to be lubricated (see note 46).

The Regiment were not granted embarkation leave but their relations were allowed to visit them; as most of them lived in Scotland, some hundreds of miles from Dover, few were able to avail themselves of this privilege. The men were allowed out of barracks only for the purpose of having their photographs taken; they were paraded and marched to the studio under the command of a sergeant.[43]

Every man was issued with a sea-kit, for which he paid out of pay advanced for the purpose. Everyone deeply grudged

*Pay Lists and Muster Rolls W.D. 12/5532.

paying for these extras for the sea voyage, "nine balls of pipeclay" were considered to be the most objectionable item on the list.[44]

On Tuesday the 4th August, 1857, the 42nd Regiment, together with the 34th Regiment, marched into Portsmouth Dockyard at four o'clock in the afternoon to parade before Queen Victoria. Her Majesty had expressed the wish to inspect those regiments in the garrison which were on the point of embarkation, and she also wished to inspect the ships in which they were to sail. At half-past four the yacht *Fairy* came up, flying the Royal Standard; the still summer air was shattered by the twenty-one gun salute of the garrison and shipping. The Queen, the Prince Consort and the Princess Royal were met at the landing place by a Guard of Honour furnished by the 42nd Regiment, who presented arms as the regimental band played the National Anthem. The Royal Marine Artillery and the 44th Regiment kept the ground, while the 42nd and 34th Regiments were paraded in extended lines. Next, Her Majesty was received by the Commander-in-Chief, Admiral Sir George Seymour; the Lieutenant-Governor, Major-General the Honourable J. T. Scarlett; Admiral Superintendent Martin, Captain Superintendent S. C. Dacres and a number of other officials. Preceding her husband and daughter and followed by a glittering concourse of officers with drawn swords, the Queen walked slowly down the ranks, dwarfed by her soldiers, who were themselves made gigantic by their feathered bonnets.

Coming to the end of the lines, the Queen, who seemed much pleased with the general appearance of her soldiers, turned and led the Royal party along the lane of scarlet cloth laid down from the place of inspection to the saluting dais, a handsome platform of polished mahogany placed near the Clock Tower, with a flagstaff from which floated the Royal Standard. The bands of the 42nd and 34th Regiments took their place and struck up a lively air as the two regiments marched past in quick time. The troops then left the ground and the Royal party walked down a scarlet-carpeted roadway to inspect the ships, which had their gangways decorated with flags and carpets. On board the *Lady Jocelyn* Her Majesty inspected the 54th Regiment and the Royal Artillery, who had already boarded in readiness for sailing with the tide.

A few days later, with the band at their head, the 42nd swung out of barracks and marched through the streets of Portsmouth to the dockyard. They were given a great send-off and a woman whom he had never seen before tucked a bottle of whisky into Hector's haversack, running by his side as he marched. The MacDonald boys had been split up, Hector and two of his brothers sailed on the *James Baines* whilst the others were on the *Champion of the Seas*, both large and fast sailing clippers.

At the dockside, with the tall masts and rigging looming high above them, they were split into separate messes each of sixteen men who marched up the gangplank in a party, on deck they were told the mess to which they were allotted and directed to it. The troop-deck was down in the bowels of the ship, it was low and dark and crowded with long tables and wooden benches that projected at regular and close intervals from the sides of the ship. The ceiling was formed of wooden battens holding dozens of hooks from which the hammocks were hung at night, like hams being smoked in a chimney. After hanging their equipment, everyone took the long climb upwards to the deck. The kilted soldiers discovered that the steep wooden ladders provided a ready source of coarse amusement for the other troops.

The men lined the rails as the clipper was towed out of the dockyard, but most of them vanished below when the ship rounded the Needles and swept into the trough of the open sea, commencing to roll and pitch in a very unpleasant manner as the wind freshened. Hector stayed on deck for about an hour, and then descended to the lower part of the ship. Already pervaded by a stale smell of disinfectant and crowded humanity, the low-ceilinged deck was a seething mass of groaning soldiers, huddled together against tables and forms, and so thickly crowded that it was almost impossible to walk without stepping on them. Hammocks and blankets had been issued, but few men had managed to master the technique of hanging them before going down with sea-sickness. Hector fought against his heaving stomach for a few minutes, but a violent lurch of the ship together with the smell of greasy cooking from the ship's galley made him one with his fellow sufferers. During the night the wind grew stronger with every hour, so that the ship rolled and tossed in a most lively fashion.

At half-past five next morning they were roused by the discordant blast of a bugle from the restless nausea in which they had tossed all night. Played by a bugler as far gone as themselves, it was perhaps the worst-played reveille they would ever hear, but few were able to pass judgement on the quality of their awakening. Those who had the strength to get up on deck found that it was hardly daylight; a heavy leaden-coloured sea was running and there was no land visible on either side. Although the ship was still rolling, the strong fresh air which swept across the taffrail blew some of the sickness out of them. Below again, milling around the primitive washing facilities, they shaved in a manner that reminded Hector of playing cup and ball with his own face. When the fall-in sounded, the men assembled by companies to answer their names; about twenty per cent of the battalion seemed to be missing.

The Regimental Sergeant-Major, who appeared to be as invulnerable to seasickness as to everything else, read out the routine for the voyage. At reveille all hands would muster on deck with hammocks and blankets which would be aired whilst the troops were below washing and shaving. Breakfast was at seven o'clock and every man would take his turn to be mess orderly to his table, to bring down the rations from the cook's galleys, to lay the table and to wash-up afterwards. There would be a general fatigue parade half an hour later when each mess would clean up its now part of the deck. At ten o'clock there would be a Commanding Officer's parade and inspection of the ship, after this the men would be free until dinner at noon. After this meal there would be another general fatigue and a drill parade. At half-past four, the tea bugle would sound and hammocks were allowed to be slung from half-past five onwards. Every man was to be in his hammock by a quarter-past eight, and at half-past the Officer of the Watch and the battalion police would go through the ship on their rounds. Drawing a deep breath, the R.S.M. looked searchingly up and down the ranks as he warned, in a solemn voice, that discipline throughout the voyage would be especially severe.

Every mess had been issued with a sack of hard ship's biscuit and breakfast consisted of these unpalatable slabs with a mug of milkless tea. Then both fit and sick alike were hounded up on deck to spend the next two hours scrubbing the decks, polishing the brass work, washing the paint and generally making themselves useful. On the Commanding Officer's parade, the men were told off into three watches and given instructions in the event of an alarm of fire or a collision. They were told that smoking would be permitted for one hour each day on the forecastle; the bugler would sound "light up" and, after sixty minutes, "out pipes". Every man had to furnish himself with a wire cover for his pipe before he was allowed to smoke.[45] Then the men fell out in their watches to practise fire and boat stations.

Enthusiastic for anything that broke into the monotony of home soldiering, no thought had been given to the nature of the conflict to which they were travelling halfway across the world. When they had settled down on board ship, the Commanding Officer, Lieutenant-Colonel Alexander Cameron, had the men paraded and told exactly why it was necessary for them to fight in India. On a pleasingly warm day the men were allowed to squat in groups on the warm deck, each group being lectured in schoolmaster fashion by an officer detailed for the purpose. They listened intently to the educated voices raised above the eternal background of creaking timbers and flapping canvas.

They were told that the entire Indian nation had not risen against the British—their enemies were to be the rebellious Sepoys of the native regiments of the Honourable East India Company's Bengal Army. Affected by a strange unrest, based partly upon superstition and partly upon the slackness of their British masters, the Sepoys had cast their loyalty to the winds when ordered to use rifle cartridges reputedly greased with the fat of animals decreed by their religion to be unclean.[46] Colonel Cameron was a fair-minded man, instructing his officers to stress that many thousands of the native soldiers of the Bengal Army remained true to their salt and were fighting alongside their British comrades at Delhi and at Lucknow, and that large numbers of native servants continued to serve their masters devotedly and in many cases assisted them to escape from the mutineers. It was the Regiment's duty, together with the ever increasing tide of British troops arriving in India, to rigorously seek out and destroy the mutineers wherever they were found. Solemnly, the men looked at each other and made unspoken oaths that they would take revenge for the vile cruelties and indignities heaped upon the European women and children at Cawnpore, Meerut and other places in Bengal.

At "eight bells"—midday—they had a dinner of bully beef, preserved potatoes and ship's biscuit. Tea later in the day consisted of half a pound of dry bread and a mug of peculiar-tasting tea, without milk. The poor rations made the dry canteen, which opened three times daily for an hour, a popular place and long queues formed that stretched halfway around the ship. There were no spirits or beer procurable for other ranks.

Within a few days everyone became accustomed to the roll of the ship and life took on the monotonous form that was to last for almost four months. The troop deck was a weird picture at night, with hundreds of hammocks swinging with the motions of the ship, bumping into each other and so close to the ground that movement was only possible on hands and knees. It was a dull, boring existence; some men read or talked while others spent hours at the rail gazing at the occasional spouting whale, sporting dolphin or porpoise, the flying fishes and other wonders of the deep. Most evenings were passed in a free and easy sing-song. Watch-duty came round regularly, and lasted for twelve hours, being practically the same as sentry-go on shore; the watch had to remain on deck throughout the night so that there were a number of men always available in the event of an emergency.

After leaving the Cape, they followed the usual sailing-ship's course, due east towards the little islands of St. Paul's and Amsterdam; in that far off parallel of southern latitude, the seas were stormy and ran high. In those days all ships bound for the Bay of Bengal followed the Western Trades as far as those islands before making a new departure and turning towards the mouth of the sacred Ganges. The days blended into weeks and the weeks into months, until the Southern Cross and other strange constellations appeared at night to warn that the northern hemisphere had been left behind.

They picked up a pilot and ran over the bar at the Sand Heads at the mouth of the Hoogly River. Knowing that they were on their last day's journey by water, everyone was excitedly lining the rails as the ship was towed up the river. The scenery on both sides of the river was interesting and attractive—fine pastures, rows of tall trees and plantations dotted with bullocks and natives. The river was full of curious little single-masted native fishing boats. As they proceeded, the signal stations on shore repeatedly signalled to them "What ship . . . what troops?" and the signallers were kept busy answering. They turned the Luff-and-be-D. Point with great speed and ran into Calcutta. The warship *Shannon* fired a salute as they passed her, and her blue-jackets manned the rigging and bulwarks of the ship and gave three hearty British cheers, to which the Highlanders loudly replied. It was about four o'clock when they came in sight of Calcutta, threading their way through dozens of anchored merchant ships. They anchored off a big *ghat*, or landing place, near the native city, amidst a vast crowd of native boats laden with fish, fruit and vegetables for sale. Everyone was immensely impressed with Calcutta, having no idea that it was such a large place or that it possessed such beautiful buildings.[47]

They remained on board the *James Baines* overnight and, in the morning, hours before it was necessary, in the usual Army fashion, the men were aroused and ordered to prepare to land. The suddenness of the orders, plus an overwhelming enthusiasm to vacate the clipper which had been their home for so long, made every man work in a fever of excitement as though he feared being left behind when the Regiment marched ashore. The crowded conditions below decks made the gathering together of kit and equipment a confused and orderless pantomime. Carrying full packs and in the same full dress uniform they wore in Britain, the men impatiently struggled up the steep wooden ladders to the deck, arriving in the open drenched with sweat. It soon dried on them in the slight breeze that came off the water, as they stood at ease for more than two interminable hours.

Although the November weather in Calcutta was considered cool, the men, weakened by weeks without exercise, quickly became distressed as they filed on to the flat barge that was towed ashore by a small steamer. Marching to Fort William through the crowded streets of the city, the heavily clad and laden Highlanders found the close atmosphere to be most trying. Almost as soon as they set foot in India, they learned that the *Champion of the Seas* had arrived two days earlier. Hector looked forward to meeting his brothers, who had been on this vessel.

At this time, there were eleven ships of war anchored in the river and over 4,000 British troops were temporarily garrisoned at Calcutta: including the 19th, 20th 42nd, 54th, 79th, 97th Regiments of Foot or portions of them, together with one battalion of the 60th Rifles and one of the Rifle Brigade. The 42nd went into barracks in Fort William, a huge place mounting 1,000 guns and commanding all the shipping in the river and the principal parts of the town. It was said to be able to house 8,000 troops

Chapter 14

When it was realised that they were to serve again under the command of Sir Colin Campbell,[48] the Highlanders of the 42nd Regiment were delighted; veterans of the Crimea regaled the younger soldiers with stories of their irascible leader. The MacDonald brothers recalled the cool manner in which Sir Colin had broken the unearthly silence at the Alma; reminded of their dead brothers, they wondered if a MacDonald would be left behind in India.

Now that they were in the theatre of operations, the 42nd found the barrack life at Fort William to be most irksome. They were not allowed out of barracks. But convinced that Colin Campbell would soon send for the 42nd, everyone worked from dawn to dusk in preparations for the fighting that lay ahead. They did not have to wait for very long; on the 23rd November there was a feverish coming and going of gallopers and a rumour rapidly spread that they would be away that night.

The MacDonalds had their doubts; in the first place, only headquarters and five other companies of the Regiment had arrived in Calcutta—the remainder were still somewhere at sea or making their slow way down the Hoogly River. In the second place, they could not believe that they were to be sent into action in this climate wearing full dress uniform, with the ponderous folds of woollen cloth that formed their kilts tucked into massive wads over their hips and without protection from the sun for their bare thighs and knees. They were still wearing their extraordinary, if picturesque, headdress. Hector shook his head:

"Only a foolish savage would choose this mass of black feathers for fighting on the plains of India . . . if it were white perhaps it would afford some protection against the sun but as it is . . ."[49]

Every soldier knew that he should have been supplied with certain items of tropical clothing on his arrival in India, but so far no one had seen anything of this apparently very necessary kit.[50]

It was not only the European soldiers who suffered from the effects of unsuitable clothing. Discussing the dress of the native soldiers, a contemporary report says:

"The Sepoys of the Company's Army were dressed in English-type uniforms—a tight coat, trousers in which he can hardly walk and cannot stoop at all; bound to an immense and totally useless knapsack, so that he can scarcely breathe; strapped, belted and pipe-clayed within an inch of his life; with a rigid basket-shaped shako on his head, which requires the skill of a juggler to balance, and which cuts deep into his brow if worn for an hour; and with a leather stock around his neck, to complete his absurd costume—when compared with the same Sepoy, clothed, armed and accoutred solely with regard to his comfort and efficiency—forms a most perfect example of what is madly called the 'regular' system with many European officers."

Following Windham's defeat at Cawnpore, the Commander-in-Chief urgently needed as many reinforcements as he could get. On the 24th November, 1857, headquarters and five companies of the 42nd Regiment, together with a wing of the 38th Regiment and a wing of the 3rd Battalion of the Rifle Brigade, with some Sappers and Artillery, making in all a force of 1,050 men, plus two eight-inch howitzers and four field pieces, left Calcutta by train for Ranigunge, 120 miles away, on the first stage of their 628-mile journey to Cawnpore. Still without tropical kit, the 42nd were permitted to make a concession to the climate by the addition of a flap of grey cloth hanging over their ears. Hector thought that it made them look rather like a lot of spaniels.

Arriving at Ranigunge, the party detrained and paraded in the station yard, where they had their first sight of the bullock-waggons that were to carry them the 300 miles to Benares; this mode of transport was called "bullock-dak". There seemed to be a vast fleet of these little covered waggons, each drawn by two bullocks; fresh bullocks were provided every ten miles and specified staging houses, known as "dak bungalows" were availalbe for resting. Two officers or six men shared a waggon; taking it in turns four men at a time rode in a waggon so that there were always two men marching by the side on foot. In this way, one third of the party, with its proportion of officers, would always be on the road and ready to fight at a moment's notice, with no man actually marching on foot for more than ten miles in twenty-four hours. It was possible to move at the rate of about thirty-six miles a day by bullock-dak, and dak bungalows provided comfortable meals and sleeping places.

The Grand Trunk Road over which they were to travel was a splendid piece of work, extending from Calcutta to Cawnpore, Lucknow, Agra, Delhi, the North-West Provinces and the Punjab. If they had been in the mood to appreciate it, there was much of the greatest interest to be seen on either side of the road. They passed mosques and beautiful Hindu temples, straggling villages and overgrown fields deserted by their owners who had fled, fearing the hasty vengeance of those with white faces upon those with brown. Every soldier in the party was stimulated by a great sense of urgency that left him no time or inclination to gaze or admire. They talked of nothing but getting to Cawnpore as quickly as possible to deal with the murderous Sepoys who had been unfaithful to their salt, and had murdered and violated English women and children. It was the thought of the women and children that most aroused the dour, bearded Highlanders; officers and soldiers who had been murdered had died doing their duty, but the horrible thought of children being caught by the ankles and their brains beaten out against stone walls brought tears to the eyes of the soldiers.

Although uneventful from the point of view of fighting, it was not an easy march. Rivers had to be crossed and sometimes it was necessary to spend hours up to the neck in water, pushing and hauling to get the bullock carts over. All ranks worked without thought for themselves; nothing was allowed to deter them from the stern purpose of revenge.

On first acquaintance, the bullocks failed to impress, having the bad habit of occasionally deciding to lie down and refusing to get up, in spite of the blows and kicks showered upon them. The drivers—nervous, frightened natives fearful of their own shadows—showed them the trick of making the animal rise to his feet. Held straight out by one man, the tail was grasped between two sticks which were then pushed two or three times briskly up and down. At once the bullock would stumble to its feet and move off dragging its cart, tail straight up in the air.

The men saw an enemy behind every brown face, whether or not its owner wore a uniform. Crossing the range of Raj Mahal Hills, travelling on that part of the Grand Trunk Road made by gangs of convicts and passing through a dense forest area, the cavalcade suddenly came to an abrupt halt. Bugles sounded and the orders were shouted along the column "Stand to your arms!" Everyone tumbled out of the little carts and fell-in on the road, facing forward. They were ordered to the ready and to cap their pieces. Around the bend of the road, in a rough sort of order, came a party of about 300 uniformed natives, armed with old matchlocks, tulwars, shields and spears; some had a bayonet on a long bamboo. Certain that they were rebels, everyone's fingers itched on the trigger; fortunately or unfortunately, however you cared to look at it, it turned out to be a false alarm. Through an interpreter, the Commanding Officer closely questioned the leader of the native party and found out that they were men in the service of a loyal rajah who were patrolling the road. Ordered to stand down, the men reluctantly grounded their arms, vexed and grumbling as their blood, hot for salutary vengeance, simmered down. After about thirty minutes parleying, the natives were allowed to pass. In single file, they edged warily past the fierce, unmoving kilted men, towering above them in their grotesque feathered bonnets.

Benares, long, straggling, and Turkish looking, commanded by a new fort built at Rajghat since the troubles of the preceding summer, was reached on the 30th November and Allahabad on the following day. This town was situated in an important position on the Grand Trunk Road, connecting Bengal proper with the upper provinces. The fort, centuries old, had been modernised and stood in the fork formed by the junction of the Ganges and the Jumna rivers; military barracks had been built within the fort. Allahabad dominated a narrow strip of territory through which the railways and roads ran north-west and south-east. The garrison were very busy making an entrenched camp to take the sick and wounded that they expected down from Lucknow as soon as that town was relieved.

At Allahabad, the party entrained again to travel on the second portion of the Great Trunk Railway. The Highlanders heard with contemptuous amusement how, in the preceding June, the mutineers had attacked the locomotives, firing muskets at the engines at a distance before advancing cautiously. Finding that the engines did not stir, the mutineers began to beat them with sticks, calling them names and abusing them. The 42nd left the train where the railway ended at Chimi; here they were ordered to commence to build an entrenched camp.

At five o'clock on the following morning, a messenger arrived in camp with a despatch from the Commander-in-Chief, ordering the column to make forced marches to Cawnpore, Lieutenant-Colonel Thorold, acting Commanding Officer, decided to allow the men to rest during the heat of the day, at the same time sorting through their kit and equipment so as to cut it down to a minimum. In the evening of the 2nd December, 1857, the column marched out and, with only the shortest halts, marched for fifty-six hours. The men found it an interminable slog, made timeless by the regular and surprising transformations of dark into light and light into dark. Later, Hector remembered little of the journey save that he trudged automatically along ever-unrolling roads, ankle deep in dust, in a little world bordered by the men who trudged to his front, to his sides and rear. Marching through the long hours of darkness produced a disembodied sense of getting nowhere, rather like marching on the spot. During the day, on the rare occasions when he raised his heavy head and looked around him, Hector discovered a vague satisfaction in realising that the surrounding countryside was slowly, very slowly, unreeling itself by the side of the column.

At one point on the seemingly endless march came an event that aroused them from their exhausting stasis, beginning as a half-hearted, reluctant head-raising at the head of the column, the men resembling creatures aroused from a deep sleep. The movement flowed sluggishly down the files as men were nudged or called into consciousness by the ranks to their front. Resenting anything that might challenge his hard-won rhythm and so bring exhaustion nearer, Hector looked around seeking the reason for the commotion.

Through grit-encrusted eyes, he saw an orderless procession of carts, some drawn by plodding bullocks, others by head-hanging horses, of palanquins, camels, elephants, waggons and doolies with curtains ominously closed. From out of this oddly-assorted concourse, women and children gazed listlessly at them—none spoke or called out, seemingly buried in an apathy beyond relief. At the front and rear of the straggling column marched men of the 34th Foot, accompanied by some native cavalry and two guns. Dotted about the column, soldiers and civilians sat painfully with stained bandages on heads, arms and legs, hunched on horses and camels. Like a flame flickering over dry grass, a single sentence rippled through the 42nd's column:

"It's the Lucknow women and children!"

Fatigue forgotten, bearded and dirty Highlanders gazed in awe at the men, women and children whose plight in the beleaguered city had thrilled, and chilled, the world. No one spoke, the few tentative, unanswered hand-waves were quickly stilled as though the spontaneous gestures were blasphemous. Slowly the two columns passed each other, the Highlanders moving hastily off the road to march in the deeper dust.

From the escort, the 42nd learned of the near-disaster of General Windham's reverse at Cawnpore. The Highlanders felt surprised that Windham "of the Redan" should have failed in this fashion.[51] No one turned to gaze after the column as it progressed in a silence broken only by the slurring plod of animal feet towards its objective. After it disappeared, heads were held higher and hands gripped muskets more tightly as vengeful thoughts seethed through minds revived from the oblivion of exhaustion.

During these intensely hot days, everyone suffered badly from the heat and the dust; swarms of flies followed them and thirst was ever-present. The long lines of men and baggage animals stirred up the dust which thickly coated the road, so that the column was surrounded by a dense pervading cloud. From head to foot, the light brown dust hung thickly on beards, moustaches and eyebrows, turning them into a troupe of incongruous, out-of-season Father Christmases. Eyes, red-rimmed with fatigue and glare, peered from slits in the white dust face-mask.

During the last hours of the march many men fell out, drained completely of the sheer physical strength that was needed to keep them in the ranks. Others, less exhausted, dropped out through foot-soreness. Nevertheless, more than seventy per cent of the column were still automatically dragging one foot before the other when they marched into Colin Campbell's Cawnpore camp at noon on the 5th December. Fresh out from England, after a hundred days at sea and with a mere four days to regain their "land-legs", the 42nd had covered the 628 miles from Calcutta to Cawnpore in eleven days—the last seventy-eight miles in fifty-six hours.

Chapter 15

By mid-afternoon, most of the stragglers had been brought into camp, their feet so lacerated and blistered that the skin peeled off with their hose as one layer.

In the early evening the men were aroused, not without difficulty, from the heavy sleep into which they had fallen as soon as dismissed at noon. After a meal, they were ordered to parade; even those whose torn feet barely enabled them to hobble, were compelled to line up alongside their comrades. Lieutenant-Colonel Thorold told them that they were to take part in the next day's attack on Cawnpore. His words were drowned in an uproar of cheering which he permitted to roll and echo for some seconds before raising his hand. They were brigaded with the 53rd, the 93rd and the 4th Punjab Rifles, under the command of Adrian Hope. After instructing them as to their task on the following day, Colonel Thorold concluded with a few stirring words and then dismissed the parade.

Leaving the parade ground in a group, the MacDonald brothers were immediately accosted by some sailors, wearing white, cotton-covered straw hats with little curtains hanging to protect the backs of their necks.[52] They all spoke at once:

"Have you come up from Calcutta . . . did you see the *Shannon*?"

"How did she look . . . was she ship-shape?"

Hector was reminded of a man enquiring after the wife he had not seen for several years. They did their best to relieve the sailors' minds and to convince them their beloved *Shannon* was in good hands. They strolled through the camp, enjoying the cool of the evening, pausing now and then to chat with other sauntering groups who hailed them as they passed. Among themselves the MacDonalds agreed that they had never seen such an unsoldierly looking lot—few of the troops sported even a morsel of pink or a fragment of English scarlet. For the most part, the infantry were dressed in linen frocks, tunics dyed a slate-grey colour called "carkey" which blended well with their sun-bleached blue trousers. On their heads they wore shakos protected by puggarees (linen covers). It seemed to be a peculiarity of carkey that no two pieces matched, so that it exhibited endless varieties of shade, fading with every washing. Officers did not seem to be confined to carkey or to anything else, each man displaying a wonderful licence and imagination in his dress. They wore coats of any cut or material, although carkey shooting jackets or jerkins with a few inches of iron curb-chain sewn on the shoulders to resist sabre cuts appeared to be the general favourite. Foot and leg wear existed in a fantastic variety of combinations, ranging from leather pantaloons to long stageboots made of a buff coloured leather, pulled up over knee breeches of leather or regimental trousers. Some officers preferred wearing their wellington boots outside their pantaloons, thus exhibiting tops of very bright colours; whilst the boots and baggy trousers of the Zouave officer were not unknown. A helmet made of felt, wicker work or pith of varying shapes with a uniform ugliness seemed to be the favourite headdress; and around it were twisted infinite colours and forms of turbans with fringed edges and laced fringes. Sometimes a peacock feather with the iris-end displayed was inserted in the hole at the top of the helmet; there were many such holes to let the hot air escape from the head.

Suddenly the MacDonalds came face to face with a group of men from the 93rd. They were wearing what bore little resemblance to acknowledged Scots uniform, some of the more eccentric wore shades of grey linen over their bonnets, most of them had discarded the kilt and were wearing faded carkey trousers. So incongruous was their dress that the MacDonalds burst out laughing.

"What are you laughing at, mate?"

Alexander MacDonald raised his hand in a placating gesture:

"Well . . . it's just that you look a bit different to when we last saw you at Dover Castle."

The men looked at each other and then down at their clothes and joined in the laughter:

"Well, of course, you ain't got your knees brown yet, have you? . . . but it won't be long before you get rid of all them wads of cloth tucked over your hips and find something to guard your legs from the sun and the insects."

Sitting on the dusty ground, their backs against earthen banks thrown up as entrenchments, the Scotsmen talked. Inevitably the conversation centred on the dreadful events that had occurred here at Cawnpore a few months earlier. Even in the half light, Hector was able to discern the compressed lips and narrowing eyes of his companions. In unrelieved monotones that made the story even more terrible, the Highlanders spoke out.[53]

"I saw the slaughter house . . . and I also saw one of the native infantrymen wash up part of the blood which stains the floor before he was hanged . . . there were dresses, clogged thickly with blood, children's frocks, and ladies' underclothing of all kinds, boys' trousers, leaves of bibles . . . strewed all over the place. There were broken daguerreotypes, hair . . . some nearly a yard long, bonnets, all bloody, and lots of shoes."

Another man took up the story:

"I picked up a bit of paper with the words on it 'Ned's hair with love'. Inside it was a little bit of hair tied up with ribbon."

"The first troops that went in saw the bodies with their arms and legs sticking out of the ground . . . they had all been thrown in a heap in a well."

"I'm not exaggerating when I tell you that the soles of my boots were more than covered with the blood of those poor wretched creatures . . . on the wooden pillars of the room were sword cuts and long dark hair was sticking, carried by the edges of the weapons . . . There were the marks of bullets and sword cuts on the walls . . . not high up, as if men had fought, but low down, and in the corners where the poor crouching creatures had been cut to pieces. Angus, tell them of the writing on the wall."

"Oh yes, on the walls were written in pencil, or scratched in the plaster . . . words such as 'think of us' . . . 'avenge us' . . . 'your wives and families are here in misery and at the disposal of savages' . . . 'Oh Oh! my child, my child'."

"Do you know, there was a row of women's shoes, with bleeding amputated feet in them, ranged on one side of the room and on the other side was a row of children's shoes filled in the same terrible way."

"It is said that when the 78th Highlanders entered Cawnpore, they found the remains of Sir Hugh Wheeler's daughter. They removed her hair carefully from her head and sent some of it to her relations and then they divided the rest amongst themselves . . . they counted every single hair in each parcel and swore to take a terrible revenge by putting to death as many mutineers as there were hairs."

Sitting in the warm darkness, under the star-spangled Indian sky, Hector felt curiously alone and detached. His mind raced over what had gone on at this very place, he pictured the besieged exposed for weeks to a scorching sun without shelter of any kind, and surrounded by the dying and the dead, their ears ringing with the groans of the wounded, the shouts of sunstruck madmen, the plaintive cries of children, the bitter sobs and sighs of bereaved mothers, widows and orphans. He thought that even such a death was far better than what fell to the lot of many, who were not even allowed to die without being made witness of the bloody deaths of all they loved on earth . . . they were insulted, abused and finally, after weeks of such treatment, were cruelly and foully murdered. Shuddering, he shook himself to cast off these terrible thoughts.

At daybreak next morning Sir Colin Campbell's entire Army was under arms; so anxious was every man to take his place in the coming fight that not a man of the 42nd was absent, even those with bleeding feet hobbled into their places in the ranks. Refreshed after a good night's sleep, Hector and his comrades were in high spirits at the prospect before them of a satisfactory day's work. They had no doubt that they would drive the enemy from Cawnpore and so convince all those who had taken part in the horrible brutalities perpetrated there, that Britain's hour had come at last. The day was clear and cool with a cloudless sky.

The British camp was in the form of a half-circle, its right rested on the river stretching from some old dragoon lines lying near the Ganges, its centre and left stretched southwestward to cover the Grand Trunk Road, and round the position originally occupied by Sir Hugh Wheeler. The city of Cawnpore lay in front of the British camp, divided from it by a canal running east and west. The larger portion of the city was on the northern side of the canal; it did not extend down to the river, being separated from it by a sandy plain about two miles in breadth, covered with officers' bungalows and compounds. This area, called the cantonments, stretched for several miles along the waterfront and on it were sited the entrenchments and fortifications of the bridge of boats, the only means of crossing the river communicating with the Lucknow road. It had been General Windham's task to occupy these defences and so protect the bridge and preserve communication with Sir Colin Campbell whilst he was relieving Lucknow. A road ran through the cantonments, to join at a few miles' distance the Grand Trunk Road which united Delhi, Cawnpore, Allahabad and Calcutta; this was the line of retreat taken by the rescued garrison of Lucknow and its preservation was therefore of vital importance.

On the evening of the 29th November, when Sir Colin had arrived from Lucknow, the mutineers had been driven from that part of the city nearest the British entrenchments. About the same time, Brigadier Greathed had occupied the Generalganj, an old bazaar of considerable extent, which lay along the canal in front of the line occupied by the British camp. Thus, the enemy were on the north side of the canal and the British on the south side, with one advance post (the Generalganj) on the canal itself. The rebels' right, facing the British left, stretched out beyond the angle formed by the Grand Trunk Road and the canal; to attack it, the British force would have to cross the canal by one or both of its two bridges. The enemy centre was in the town of Cawnpore itself, where he occupied the houses and bazaars which overhung the canal; they were strongly fortified and loopholed. It was a part of the city riddled with strongly barricaded narrow lanes running from the main streets. The left wing and centre of the enemy position was held by regular and irregular troops under the Nana; their line of retreat was along the Grand Trunk Road to Bithur.

The Sepoys were divided into two distinct bodies, that which held their right flank was composed of the Gwalior Contingent, the Rani of Jhansi's followers, and the mutinous regiments that had been stationed in Bundelkand, Central India, and Rajputana; their line of retreat was by the Kalpi Road. It was a force of about 25,000 men with forty guns, under the command of Tantia Topi; they were not all disciplined soldiers but all were experienced in the use of arms and accustomed to fighting.

The entire line of the rebel force extended from the Ganges through the city of Cawnpore, and along the canal to the west of the city wall, which was parallel to the canal. The camp of the enemy was pitched two miles in the rear of his right position, and covering the Kalpi Road, which afterwards formed his line of retreat. It appeared to be a very strong position but, after considerable study, Sir Colin Campbell detected its weakness—between the enemy centre and right there was the wall of the city separating one portion of his force from the other so completely, that, in case of emergency, the Sepoy army had no means of transferring troops from one flank to the other.[54]

The enemy were very strongly posted in their centre and left and could only be approached through the city by way of the difficult broken ground, covered with ruined houses, stretching along the river bank.

While the men were eating their breakfast, and the tents were being struck, packed and sent to the rear, Sir Colin had been carefully explaining his plan of operations to the officers commanding his Brigades. The method of attack was to make a feint on the enemy's left and centre, but to direct the real attack on their right, thus hoping to dispose of Tantia Topi's force, before reinforcements could be obtained from any other part of the line.

Considerably outnumbered, Colin Campbell's force consisted of about 5,000 infantry, 600 cavalry and thirty-five guns. The infantry was divided into four brigades:

The 3rd Brigade, commanded by Greathed
- The 8th Regiment
- The 64th Regiment
- The 2nd Punjab Infantry

The 4th Brigade, commanded by Adrian Hope
- The 42nd Regiment
- The 53rd Regiment
- The 93rd Regiment
- The 4th Punjab Rifles

The 5th Brigade, commanded by Inglis
- The 23rd Regiment
- The 32nd Regiment
- The 82nd Regiment

The 6th Brigade, commanded by Walpole
- The 2nd and 3rd Battalions of the Rifle Brigade
- A wing of the 38th Regiment

Commanded by Little, the cavalry consisted of the 9th Lancers and details of the 1st, 2nd and 5th Punjab Cavalry and Hodson's Horse. The artillery included Peel's Naval Brigade, the troops of Blunt and Remmington, the batteries of Bourchier, of Middleton, of Smith, of Longden, and of Bridge, under the chief command of Dupuis. General Windham was given command of the entrenchment, being ordered to open fire with every gun at nine in the morning. At the same time, Greathed, supported by Walpole, was to threaten the enemy's centre.

At exactly nine o'clock the bombardment commenced; it was reported as being a "tremendous fire"* and a "great

*_Daily Life during the Indian Mutiny_, by J. W. Sherer. (1898).

artillery duel".* Two of Captain Peel's naval guns were under Windham's command and the artillery cannonade has been described by Mate Garvey.†

> "We took our time from the right, and such a crash of artillery you never heard; houses fell, trees disappeared, and the air rang again with the whistling of shot, fizzing of shells, etc. It was noble fun. In a little more than an hour I fired seventy-five rounds from each of the guns in my battery."

It was remarked at the time that this tremendous volley of fire drew but a small return from the enemy. Occasionally arising above the roar of the guns could be heard the sharp rattle of musketry from Greathed's troops along the bank of the canal. Whilst this was taking place, the infantry columns were filing from the entrenchments to take up their position out on the British left; they were in the rear of the old cavalry lines which effectively masked them from the enemy's observation. Progress seemed irritatingly slow to the 42nd, the columns being continually halted as the troops in front of them converged on the narrow openings in the entrenchments which led out to the sandy plain to their front. During one of these halts Hector found himself only few yards from a convulsively leaping battery of guns, whose repeated flame-tinged roars split the still warm air and caused his head to ring. Many of these guns were being worked by native artillerymen, that nearest to Hector was a battery of Madras Artillery. One of the crew was a little fellow, wiry and strong, whose activities and energy indicated absolute enjoyment of the task in hand. It seemed queer to Hector that these coloured men should be firing upon their own race; perhaps his surprise was mirrored upon his face because in between rounds, the little native spoke to him in a quaint, sing-song voice:‡

"I daresay, you have never seen a native soldier like me . . . we are very much nearer the British than those fellows up there . . . there is very little difference . . . we can eat any meat we choose and drink wine!"

Stifling his prejudices against faces that were brown, Hector called out to him:

"Can you fight like one? The British . . . particularly we Scots . . . are very fond of fighting!"

*_The Indian Mutiny of_ 1857, by Colonel G. B Malleson (1891).

†_The Devil's Wind_, by Major-General G. L. Verney.

‡_Daily Life in the Indian Mutiny_, p. 142.

The little native's brown eyes sparkled and he threw his arms in the air:

"Fight! I should think so! We are just British over again—only a different colour!"

At last the infantry brigades of Hope and Inglis were drawn up in contiguous columns on the plain of the cantonments; Hope's brigade on the north side of the Grand Trunk Road behind the cavalry stables.

Reinforced by the 64th, Brigadier Greathed's three regiments at the Generalganj bazaar engaged the enemy in a brisk attack. Walpole's brigade, covered by Smith's Field Battery, crossed the canal by a bridge immediately to the left of the Generalganj, cleared the canal banks and advanced, hugging the walls of the town. At every gate he reached, Walpole left a force which was to throw back the head of any column which tried to debouch to the aid of the Sepoy right wing.

On the British left, Peel's and Longden's heavy guns, together with Bourchier's and Middleton's Field Batteries, opened up on the brick-kilns and mounds which the enemy were holding in strength on the British side of the canal. Deployed in parallel lines, Brigadier Hope leading one line and Brigadier Inglis leading the second, the infantry advanced from their cover behind the cavalry lines, preceded by the 4th Punjab Infantry in skirmishing lines. Farther to the left, the cavalry and Horse Artillery were directed to cross the canal by a bridge a mile and a half westward, to threaten the enemy's rear and to fall upon him as he retreated along the Kalpi Road.

Coming out on to the open plain, the 42nd were in support in the centre behind the 53rd Regiment. Instead of seeing the battlefield stretched out before him as he expected, Hector could only see the steadily advancing backs of the infantrymen to his front, partially obscured by clouds of dust and smoke which billowed across the plain. Looking to his right where vision was clearer, he caught a glimpse of the dark green of the Rifle Brigade battalions crossing the canal. Although the air was filled with the noise of crackling musketry and roaring guns, with roundshot plunging through the ranks or ricocheting over their heads, Hope's brigade marched steadily forward as though on parade, without the slightest confusion or apparent concern. They were moving against some brick-kilns and mounds on the British side of the canal, which were strongly held by Sepoy musketeers who could only fire at a slow rate but were in such large numbers that their volume of fire was heavy. The 4th Punjab Infantry, supported by the 53rd Foot and the skirmishers of the 42nd charged the enemy in grand style, drove them from the mounds and kilns and back over the bridge to the far side of the canal. Here the natives were reinforced and, from a strong position amongst more brick-kilns, they poured a withering fire of shot, shell and bullets, covering the bridge and causing losses as the infantry attempted to rush them.

The dust and smoke made it difficult for the 42nd, coming up behind the rest of the brigade, to understand the reason for the hold up. Immediately in front of Hector MacDonald, Lieutenant-Colonel Thorold, commanding the Regiment, was having difficulty controlling his horse, the animal was cavorting and turning, frightened by the noise. Suddenly its perambulations were dramatically halted as a round-shot brought the animal to the ground, to sweep on through the line and kill Private Mark Grant, marching immediately next to Hector. Spattered with blood and shaken by his narrow escape, Hector pulled himself together and moved forward again with the line; in front of him the gallant old Colonel sprang to his feet, picked up his sword and marched in front of the Regiment as though nothing had happened.

The order was given for everyone to lie down in extended order, short of the bank of the canal. For a few minutes the long lines of infantry lay on the hard, dusty ground; round-shot bounced through their ranks and bullets whined overhead. Suddenly the rumble of heavy wheels could be heard from behind them. Raising their heads and looking over their shoulders, the infantry saw the astounding sight of Captain Peel of the Royal Navy running hard at the head of about forty sailors, dragging a heavy twenty-four-pounder gun and limber. Ignoring the heavy fire directed upon them, the long lines of sailors ran the gun on to the very bridge itself; Peel's voice rang out above the din "Action Front!" The gun was swung round and immediately went into action, the double crews of sailors loading, sponging and firing frenziedly.

Without waiting for orders, the infantry leapt to their feet, cheering madly. Highlanders, Line infantry and native troops rushed for the bridge and the canal. Some waded through the shallow water whilst others edged their way past the gun, to drive the Sepoys before them at the bayonet point. The enemy abandoned their guns, turned and fled. Bourchier's Light Field Battery of the Royal Artillery passed through the ranks of the leading infantry at a gallop, to unlimber and open fire. On the far side of the canal, Hope and Inglis reformed their brigades and moved on at the double to the camp of the Gwalior Contingent. They were accompanied by all the guns of the *Shannon*, dragged by their enthusiastic blue-jacket crews, with the ever-present Captain Peel at their head. The rebel camp came into sight, the guns unlimbered and fired showers of grape through the tents, then it was rushed. Evidently the enemy had not expected to be defeated in this manner—Sepoys were killed whilst cooking their chupatties on small fires and wounded men lay about in all directions; in one place a number of patient bullocks stood fastened to carts.

It was now about one o'clock and the enemy were in full flight along the Kalpi Road. Sir Colin Campbell wished to follow the enemy up at once, but the cavalry and Horse Artillery had been delayed and were not on the scene. Sending General Mansfield with a small force round to the north of Cawnpore to threaten the road along which the Nana's troops must retreat, Colin Campbell decided to follow them up himself with his escort and Bourchier's battery of Horse Artillery. In the rear when the forward movement began, the 42nd were now the leading infantry regiment in the pursuit, outstripping even the supple men of the 4th Punjab Regiment. Later, when the cavalry and Horse Artillery turned up, the pursuit of the disorganised enemy went on for fifteen miles. The infantry, accompanied by the Naval Brigade dragging their guns, carried on the pursuit for ten miles in the heat of the day. Slaughtered on all sides, the rebels threw away their arms and accoutrements and dispersed all over the country, hiding themselves in patches of jungle. With night coming on, the wearied forces returned to Cawnpore, bringing with them seventeen captured guns. The 42nd had been up with the pursuit throughout, the strength and courage of their young men was remarkable; many of them were mere lads who had never seen a shot fired before, yet during the whole of this day's action and long march not a single man fell out or was heard to complain of his hardships.

General Mansfield, who had been sent to threaten the enemy's left wing, spent the afternoon struggling over broken ground and through enclosures, driving part of the enemy before him. Unfortunately he allowed large bodies of the enemy's infantry and cavalry to carry their guns away to the west.[55] At sunset, finding himself in a relatively isolated position and conscious that there were considerable numbers of the enemy still in occupation of the town and the old cantonment, Mansfield strengthened the pickets all round his position and bivouacked his troops for the night, where they were left undisturbed by the enemy.

In spite of his resounding victory, Sir Colin Campbell realised that only one half of Tantia Topi's force had really been dealt with and the other half, with their guns, still remained intact. On the following morning, the 8th December, Campbell ordered Brigadier Hope Grant to march to Bithur, to where it was thought likely that the Nana's troops would retire. Grant was told to use his own discretion and to act according to circumstances and, if it should appear to him to be desirable, to advance farther to Serai Ghat, a ferry over the Ganges about twenty-five miles above Cawnpore. The column that marched out consisted of 2,800 men and eleven guns, formed of the following:

42nd Highlanders	—	403
53rd Foot	—	413
93rd Highlanders	—	806
4th Punjab Rifles	—	332
9th Lancers	—	327
5th Punjab Cavalry	—	85
Hodson's Horse	—	109
Foot Artillery	—	139
Horse Artillery	—	83
Sappers	—	100

The column left Cawnpore early in the afternoon of the 8th and, after marching thirteen miles, was halted for rest and refreshments. At midnight they started off again and marched to Sherrajpur, where the force bivouacked until daybreak. Informed that the enemy were attempting to cross the Ganges by the Serai Ghat ferry, Hope Grant advanced with his main body and found the enemy assembling on the bank of the river, loading guns on to boats. Grant immediately ordered up his cavalry and guns; only the exertions of tired horses and weary men prevented the artillery from being lost in quicksands at the river edge. An artillery duel took place and, after half an hour's firing, the enemy's guns were silenced. A force of the rebel cavalry charged in an attempt to capture Grant's guns but were dispersed in a counter-charge by the 9th Lancers, the Punjab Horse and Hodson's Horse, who cut the enemy up and captured a number of standards. The Infantry Brigade supported the advance of the cavalry but the enemy had retreated before they could come into action. Fourteen brass guns, and an 18-pounder with limbers and waggons were captured, together with a large quantity of stores and ammunition. Although the enemy were firing grape from thirteen guns at ranges of about 500 yards, not a single casualty was caused on the British side.[56]

The captured guns were brought away by the infantry, after a great deal of trouble in extricating them from quicksands. The troops had been marching and fighting for thirty hours with few and short intervals for rest and had scarcely eaten for twenty-four hours, so that it was not until dusk on the 9th December that they were finally able to have a meal and to rest.

Hope Grant's column encamped near the Serai Ghat on the 10th and on the 11th marched back to Bithur, where Adrian Hope's Brigade, including the 42nd, remained to search for treasure reported to have been buried near the palace, which they destroyed during the search. A large amount of treasure was discovered in a tank with a flow of water so great that 200 men were required to bale it out by night and day so as to keep it sufficiently low for the Sappers to work. The Grenadier Company of the 42nd, when destroying some baggage carts, found a very large gong which was kept as a trophy by the Regiment.

The remainder of the Regiment—numbers 2, 4, 5, 6 and 7 Companies, under the command of Major Wilkinson, joined at Bithur on the 22nd December, 1857. Lieutenant-Colonel Cameron and Major Priestley, who had been left at Calcutta, joined Headquarters Company on the 12th December.

Chapter 16

Putting Cawnpore into an efficient state of defence, the Commander-in-Chief appointed Brigadier Inglis (of Lucknow fame) to the command; General Windham was posted to Ambala. On the 24th December, with a force of about 8,000 men, Sir Colin Campbell commenced his march on the Great Trunk Road towards Fatehgarh (the British cantonment of Furruckabad). The force covered thirteen miles on that day, halting at noon. Christmas Day was observed by a parade service, afterwards the men were allowed to do as they liked. Under the circumstances, it was a happy day, everyone "chummed" together, each man contributing whatever he could to the common pool of food for Christmas dinner.

Covering about thirteen miles each day, the march continued for another three days through flat, well-cultivated country dotted by small woods. On the 28th December they reached Meerunka Serai, where they were joined by Brigadier Hope and his column from Bithur.

The spectacle provided by an Indian Army on the line of march fascinated Hector, who had never before seen such a colourful mixture of men and animals, whose plodding progress through the thick dust stirred up an ever present cloud that lay along the lengthy column like a cloak. Each day's march commenced in darkness and the sleep-drugged men marched automatically for the first hour in a state of irritable silence. The first streaks of dawn brought with them the welcome day-heralding notes of the bugles sounding the "halt", the still chilly air being momentarily shattered by the metallic lilt that rapidly cascaded from the front of the column to bounce like a ball from regiment to regiment, hanging upon the air at the rear of the force before reluctantly dying away. As though vying with each other in some announced competition, brass-voiced officers and N.C.Os bellowed their orders, causing cavalrymen to dismount and the infantry to pile their arms in the middle of the road, then the entire army dispersed on either side of the road and took breakfast. The men were rolling up their overcoats and strapping them to their packs, munching their meagre meal as they did so; welcome an hour before when they began the march in the chill and dewy night, the coming of daylight did away with the need for such protection. The officers may have fared better with food as it is recorded that their "... favourite refreshment ... is bread, cold tongue and brandy-pawnee, which find their way out of innocent-looking holsters. ..."*

Carried from bugler to bugler, the rippling notes that brought their rest period to an end came all too soon. Arms were unpiled and everyone fell in to the ranks; now thoroughly awake, the men were cheerful and noisy. The day was made lively and the route easier by the cheerful uplifting music of the bands—drums, fifes, bugles and bagpipes brought a spring to the step and delayed the inevitable foot and bodily aches as the march proceeded, broken only by two more rest periods.

The sun rose, bringing with it the intense heat that transformed each day's march into a wearying replica of the miles marched on the previous day and the miles to be marched to-morrow. The dust, in a thick cloud extending the length of the column and at a height of about ten feet, took on a progressively increasing and stifling intensity. Soon the bandsmen were too choked and dry to blow and the column plodded, heads down, in a state of silent endurance. The road was long and level with few rises and falls, bordered on either side by wide stretches of grass and groves of trees. From the dust bowl of the road, it looked cool and inviting, but even this haven was soon to vanish as the camels and elephants were sent to march clear of the road, causing the dust to spread over an even wider area.

Arriving at the halting place at the end of the day's march, the men fell-out, piled their arms and sat down on the grass. After about half an hour the elephants plodded in, the tents they carried were unpacked and pitched and those men not detailed for a duty lay down in the tents to sleep. It was sometimes as long as three or four hours before the hackeries trundled in, bearing the baggage and cooking utensils. Then the men arose to wash and clean themselves up whilst a meal was being cooked. On one occasion, for various reasons the march was badly delayed so that they did not reach their camping ground until about 9.30 p.m., where the 42nd were allotted an area in a ploughed field. No baggage or provisions had arrived and the ravenously hungry Highlanders had eaten

*_The Devil's Wind_, p. 107.

every crumb in their haversacks. Wandering off, the MacDonalds came across a group of Indian camp-followers crouched low over a small fire, making chupatties. The natives asked two rupees each for the chupatties; this started off the haggling without which no deal was ever concluded in India. Whilst the arguing was going on, two of the 93rd came strolling up:

"Don't argue with them . . . take the bloody things and we'll all have a bite to eat . . . kick their arses if they give any trouble!"

Undecided, the MacDonalds looked at each other and then down at the now alarmed natives. Slowly they shook their heads and returned to the bargaining. Cursing, the two 93rd privates moved off. Hector was pleased by his brothers' attitude; although the 42nd had not been in India very long, Hector had formed his own opinion of the natives of the country. They seemed quite easy to get on with and the better class of Indians had a dignified way of expressing gratitude and honesty, going to great lengths to show their appreciation of the most trifling acts of kindness offered them by the white soldiers. Hector had noticed that English residents, possibly justified in the light of events, were very prejudiced against the natives, but he was inclined to think that the mutiny may have been caused by the contempt so openly shown by the British towards the natives they governed.

Eventually three chupatties were bought for a rupee each and divided between them. At midnight the elephants arrived with the tents which were pitched in total darkness; there was not even a candle available and everyone settled down, famished, to wait for the arrival of the hackeries. They did not come in until about four o'clock, when the men hastily aroused themselves, and soon every tent was ablaze with light, and roaring fires lit up the sky on all sides as a meal was cooked and eaten whilst the first streaks of dawn appeared.

Usually, the men settled down to sleep at about eight p.m. on the conclusion of a day's march and rose next morning at about five, drinking a quick cup of coffee whilst packing up their kit and then marching off before light.

Tiring of walking, a field officer of the 42nd bought himself a camel, and so became probably the first man ever to attempt to ride the humped beast whilst wearing a kilt. The camel is not an easy beast to ride and, to the delight of the men in the ranks, the officer, far from proficient, consistently slipped backwards over the camel's tail whilst clutching desperately with both hands at its hump. Time and again he slid back, to fall sprawling on the grass amid shouts of laughter. Finally he tired of the self-imposed task, sold the camel and resumed his plodding place at the head of his company.

On the 1st January, 1858, Brigadier Hope was ordered to take out a small column to cover the Sappers repairing the suspension bridge over the Kali Naddi near Fatehgarh. He took the 53rd and 93rd regiments, leaving the 42nd in camp. A detachment of Peel's Naval Brigade went forward with their guns to support Hope. The sailors were delighted to be able to assist in the work, and repaired the bridge by replacing with ropes some of the ironwork which the rebels had begun to destroy. Going forward with his staff to inspect progress, Sir Colin Campbell sent back an urgent message ordering the rest of the force to come up with all speed, for the enemy had returned and were now in strength on the other side of the river. The rebels had occupied the village of Khudaganj, just across the river and only 300 yards from the bridge. From here they opened up a vigorous musket fire, covered by several heavy guns. Only the skirmishers of the 53rd and two or three supporting companies were across the river to oppose a native force considered to be about 5,000 strong.

The main body of the army arrived at about eleven a.m. and, led by the infantry, began to cross the bridge. It was a tedious operation as there had not been time fully to repair it, and in one place planks had only been laid for half its width so that horses had to be led and infantry had to pass over in sections. The enemy had got the exact range and several casualties occurred on the crossing. Campbell had pushed the 53rd Regiment across the bridge with strict orders to remain on the defensive, to allow the cavalry to get behind the enemy and cut off their retreat to Fatehgarh. Soon all the 53rd were on the enemy's side of the river, keeping up a withering fire from behind the cover of mounds, ridges of earth and tufts of tall, coarse grass. The Lancers and a body of Sikh cavalry crossed the bridge and took up a position on their left.

There was a feeling throughout the Army that Sir Colin Campbell was inclined unduly to favour the Highland Brigade, and the 53rd (at that time largely composed of very belligerent and very tough Irishmen) got hold of the idea that Sir Colin was going to allow the honour of delivering the assault on the village of Khudaganj to the 93rd Highlanders, who were seen to be moving forward. Sir Colin and his staff were waiting near the bridge for the attacking party to form when suddenly the "Advance" was sounded by a little drummer boy of the 53rd, who stuck himself up on a mound and blew the "Advance" and the "Double" on his bugle with all the breath in his lungs. With a tremendous cheer the 53rd leapt to their feet and charged forward. Sir Colin Campbell was furious, but the 53rd could not be brought back and there was nothing for it but to support them. Up the gradually sloping ground towards Khudaganj rushed the impulsive 53rd, followed by the 93rd Highlanders; Greathed's Brigade took a line to their left and the cavalry and Horse Artillery mounted up ready for action. As the attackers neared the village the rebels hastily limbered up their guns and retired, presenting an opportunity for mounted troops such as does not often occur. With Hope Grant leading, the 9th Lancers and the Sikhs crashed home into the rebels, capturing seven guns and killing large numbers of them in a few minutes. They broke and fled in all directions, and in the five-mile pursuit that followed large numbers of them were cut down and many guns were captured.[57]

After the fighting had died down, the 53rd and the 93rd re-assembled in Adrian Hope's Brigade area. Almost at once Sir Colin Campbell came riding up, obviously in a furious temper and bent on letting the 53rd know exactly what he thought of their impulsive action. Exercising his well-known talent for invective to the full, the Commander-in-Chief commenced to berate the 53rd. Resting on their arms, the 42nd stood by and listened, highly amused. To their delight, every time Sir Colin began a sentence his words were drowned by the Irishmen loudly crying:

"Three cheers for the Commander-in-Chief, boys!"

It was soon obvious that the 53rd were determined not to give Sir Colin a hearing and, having just been winded by a blow in the stomach from a spent bullet and not in his usual good voice, the Commander-in-Chief finally turned away laughing.

Later in the day the cavalry returned to camp, almost every man carrying some trophy. The 9th Lancers came in bearing three standards, with the Sikh Cavalry behind them. Waving their lances in the air, the Lancers sent up cheer after cheer, backed up by the Sikhs who brandished bare tulwars over their heads. The 42nd and the other regiments of the Highland Brigade ran down and cheered the victorious cavalry, waving their feathered bonnets in the air. Riding back to camp through the tents of the Highland Brigade, Sir Colin Campbell said that the cheering and enthusiasm of the men exceeded anything he had ever seen before.

Next day the column marched to Fatehgarh. Dead bodies were strewn on either side of the road and in the fields could be seen the tracks where the Sepoys had fled, pursued by the relentless cavalry. Here and there were patches of trampled ground where melées had evidently taken place. Some of the wells they passed were choked with Indian corpses. The column marched in to Fatehgarh at four in the afternoon and encamped on the Parade Ground. The enemy had abandoned the fort and town and had left untouched the valuable gun-carriage factory, to the delight of Captain Peel of the Naval Brigade who would now be able to mount his 64-pounder guns from the *Shannon*.[58] The rebel camp had been abandoned in haste and was left full of articles plundered from Europeans; there were ladies' boots and shoes, dresses and children's clothing strewn about all over the camp.

The army remained at Fatehgarh for nearly a month. Sir Colin Campbell had asked a lot of his troops during his advance on Fatehgarh, being determined to push on and imbuing everyone in the camp with his own enthusiasm. Forced marches with irregular meals, lots of hard work and rough encampments on the open plain amid constant dust and heat had taken a heavy toll of everyone. Although glad to rest for the next few days, they were soon refreshed, however, and the men began to chafe at the unaccountable delay. Before long the camp was a buzzing hive of complaints, irritability and boredom. Vast amounts of supplies had come up and everyone was living in extremely comfortable conditions. The 42nd were in square, coarse canvas tents, lined with blue cotton and supported by a single pole; the roofs were double with the upper one spreading out on two opposite sides into large eaves. On either side of the tent were doors hung with green blinds made of finely split bamboo. Life was comparatively leisurely with a late reveille and breakfast at about nine. Most men were glad to take a daily bath, utilising the services of a *bhisti* (water carrier) who poured water from his pigskin container on to the back of the crouching bather. The officers were particularly well attended, each one having a retinue of at least seven servants—a headman, a *kitmager* (cook or butler), a valet, a *syce* to look after the ponies, a *bhisti* who provided water for cooking, drinking and bathing, and two grass cutters who looked after the ponies under the directions of the *syce*. It was possible to obtain the services of these people for about forty pounds a year. Even when campaigning, the officers were constantly being attended by their servants to the extent of having coffee in bed and being shaved without even being woken up!

The camp became so settled that soon there was a regular service of *doodwallahs*, young women in white robes and with bright coloured shawls around their heads, jingling bangles on their ankles and wrists, swaying gracefully through the camp with a shining brass chatti on their heads, calling in a musical voice "buckrie dood" (goat's milk).

One day in the middle of January, a General Parade was ordered to witness the execution of a rebel rajah and his son, who were known to have roasted white prisoners alive. The regiments formed up on three sides of the parade ground, two guns were placed in advance of the men forming the base of the square, their muzzles pointing outwards towards the open side. Then the prisoners were marched into the area under a guard of armed police and an escort of the 53rd. The sentence of the Court was read to the prisoners. Apparently unmoved, they stood quietly with expressionless faces. Head held high, the old man walked across to the guns with a firm stride, his snow white hair and venerable appearance arousing compassion in the ranks of the watching soldiers. His son was less calm and had to be assisted by two policemen, one holding on to each arm. Reaching the gun, he shrank back and began to struggle so that he had to be held in position with his back pressing against the muzzle whilst the cords that lashed his body to the wheels were fixed in position. His father, after one disdainful glance at his son, waved aside the police and stood with his back firmly pressed against the gun muzzle whilst the lashings were made fast around his body. Then everyone withdrew, leaving the lashed men incongruously erect in front of the guns. The younger man was struggling in his bonds and arching his back as though to minimise the effect of the charge that was soon to destroy him. A deathly silence lay like a pall over the rigid assembly, to be startlingly broken by the clear, high-pitched voice of the old man crying out the same sentence over and over again. Later, Hector was told that he was praying that his surviving children might be spared to burn them all. It was a panorama that seemed to last for an eternity and which remained vividly in Hector's mind for the rest of his life. Suddenly, the officer commanding the artillery, shouting loudly enough to drown the age-weary voice of the old man, cried:

"Division! Ready! Fire!"

Aware as he was that two human beings were about to be blown to pieces before his eyes, Hector MacDonald found himself ill-prepared for what followed. The warm, still air was shattered by two crashing explosions so close together that they merged into one, accompanied by a billowing cloud of greasy smoke that hung in the air, shredding reluctantly as though to screen the scene. Like a dust storm, in a cloud formed of shreds of clothing, burning muscle, frizzing fat and lumps of coagulated blood, the torn and shattered remains of the old man were strewn over the parade ground. Being tied, his legs and arms fell close to the cannon mouth; the head and upper part of the body was blown about 50 yards. The face was quite untouched.

Still struggling in his ropes when the order to fire was given, the younger man slipped from his lashings just before the explosion, to hang suspended below the cannon's mouth. His shoulder was blown away and his arm was set on fire. An officer ran forward and placed a pistol to the man's head. Three times the cap snapped and three time the pistol failed to fire. On each occasion the wretched man shrank from the expected shot. A quick order sent a man doubling from the ranks, to fire his musket into the back of the native's head. The blood poured out of his nose and mouth like water from a briskly handled pump. It was the most horrible sight Hector had ever seen. During his life he saw death in all its forms but he never saw anything to equal this man's end.

The air was filled with the staccato shouts of officers and N.C.Os calling their men to order before marching from the parade ground. Back in quarters, the subdued men removed their equipment and stretched themselves out sombrely on their beds. After a few minutes, Hector raised his head and glared round at the other men lying motionless in the shadowy tent.

"Why do they have to do it that way . . . why can't they hang the poor buggers . . . it's not civilised!"

On the far side of the tent, an old soldier who had served in India before, answered him without raising his head from his pillow so that his words, in a flat monotone, were spoken up towards the tent roof:

"It's a quick death . . . they feel no pain . . . takes the heart away at once. It's about the only death that has any terrors for the natives, if he's hung or shot he knows that his friends or relatives can claim his body and will give him the funeral rights required by his religion. But if he is sentenced to death in this form, he knows that his body will be blown to a thousand pieces and it will be impossible for his relatives to pick up all his pieces . . . they can't bear the thought that perhaps a hand or a foot of someone of a different religion to himself will be burned or buried with the remainder of his own body, because that's contrary to his religion."[59]

Chapter 17

On the 6th January the Commander-in-Chief was on the banks of the Ganges at Fatehgarh. With him were the brigades and columns of Hope Grant, Adrian Hope, Walpole, Windham, Seaton, Greathed and Little. Inglis, with a movable column, was restoring order in a part of the Doab between Cawnpore and Etawa, while Outram was still at the Alum Bagh. Waiting for more troops from Calcutta and for vast stores of warlike material from the upper provinces, Sir Colin scarcely moved from the spot during the remainder of the month.

On the 27th of the month, Brigadier Adrian Hope took a small column out from Fatehgarh, consisting of:

9th Lancers (one squadron).
Hodson's Horse (200).
Bengal Horse Artillery (one troop).
Bengal Field Artillery (four guns).
42nd Highlanders.
53rd Foot.
4th Punjab Rifles.

The lucky men selected to go with Brigadier Hope were delighted. Not only was camp life boring but it seemed to inspire officers and N.C.Os to devise arduous drill parades and similar activities. The column marched through Kushinabad to Shamshabad, where they found the enemy in considerable force, on the edge of the plateau overlooking the plain stretching towards the river. The mutineers occupied a commanding knoll on which was a Moslem tomb surrounded by the remains of an old entrenchment where the rebels had raised a sandbag battery. Their front was defended by a ravine impassable for cavalry or guns. Brigadier Hope deployed his force and the infantry moved over broken ground towards the enemy camp. As soon as they came within range, the rebels opened upon them with a well-directed fire of roundshot. However, the enemy guns were soon silenced by the Horse Artillery, who had gone out to a flank. During this period,

Hope had marshalled his infantry in a hollow where they had been screened from view; as soon as the enemy guns ceased firing they rushed from their position to the camp and captured it without loss. As usual, the enemy turned and fled, to be hotly pursued by Hope's cavalry. Several guns and a large quantity of ammunition were captured. Before being hanged, some of the prisoners revealed that the force consisted of two of the mutinied Bareilly regiments, accompanied by a motley group of rebels seeking plunder.

On the following day, the force had a fierce encounter near Farakabad. Scouts had been sent out seeking the enemy and, just as the men were taking breakfast, a cavalry patrol came pounding in to the camp with the news that about 5,000 rebels with four guns had been discovered a few miles from the city. Bugles blew and a force was called to arms—it consisted of the 42nd and 53rd Foot, the 4th Punjab Rifles, two squadrons of the 9th Lancers, two squadrons of Hodson's Horse, a Horse Battery and two Troops of Horse Artillery. It was a densely foggy morning and the column proceeded cautiously to avoid stumbling upon the mutineers or being taken by surprise. After an eerie, nerve-racking march, they knew that they had found the enemy when round-shot started plunging amongst them from guns planted in an old mud fort, situated on rising ground.

The artillery went forward to engage the enemy whilst the cavalry deployed to out-flank the position. Suddenly, more by luck than judgement, the enemy's artillery fire blew up two tumbrils of ammunition at a moment when the 42nd were deployed from column into line, preparatory to attacking. The misty air was torn by two roaring explosions accompanied by sheets of flame; bullets, shells and rockets screamed and ricocheted in all directions. Flung from his feet by the earth-shaking explosions, Hector lay huddled with his head wrapped in his arms whilst debris clattered all around him. When it ceased, he cautiously raised his head and peered through the smoke and fog-laden air. On all sides men were lying where they had been thrown, some were raising their heads, others shaking arms and legs as though to confirm that they were still attached to their bodies. As always after any action or danger, Hector sought out his brothers. A soldier has to look after himself and rarely, if ever, considers that he might be the one to be killed—it is always going to be the unfortunate man on your right or left who will fall to the ground. To have a brother serving in the same regiment brought a nagging sense of anxiety—to have five brothers with you made one almost intolerably vulnerable.

More than twenty men were killed and a large number wounded by the blowing up of the tumbrils.[60] The artillery and outflanking cavalry forces soon dispersed the rebels, who fled in all directions leaving behind their guns. The infantry did not come into action at all.

On the 1st February, Sir Colin Campbell broke up his camp at Fatehgarh and commenced the return march to Cawnpore. Escorted by the 9th Lancers and a troop of Bengal Horse Artillery the Commander-in-Chief with his staff pushed on in advance of the army and, proceeding at a rate of twenty-five miles per day, they arrived at Cawnpore on the 4th February. With all speed, the main body of troops at Fatehgarh followed the Commander-in-Chief; Adrian Hope's Brigade, containing the 42nd, reached Cawnpore on the 7th. They had marched back over the Kali Naddi, where they had beaten the Sepoys on January 2nd; it was a route marked by piles of bones and grinning skulls, picked white by the jackals. On the 11th February the Army, now larger than any which had, up to that time, appeared against the rebels, began to cross the Ganges from Cawnpore into Oude. In spite of the fact that a second bridge of boats had been constructed, the vast numbers of animals, vehicles and people that marked an Indian army made the crossing a slow and difficult one that lasted several days.

Russell of *The Times* graphically described the march:

> "Daylight was still striving with the moonlight for mastery, and casting a sort of neutral tint over the camping-ground, on which blazed the flames of many watch-fires, when the heads of our columns began to cross the bridge of boats at Cawnpore. There was but a waste of baked earth where, at sunset, had been a camp—only a few tents belonging to the commander-in-chief and the head-quarters' staff, were left behind; and for hours the bridge echoed to the tramp of men and horses, the rumble of artillery, and to the tread of innumerable elephants and camels and oxen. The Ganges is at this season at its lowest, and the bridges are not, I should think, more than 300 yards long; one is used for the exit, the other for the entrance of Cawnpore. They lead to a level sandy plain, overflowed by the Ganges for several

hundred yards in the rainy season, on which there were now moving, as far as the eye could reach, the strings of baggage animals and the commissariat carts of the army, with their fantastic followers. The road has been much cut up by the passage of artillery, and in some places is only to be distinguished from the land at each side by the flanking line of telegraph-posts. The country, as we go on, is as level as a bowling-green, but on all sides the horizon is bounded by the groves of mangoes. The country is green with early corn; but close to the roadside the presence of our hosts has made itself visible, and the trees are stripped of their branches, and the fields trampled and brown, the young crops being used as food for animals, and the boughs and branches as provender for elephants and camels. The villages by the roadside, built of mud, but rather better than those in Bengal, were deserted and in ruins, and, except in the wake of the army, not a soul was visible. The dust flew in clouds—a light choking powder, which filled eyes and lungs and mouth, and rendered all the senses unpleasant. It was with great satisfaction, therefore, that I learnt, after a little purgatory of some three and a-half hours, that we were approaching Oonao (pronounced Ohnow), where Havelock fought and beat the enemy on two successive occasions in his advances to Lucknow. It is about eleven miles from Cawnpore, and it presents an irregular outline of mud houses, with high mud walls which in the distance looked like those of a fortress. Above them peer the minarets of some small mosques, and there are thick groves of mangoes and orchard trees all around it. The road passes it on the left; and in half-an-hour more we saw before us a wide plain, destitute of trees, over which the crowds of vultures and kites that ever follow a camp were wheeling in great flocks, telling us that we were near our resting-place. Through the clouds of dust we could distinguish our tents in the distance. Camels and hackeries and elephants came pouring in all day till late at night, and the sun set through a thick veil of dust, through which might be seen dimly the fleet of camels steering their course steadily along the line of the main road towards Lucknow.

Next morning was very like yesterday morning: if possible, there was more noise and dust. The first bugles went at two o'clock, and at 3.30 the camp was struck, and the force under Walpole was again in motion. It was a strange scene—

not to be described or imagined. The moon was shining brightly on the vast array, when in motion, became comparatively silent; but the ground, indeed, thundered with the beat of many feet, and now and then the shrill neigh of a charger provoked a thousand responses. The camels, looming to a gigantic size in the light, passed noiselessly like spectres. As we approached the road—narrow for such a host—the clamour uprose again, and doolies, hackeries, ox-carts, and baggage animals became involved in immense confusion, which was not diminished by the efforts of the baggage guard to restore order by commands issued in the vernacular, and enforced now and then by the aid of a musket stock. At last we got into files upon the road, and rode on in clouds of dust. Presently in front we heard the joyous clash of a brass band, playing a quick step, and, getting off the road, we managed to join our old friends of the Rifle Brigade and renewed acquaintanceship with talk of old marches in the Crimea. As the sun rose upon one side and the moon set upon the other, the spectacle assumed a weird, unearthly aspect, which not all the hard reality around us could quite destroy. We were marching over historic ground. We trod the very earth which had felt the tread of Havelock and Outram's gallant little columns, and before us were positions made memorable by their valour. Oonao was succeeded by Busheerut-gunge; and at every few hundred yards spots were pointed out, even trees identified, as the places where 'We caught sight of the enemy's sowars', or 'where Havelock gave the men such a wigging for straggling a little in the ranks'. Through dust and smothering pillars of pulverised earth we went on; but, fast as we went, we heard that an hour before, Sir Colin, with General Mansfield and a small staff, accompanied by his little escort of irregular horse and a solitary English lancer, had dashed on towards Bunthura. They had started from Cawnpore soon after midnight, and at a swinging gallop had passed through the regiments on the march. It was nearly eight o'clock in the morning when we debouched upon another wide plain, passing the camp of another battalion of the Rifle Brigade and some Punjabee infantry, and pitched our tents at Nuwabgunge for the day. The heat was very great, and as there was nothing to see but clouds of dust, nothing to feel but dust—dust everywhere, in eyes, in nose, on clothes, in tea, on plates, on meat and bread, in water, in the tent, outside the tent."

Probably the largest British army to have taken to the field since Waterloo in 1815, it was accompanied by a vast train of native camp followers, many of whom had brought their families with them. There were at least 200 guns, ranging from siege guns down to the light Horse Artillery pieces. The sixty-five-hundredweight guns of Peel's Naval Brigade were monsters that required solid shot weighing sixty-eight pounds each, hollow shot of fifty-six pounds and shell of fifty-one pounds. This necessitated an ammunition and baggage train for the Naval Brigade of at least 800 bullocks. The ammunition for the remainder of the force was carried in 1,500 carts.

Adrian Hope's Brigade marched with Peel's sailors and at Unao, when the Highlanders passed the parked Naval guns by the side of which Peel and some of his officers were standing, the Highlanders were delighted to show their great admiration for these sailors so far from the sea, by marching to attention, with eyes right and the band playing *Auld Lang Syne*. On another occasion, the Naval Brigade were able to reciprocate by going out to meet the 93rd Highlanders when they came into camp. The sailors lined both sides of the road and their fiddlers placed themselves at the head of the Highland Regiment and played them to the camping ground. Doctor Munro of the 93rd recorded:*

> ". . . the blue jackets saluting us with cheers and with many singular pithy nautical phrases expressive, I believe, of esteem and used by sailors as terms of endearment, but which I think I had better not repeat here. It was a most amusing scene. The strange musicians moved along with a rolling gait, raising their feet high and stamping on the ground, while they fiddled away with an energy meant, no doubt, to show their desire to make their reception of the 93rd as demonstrative as possible. Our men accepted the compliment thus paid them by their sailor comrades, but found it impossible to restrain their laughter at the novel sight of a Regiment of Highlanders marching with a Band of Fiddlers at its head."

Slowly the army straggled along the road to Lucknow, at times stretching along the whole length of the route. It was a troublesome march, transporting the guns through the muddy nullahs and up the steep banks was very difficult. The heavier

**The Devil's Wind*, p. 124.

guns were each drawn by twenty-two bullocks or two elephants and when they stuck in the mud it meant that all the infantry in the area of the gun had to fall out of the line of march and assist in pushing, pulling and dragging the ponderous weapon on to dry ground. Seemingly never able to pull together, the bullocks were usually taken out of their traces, then the wheels and drag ropes were manned by blue jackets and soldiers while elephants pushed from the back. In spite of such back-breaking work, the Highlanders rather enjoyed these diversions and found the activities of the elephants something at which to wonder. The huge, ponderous beasts viewed the scene from their little piggy eyes and then, seizing the exact moment when the gun was coming to a standstill and their help was most needed, they placed their foreheads against the muzzle of the gun and shoved until the weapon safely landed on top of the bank.

If affection was felt towards the elephants no one liked the camels, gurgling and grumbling beasts with a bad habit of biting innocent, well-meaning people who were trying to take an interest in them. Ungainly and disagreeable, querulous and morose, they delighted in their ability to make the most horrible noises with their throats, jaws, tongues and stomachs; and although capable of marching for days, with the nose of one fastened to the tail of the other in an endless procession, they spat viciously at anyone approaching to offer them a piece of bread or to rub their rugged sides.

By the 1st March, the main body of the army, including the siege-train, Engineer party and Naval Brigade, with ammunition and stores of all kinds, had collected at Bhantria, a large plain on the road to Lucknow and about nine miles from the city. On the 3rd March the 42nd retired to bed as usual at eight o'clock, but at eleven they were aroused and told that orders had been received to march at once. Before they had been awakened, the native servants had packed up everything in the tent except the clothes they were to wear, knocking out all the tent pegs except four to keep the tent from falling. Grumbling, the drowsy Highlanders dragged on their clothes and equipment. Whilst they were dressing, the natives had carried out their charpoys (light bedsteads), rolled up their bedding and, as the last Highlander stepped reluctantly from the tent, the remaining pegs were driven out by the *calassies* (tent men) and down came the tent. Each man was given a cup of hot coffee and a chupattie and then they were called on to parade.

"42nd! 42nd! . . . Attention! Fours Right! By your left Quick March!"

The band at the head of the Regiment played a lively tune that drove weary and obstinate feet into the correct step in company with the 93rd Highlanders and the Naval Brigade. Although their journey was only seven miles, it lasted twelve hours because of the narrowness of the roads, which were in an extremely bad state. Twice they lost their way in the darkness and numerous hold-ups occurred as the Naval Brigade struggled to manoeuvre their huge and ponderous guns through the tortuous approaches to the ancient fortress of Jellalabad. The column did not reach the camping ground in the rear of the Dilkusha Palace, which had been captured from the enemy on the previous afternoon, until half-past ten on the morning of the 4th March.

Sir Colin Campbell's intention was to form a camp near part of the Dilkusha Palace at the eastern-most extremity of the city, just beyond reach of the enemy's guns. The role of this formation was to protect the enormous siege-train and the countless appendages of the Indian Army on their journey from Bhantria to the Dilkusha. William Russell wrote that no language could correctly convey an idea of the vastness of the number of elephants, camels, oxen, horses, camp-followers and vehicles that daily demanded the Commander-in-Chief's attention.

> "Who can really bring before his mind's eye a train of baggage animals twenty-five miles long, a string of 16,000 camels, a siege-train park covering a space of 400 by 400 yards, with 12,000 oxen attached to it, and a following of 60,000 non-combatants? Even the doolies, or litter-carriages for wounded men, constituted a formidable item. To each company of a regiment there were ten doolies and to each doolie were six coolies or native porters; thus there were nearly 500 doolie carriers for each average regiment; even with this large supply, if the sick and wounded in any one regiment exceeded 800 men, there would be more than the doolies could properly attend to."

Lucknow lay on the right bank of the River Gumti, which changed its course towards the south after winding round the Martinière and the Dilkusha. A long series of palaces and gardens extended between the most crowded part of the city and the river, occupying an immense area so that, for at least five miles, this string of large buildings formed a belt between the river and the dense streets of the city. Between November and March the rebels had fortified the city in great strength, without extending their defences across the river. Although not enclosed, like Delhi, by a fortified wall, Lucknow's many square miles of narrow streets and high houses, occupied by a large military force in addition to its ordinary population, constituted a formidable stronghold. Rightly judging that the English commander would avoid a hand-to-hand contest in the streets and would direct his attack towards the south-eastern suburb, the rebels spared no labours in strengthening this side of the city. They treated the courts and buildings of the Kaiserbagh as a sort of citadel, interposing a triple series of obstacles between it and the besiegers. The first and outer line extended from the river to a building known as Bank's House; the canal formed the wet ditch of this line and within the canal was a rampart of elevated earth-works. The second defence consisted of an earth-work beginning at the river side near the Moti Mahal, and the third and interior defence was the principal rampart of the Kaiserbagh itself. All these lines consisted of well-constructed earth parapets or ridges, fronted by wide and deep ditches and strengthened at intervals by bastions. The enemy had also loop-holed and fortified every house and enclosure, constructed strong counter-guards in front of the gateways and placed isolated bastions, stockades and traverses across the principal streets.

At the beginning of March it was believed that the city was garrisoned by 30,000 mutinous Sepoys and 50,000 peasants from the country, with desperate characters from the villages who had joined the regular Sepoys, together with the armed retainers of chieftains. It was estimated that the enemy defended their works with nearly one hundred guns and mortars.

The plan of attack decided upon by Sir Colin Campbell owed much to the reconnaissance of Brigadier Robert Napier R.E. (Chief of Staff to Outram and later Commander of the Engineer Brigade before Lucknow) who advised the attack being made on the east.[61] Not only did that side offer the smallest front but it also afforded ground for planting the artillery, which the west side did not. And it was the shortest approach to the Kaiserbagh, a place in which the rebels placed the greatest importance. Further, the British knew their way round the east side of the town and were little acquainted with the west. Napier also recommended that the attack should be accompanied by flank movements in the north, with the object of taking in reverse the first and second line of the enemy's defences.

While the army was establishing its camp near the Dilkusha, the Engineers had been collecting materials to build bridges across the Gumti, near the Bibiapore, where the river was about forty yards wide. Here, Campbell intended to push a strong force across with the object of enfilading the rebels' defences and so assisting the advance of the main columns. The enemy began to assemble in large numbers on the opposite bank as though to oppose the operations, but were soon dispersed when the British artillery came up and opened fire upon them. The bridges themselves were patchwork affairs made from a collection of empty beer casks, lashed by ropes to timber cross-pieces and floated off one by one to their positions, finally being crowned by a roadway of planking.

On the 6th March Major-General Sir James Outram crossed the river over these bridges with 6,000 men, both infantry and cavalry, heavy guns and mortars, ammunition waggons, carts and ambulances—he suffered not a single accident to man or beast.

For two days and nights the road from Bantria to the Dilkusha had been filled with an apparently endless procession of soldiers, guns, waggons, beasts of burden and all the other impedimenta of an Indian Army on the march. The soldiers were most enthusiastic and looked forward to having another go at the enemy. An eye witness wrote:[62]

> "Most of the Regiments were in a highly efficient state, but the Highlanders were most conspicuous, not only for their costume but for their steady and martial air on parade and in the field. As they marched off in the early grey of the morning, with their pipes playing '*The Campbells are Coming*' one caught a vision of the interior of Lucknow through the dancing sheen of their arms; the Chief inspected them and seemed proud of his countrymen and it was only natural he should be so."

Out in the open country Campbell's force had been much annoyed by enemy artillery fire. So, without much difficulty, they advanced and captured the Dilkusha itself where they established an advance picket with heavy guns placed in battery to oppose the enemy's artillery. In this way a secure base with its right resting on the river was obtained for further operations. Sir Colin Campbell was conscious of a good day's work, not in conquest but in the preparations for conquest.

The Dilkusha Palace, built in the Italian style, still retained much of the splendour that belonged to it in more peaceful days, when it was the heart's delight of its sensual monarch. The 42nd, who garrisoned the Palace, could see from its flat roof the chief buildings of the city together with the enemy's extensive defensive preparations. As soon as anyone appeared on this roof the Sepoys in the Martinière put up a flurry of musketry, but the distance between the two buildings made it ineffective.

Chiefly through the energy of Lieutenant Patrick Stewart, the Commander-in-Chief was able to carry an electric telegraph with him from camp to camp; poles being set up and wires extended wherever he went. Through a drawing-room window of the Dilkusha Palace itself; a wire made its appearance and was stretched over a row of poles along the line of route which the Commander-in-Chief and his troops had followed. The wires even followed out from over the river and made their appearance on the left bank. No sooner did Sir Colin advance a few miles, than Stewart followed him with poles and wires, galvanic batteries and signal apparatus, conquering the most appalling difficulties to set up a talking machine close to the very enemy themselves. It was claimed that wherever he lay down his head at night, Sir Colin could touch a handle and converse with Lord Canning at Allahabad before he went to sleep.[63]

During Outram's operations on the left bank of the Gumti, a very heavy fire was kept up against the Martinière by mortars and guns placed in position on the Dilkusha Plateau. The Naval Brigade were prominent throughout the day, commanding four great guns on the road and battering away at the Martinière and a cluster of small houses near the building. It was during this day that Captain Peel, the commander of the Naval Brigade, was injured whilst ordering his guns into position to make a breach in the wall of the Martinière. With his usual indifference to danger, the naval commander stood up in plain view on a small knoll to get a better view of the target, becoming a mark for the Sepoys lining the rifle pits in front of the building.

"One could see their fellows laying their muskets along

the top of the rifle pit, then puff, a little white smoke, then bang! whew-ew-iz! then sput! against some stones the bullet fell flatte ed close to our feet. At last, one bullet, more true than the others, struck him and he fell saying 'Oh! They've got me.' "*

At two on the afternoon of 9th March, columns of infantry, with bayonets glittering in the sun, advanced from their camp behind the Dilkusha. Sir Colin Campbell's instructions read:

"Sir Edward Lugard will employ for the purpose . . . the 4th Brigade with the 38th and 53rd Regiments of the 3rd Brigade in support. The 42nd Highlanders will lead the attack, and seize, as a first measure, the huts and ruined houses to the left of the Martinière, as viewed from the Brigadier-General's front. The men employed in the attack will use nothing but the bayonet. They are absolutely forbidden to fire a shot till the position is won. This must be thoroughly explained to the men, and they will also be told that their advance is flanked on every side by heavy and light artillery, as well as by the infantry fire on the right . . ."[64]

At three o'clock, under a heavy musketry fire from the enemy, the 42nd and 93rd Highlanders, together with the Punjab Infantry, marched steadily out from the shelter of the Dilkusha. Led by Major E. R. Priestley, four companies of the 42nd advanced in extended order; the remaining five companies moved forward in line with Lieutenant-Colonel Cameron at their head. Although under heavy musketry fire from the Sepoys, the infantry reached the cover of a wall two hundred yards from the Martinière without a man being hit. After a moment to gather themselves, the order was given—"Advance in double-time!" Three loud cheers drowned the sounds of battles and the pipers struck up '*The Campbell's are Coming*' as the regiment rushed into the open and across the field that lay in front of the Martinière. Hardly a shot was fired at them as the alarmed enemy left their positions and fled to the rear of the building, so that the position was captured by the 42nd without losing a man. The sight of the glittering bayonets thrust belligerently forward by these terrible men in kilts appeared to frighten the enemy more than all the guns and howitzers, mortars and rockets. In fact, the European soldiers had a saying:

"A bayonet charge is more than the Pandies can bear!"

**The Devil's Wind*, p. 129.

As soon as they had occupied the Martinière, heavy fire was opened upon them from the next line of defences in its rear. Taking what shelter they could, the infantry returned the fire for some time, then Lieutenant-Colonel Cameron was ordered to position his five companies in a small collection of houses some 300 yards to the right of the Martinière. Moving out into the open, the men came under a heavy fire from the parapet of the nearby canal; several men fell before the houses were reached. From this position it was possible to see that part of the parapet was undefended, having been enfiladed by Outram's guns from across the river. After they had regained their breath, the 42nd's five companies, together with the 4th Punjab Rifles under Major Wyld, rushed out to the base of the high canal parapet. The infantry laboriously scrambled up to the top of the parapet in steps cut with their bayonets in the baked mud. Then they made ground to their left and cleared the Sepoys from the position nearly as far as Bank's House. Losses were very light, probably because the enemy were in the process of abandoning the position.

In the early evening Outram's C.R.E.,* Major L. Bicholson, noticed that the enemy appeared to be withdrawing and sought to pass the information on to Brigadier Hope, so that he could order his Highland Brigade to assault the weakened defences. Thomas Butler, a young subaltern of the Bengal Fusiliers, volunteered to swim the river and to pass any information on to Hope. For this feat, Butler, who had already distinguished himself at the capture of Delhi, was awarded the Victoria Cross.

The remainder of the 42nd were brought up and orders were given to occupy Bank's House with its surrounding gardens and houses. After a round of cheers that the Highlanders were still able to produce from dry throats, the attack went in and the place was carried with little loss. The enemy made no attempt to stand, although their troops surrounding the area maintained a heavy fire from the loopholed walls and roofs of houses.

During the attack on the Martinière, Lieutenant Frances Farquharson of the 42nd showed great bravery and spirit in leading a portion of his Company to storm a bastion mounting two guns, so that the advanced positions held during that night were rendered secure from the fire of enemy artillery. Unfortunately, on the following morning Lieutenant Farquharson was severely wounded while holding an advanced position.

*Commander, Royal Engineers.

Later he was awarded the Victoria Cross for his conspicuous bravery.

The capture of Bank's House enabled Sir Colin Campbell to commence the second part of his operation, which involved using the great block of houses and palaces extending to the Kaiserbagh as an approach, instead of "sapping up" towards the second line of works. The first building that had to be stormed was the Begum's Palace and, on the 11th March, a long and heavy bombardment took place. Manhandling their heavy guns, the sailors gradually brought them closer and closer to the massive palace wall until at last they were within 150 yards. The huge shot went through all three walls of the Palace's surroundings. At four o'clock in the afternoon, the walls had been sufficiently breached to make storming practical and the 93rd Highlanders, the 4th Punjab Rifles and some Gurkhas formed up to storm the breaches.

Doctor Munro of the 93rd, who was with the storming party, described the scene:*

"Behind some ruined buildings and battered walls, nearly opposite the breach, stood some 800 men throughout whose ranks reigned a silence as deep as death. Each man stood leaning on his rifle, wrapt in his own thoughts . . . Suddenly there was a slight movement in the ranks, just enough to break the previous stillness. Officers moved quietly to their places, men stood erect, pressed their bonnets firmly down upon their heads, stretched their arms and limbs and then, grasping their rifles tightly, stood firm and steady.

Thus they remained for a second or two, when the tall form of their favourite leader, Adrian Hope, appeared, and his right hand waved the signal for assault. Then a cry burst from their ranks. It was not a cheer, which has a pleasant ring in it, but a short, sharp, piercing cry which had an angry sound that almost made one tremble. I never heard the like before and never since.

With the leading party and amongst the foremost stormers was Pipe-Major McLeod who, entering the breach, tuned up at once and pacing up and down within the inner court of the enemy's works, played the Regimental Gathering while the fight raged fiercely round him, thinking, as he said afterwards, that 'the lads would fight all the better when they heard the music of the pipes'."

**The Devil's Wind*, p. 132.

The 93rd rushed forward from their cover, led by Captain Clarke, who ran up to the breach waving his sword and shouting out: "Come on the 93rd!" Cheering loudly and continuously, the kilted Highlanders swarmed forward, some hoisting their bonnets on the points of their bayonets; they swarmed down into a deep ditch, up again and disappeared behind the wall. On all sides could be heard the cheers of soldiers swarming into the Palace, the cries and moans of wounded and dying and the sharp reports of musketry. Little could be seen by those watching from outside. Now and then a Sepoy was observed clambering over a roof or along the wall of a house, before falling back shot by the soldier who would appear in pursuit on the wall or roof behind him. Very heavy losses were inflicted upon the enemy as they beat a hasty retreat from the building in an attack later reported by Sir Colin Campbell as "the sternest struggle which occurred during the siege".

Coming up in support, the 42nd entered the Palace with the fighting going on ahead of them. Looking around him, Hector marvelled that an entry had ever been affected—the thick walls were profusely loopholed for musketry and there were numerous bastions and earthworks with a deep ditch around the high earthen rampart. It seemed as though the Sepoys had again been paralysed by the sight of the bayonet. From court to court of the huge pile of buildings they pushed on, past scenes of dead Sepoys, blood-splashed pavements and parties of excited Highlanders, seeking the enemy's hiding places. Groups of plunderers were searching the dead, lying heaped on top of each other amid the ruins of rooms brought down upon them by shell fire. Dense smoke hung lazily on the still air, accompanied by a pungent and overpowering odour. It was caused by the thickly quilted cotton tunics and bed coverings of the Sepoys being set alight by gunfire, causing the bodies to burn and smoulder. In many of the rooms it had been necessary to throw bags of gunpowder to flush out the stubbornly resisting mutineers, which had also caused fires. In some of the rooms Hector could see, through the dense smoke, piles of bodies smouldering and sometimes convulsively writhing.

The Palace had consisted of innumerable rooms and salons ornamented with splendid mirrors and chandeliers, but now everything was lying underfoot, smashed and trampled by the men who had gone before them. It was rumoured that the first men in found large numbers of Kashmir shawls, valuable silks and even a few gold mohurs. On all sides soldiers were leaving the battle in search of loot; unable to find gold, silver and gems, some men were laden with shawls, cushions, umbrellas, pictures, looking-glasses and even musical instruments. Highlanders and Punjabis roamed about once gorgeous salons and *zenanas*, tearing, stabbing and slashing at furniture and panels in their search for valuables. Swift retribution was taken on small groups of panic-stricken fugitives who fled from room to room until splendour and blood struggled for mastery in many of the courts and rooms of the palace, carpeted with broken glass that crunched under the heavy feet of the seeking infantry.

A large number of the casualties among the attackers occurred during the pursuit of Sepoys through the dark rooms and passages of the various buildings that were stormed. From their hiding places, the Sepoys could see their pursuers advance and fired upon them from close range. However, in all of these minor affrays, cold steel proved the master.[65]

Colin Campbell knew that neither his English troops nor his native infantry would have hesitated to rush forward and storm any of the buildings that lay ahead. But he also knew that the loss of men was more difficult to replace than guns and missiles at such a time and in such a country. Well supplied with heavy guns, Sir Colin Campbell acted sensibly by employing them and the Engineers before sending his men in.

After the Begum's Palace fell, progress was made towards the next large building, the Imambara, by sapping through a mass of intermediate buildings rather than by open assault. So many and so intricate were these buildings, that three days were occupied in the operations. It was work of a formidable character, for the flat roofs of many of the houses were covered with two or three feet of earth, baked in the sun, and loopholed for musketry. Every such house had to be scrutinised before an advance could be made towards it, then the Sappers dug their passages, either actually underground or through the lower portions of walls and enclosures surrounding the buildings. By the 13th, these approaches were so far completed that a large number of guns and mortars could be brought forward and placed in position for bombarding the Imambara and the other buildings that stood around it.

The 14th March was one of the busiest days of the siege. The Engineers had made passages for the heavy guns and mortars to be brought forward to bombard the Imambara. After a heavy cannonade, the storming columns pressed forward and took the building with little loss. Closely pursuing their advantage, they entered the Kaiserbagh, the main stronghold, on the heels of the fleeing enemy so that this position, looked upon by the rebels as their last and most powerful citadel, was taken with little loss. Disconcerted by the sudden arrival of their panic-stricken comrades, its garrison were paralysed into putting up little resistance. And so the great Palace changed hands, with smoke and blood and cries of war strangely mingling in the magnificence of mosques, corridors, courts, gardens, terraces, salons, mirrors, gilding, chandeliers, tapestry, statues, pictures and costly furniture, all jumbled together in a strange kaleidoscope of oriental and European splendour.

The Kaiserbagh had been so quickly conquered that the officers lost control of the movements of the troops under their command and the hours that followed were never recalled by Hector and his brothers with anything but shame. In a situation where lust for prizes and plunder overcame heroism, brave and faithful (although poor and unlettered) soldiers suddenly found themselves masters of splendid palaces containing vast stores of oriental and European luxuries, with very little check or supervision by their officers. At first, in a spirit of triumphant revenge, costly articles too large to be carried away were broken and smashed; glass chandeliers were hurled to the ground, mirrors shattered into countless fragments, statues mutilated and overturned, pictures stabbed and shredded and doors of costly wood torn from their hinges. At last the troops, tiring of destruction, forced their way through courts and corridors strewn with Sepoys' brass *lotas* (drinking vessels), charred charpoys, clothing, belts, ammunition, muskets, matchlocks, swords and pistols—all evidence of precipitate flight. Fired with lust and greed, the men moved at an ever increasing pace through rooms full of their comrades rummaging and dividing plunder amongst themselves. In one splendid salon a party of Sikhs had built a fire of delicate furniture on the floor and were melting down gold and silver lace for easier transportation. In a far corner of the room another group were quarrelling over shawls, lace, pearls and embroidered gold and silver.

Everyone felt himself permitted to retain what he could capture, and in this saturnalia it was believed that some of the troops appropriated enough treasure to render them independent of labour for the rest of their lives. Many of two British

Line regiments found, in a treasure room, caskets and boxes containing diamonds, emeralds, rubies, pearls, opals and other gems made into necklaces, bracelets and girdles, together with gold mounted pistols and jewel-hilted swords, saddle cloths covered with gold and pearls and Japanned boxes filled with crystal and jade vessels. It was not long before coolies, syces, doolie-bearers and grass cutters were irresistibly drawn to the scene, running hither and thither laden with costly clothing, swords, firelocks, brass pots and other articles larger in bulk than the soldiers could dispose of.

In all his wildest dreams, Hector MacDonald had never imagined such splendour existed. In room after room of lavish magnificence he saw despoiled pictures, glass and china lying among torn once-priceless silks and cashmeres. Most of the more transportable items of plunder had been taken when the 42nd arrived at the Kaiserbagh. Hector secured a couple of jewelled tulwars which he later sold to an officer for a sovereign. When there was more time and opportunity, some of the soldiers held a kind of mock-auction, at which camp followers and officers bought treasures for a mere trifle; there was not much ready cash among the conquerors.

Edmund Verney of the Naval Brigade* recorded that:

> ". . . the Sikh soldiers evolved a simpler and better method of looting than the simple English—the Sikhs are very knowing fellows; a Sikh sergeant will watch a party of Europeans enter a house for the purpose of plundering, and immediately he plants sentries all round. As each man comes out, he is told that there are strict orders against looting and that he must disgorge his plunder. This, of course, he does with very bad grace, and walks away sadly crestfallen. As soon as the whole party has gone off, the sergeant calls in his sentries, divides the loot, keeping a lion's share for himself, and they all go on their way rejoicing."

By the morning of the 17th March, Sir Colin Campbell was the undoubted master of Lucknow, although there were still isolated buildings in which small bands of the enemy were holding out. For some days afterwards, the deserted and half ruined houses served as hiding places for fanatics and looters. Many officers and soldiers were shot by the concealed enemy long after the great buildings of the city had been conquered.

Campbell did not wish the people of Lucknow to regard him

The Devil's Wind, p. 140.

as an enemy so, by a proclamation and other means, he encouraged those who had not been in complicity with the rebels to return to their homes. Until the ordinary relations of society were reintroduced, anything like civil government was impossible and it was essential in the meantime that the deserted homes should be spared from reckless looting. The Commander-in-Chief's intentions were mainly thwarted by the plundering and violence of the camp-followers, whose numbers rendered them uncontrollable in a large, rambling, straggling city of tortuous streets and intricate lanes as was Lucknow. Soldiers, both white and native, roamed the city in bands seeking valuables, frequently coming into collision with each other. To prevent these occurrences, the Commander-in-Chief issued more stringent regulations to restore order amongst his troops. An hourly roll-call was ordered and no soldier was allowed to enter the city without a written order. Pickets were placed in the principal streets to compel the camp-followers to disgorge the plunder which they had collected. Any armed camp-followers found in the streets or houses were seized and hung up; no soldier was permitted to wear his side-arms except when on duty, and triangles were set up at proper places for the summary punishment of minor offenders. Very quickly, the shooting and hangings prevented further excesses, although few of the native inhabitants returned to the city. Perhaps they were wise to act in this fashion for such was the mood of the European soldiers that no native was safe. With relish many of the men told stories of vengeful acts, not all of which were allowed to go unpunished. Hector heard of two privates in another regiment who, when searching a trembling native, had been told in perfect English by another native that they should act as protectors and not oppressors of the inhabitants of Lucknow. Unfortunately, he added that if any officer knew what they were doing they would be punished. This sounded like a threat and his knowledge of English alarmed the two soldiers so they put their muskets to his side and shot him. Later the men were identified, arrested and severely punished. On the day following the storming of the Kaiserbagh, Hector and his brother Angus came upon a noisy crowd of soldiers roughly handling two natives, not knowing them to be bullock drivers employed by the British who had been wounded and were in search of medical aid. As they were ragged and smeared with dust and blood, the soldiers could see them only as rebels and beat them to death.

During the whole of the operations at Lucknow, the 42nd Regiment had lost five men killed and forty-two wounded. Campbell's casualties from the 2nd to the 21st March were sixteen British officers, three native officers and 108 men killed; fifty-one British officers, four native officers and 540 men wounded with thirteen men missing. It was estimated that the enemy's loss could hardly have been less than 4,000.

Chapter 18

Although troops wandering around by themselves were likely to be attacked in the street, things were now quiet and the inevitable boredom set in. Like the other European troops, the 42nd were troubled by the heat of the Indian equinox, although it was much less than that of summer. Everyone was eager to get rid of their irksome uniform, for the newly arrived regiments, including the 42nd, had fought in practically full dress.[66]

Camp conditions were far from pleasant, as indicated in a letter from an Assistant-Surgeon of Brigadier Franks' division:*

> "Though we are all in the town, our camp and hospital are still in the old place. While I write this in my tent in camp, the thermometer is at one hundred degrees; not a breath of wind, and the flies—I can pity the Egyptians now—the tent is filled with them, and everything edible covered with them. We drink and eat flies, and in our turn are eaten by them. They nestle in your hair, and commit the most determined suicides in your tea or soup. Old-fashioned looking crickets come out of holes and stare at you; lizards run wildly across the tent; and ants by the thousand ply their wonted avocations utterly unmindful of your presence. When night arrives, it becomes a little cooler, the candles are lit, all the flies (save the suicides) have gone to roost upon the tent-poles, and you fancy that your troubles are over. Vain hope! the tent-doors are open; in flies a locust, hops into some dish, kicks himself out again, hitting you in the face, and finally bolts out at the opposite door. Then comes a flock of moths, all sizes and shapes, which dart madly at the lights. At last you put out your candle, and get into bed, when a new sound commences. Hum, hum, something soft and light settles on your face and hands; a sensation of red-hot needles intimates that the mosquitoes are upon you. The domestic flea and bug also abound; their appetites quite

**The Revolt in India* p. 426.

unimpaired by the climate. Jackals and pariah dogs yell and howl all night. Day dawns, and you have your flies down upon you lively as ever. This will give you some idea of our tent comforts."

Similar views were expressed by Edmund Verney of the Naval Brigade:*

"... we have suffered from a plague of flies. I have never before appreciated how terrible a thing a plague of flies could be; they have been bred by the innumerable dead bodies of men and animals. The moment one sits down they settle on every exposed part of the body; they drown themselves in tea and gravy, immolate themselves on the ends of cigars, accompany to one's mouth all one's food and render sleep next to impossible. Indeed, the only way to obtain rest is to get under a mosquito curtain; at about sunset the mosquitoes relieve the guard and the flies have their watch below."

Sitting at the entrance of his tent in the early evening of the 23rd March, Hector looked up to see two men of his company hurrying towards him. Coming up, they stood looking down without speaking. Hector stared up at their serious faces, looking from one to the other.

"Well! . . . What is it? . . . D'ye want me?"

The two men looked at each other and one answered haltingly:

"Hector . . . y'brither Angus . . ."

Slowly, Hector rose to his feet.

"Angus? What's wrong with him? Is he hurt?"

"No . . . he's not hurt . . . ye better come with us."

Hector hurried after the two Highlanders, through the camp before plunging into the warren of shattered and tumbledown native houses that lay beyond. Turning a corner, they came upon a big Highlander with a red beard, lying motionless on the dusty ground, his head on his arm. A red and white spotted handkerchief had been roughly propped on three sticks to make a little shelter for his face. A few feet away, sitting on a low brick wall with his head in his hands was Ian MacDonald. Hector knelt down by the side of his brother Angus and putting out his hand he shook his shoulder, knocking over the little handkerchief-shelter as he did so.

**The Devil's Wind*, p. 139.

"Angus! Angus . . . wake up . . . come on . . . what's wrong with you?"

One of the two Highlanders bent forward and gently put his hand on Hector's shoulder.

"It's nae guid, Hector . . . we've tried to rouse him . . . I fear he's dead."

Hector stared into the bronzed and bearded face of his brother . . . dead? . . . he couldn't be dead. He straightened up and turned to Ian, still sitting in the same position with his head in his hands. Hector shook him angrily.

"Ian! What happened? Come on, wake up . . . what happened to Angus?"

Making a great effort, Ian MacDonald raised his head and drowsily opened lustre-less eyes; his lips were slack and saliva bubbled at the corners of his mouth.

"We . . . Angus and me . . . found some grog . . . och, Hector . . . we haven't had any for so long . . . it was hot . . . the sun beat down on us and then Angus fell over . . . he couldn't get up and I couldn't help him . . . so I made a little shelter for his head and I don't remember any more until the lads here woke me up!"

The two Highlanders nodded:

"We had a terrible job with Ian but we could do naught for y'brither Angus . . . like that laddie in the 93rd, he passed away in his sleep in apoplexy."

Slowly, they turned on their heels and vanished, leaving the brothers alone. Hector stared at Ian and saw fat tears well from his bleary eyes:

"Don't look at me like that, Hector! It wasn't my fault . . . it could have been you or Alex with Angus when he found the grog!"

Unable to speak, Hector shook his head and turned away.

The two Highlanders came bustling up carrying a charpoy. Carefully and gently, they picked the big heavy No. 1991 Private Angus MacDonald up by his feet and his shoulders and laid him on it, covering his face with the spotted handkerchief

Chapter 19

The fighting at Lucknow was over, there was nothing left for the troops to do and much serious work to be done elsewhere. Sir Colin Campbell broke up his Army of Oude into separate formations, regiments being reorganised into brigades and divisions and new brigadiers appointed where necessary. Many of the soldiers left Lucknow with memories coloured by the knowledge that it was a place where such extraordinary gain had fallen to the lot of many among their number. Hector and his brothers were glad to shake the dust of the cursed place from their boots. They marched out, conscious that a MacDonald had been left behind just as two brothers were buried in the Crimea.

The policy of the Commander-in-Chief had left open a road of escape through which the greater proportion of the rebellious garrison of Lucknow had escaped into the difficult regions of Rohilkand.[67] To deal with such large numbers of mutinous Sepoys, rebel leaders and desperate men it was necessary for a force to be sent to Rohilkand. So, on the 10th April, a division under the command of General Walpole, marched out from Lucknow en route for Bareilly, about 150 miles away. The force consisted of:

H.M.'s 42nd Regiment.
79th Regiment.
93rd Regiment.
Two Battalions of the Rifle Brigade.
The 1st Bengal Europeans.
Two Regiments of Native Infantry.
H.M.'s 7th Hussars and 9th Lancers.
Three Regiments of Punjab Cavalry.
The Naval Brigade from H.M.S. *Shannon*.
Various detachments of Artillery and Engineers.

Everyone knew that this Division would have hot work before it—Bareilly was the principal rendezvous of the insurgent chiefs of the north-west—the Nana Sahib, Kahn Bahadur, the Nawab of Fateghar and others. In addition, the powerful sun of the month of April would be pouring down on the heads of the troops. It was very frustrating to the European soldiers to feel their bodily strength failing through heat at a time when their spirits were as heroic as ever. Everyone tried to push into the back of his mind the knowledge that they were about to fight a campaign in the hottest weather when exhaustion and sun so devastated the European constitution. During the mutiny the English had observed the mobility of the native rebel troops—a man who can live upon rice, parched corn and water and to whom it is a matter of indifference whether he is clothed or not, has a remarkable freedom of movement and a complete disregard for logistics. The lithe, supple-limbed Hindu, carrying no superfluous flesh, could cover great mileages, particularly when retreating.

Nevertheless, of two evils it was better than being left behind in Lucknow, where the month of April had opened with a distressing degree of heat so that a temperature of 100°F under the shade of a tent was not at all unusual. Hot winds bearing clouds of dust distressed every organ of sense. There were putrefying bodies yet unburied in the streets, pools of recently dried blood lay everywhere and no one dared to guess at the foul and insanitary things that lay hidden within the many courts and labyrinths of the devastated palaces of Lucknow. William Russell wrote:

> "Of the dust it is quite beyond the powers of writing to to give a description. It is so fine and subtle, that long after the causes which raised it have ceased to exert their influence, you may see it like a veil of gauze between your eyes and every object. The sun, while yet six or seven degrees above the horizon, is hid from sight by it as though the luminary were enveloped in a thick fog; and at early morning and evening, this vapour of dust suspended high in the air seems like a raincloud clinging to a hillside. When this dust is set rapidly in motion by a hot wind, and when the grosser sand, composed of minute fragments of talc, scales of mica, and earth, is impelled in quick successive waves through the heated atmosphere, the effect is quite sufficient to make one detest India for ever. Every article in your tent, your hair, eyes and nose are filled and covered with this dust, which deposits a coating half an inch thick all over the tent."

Another thing that irritated the troops was the fact that the enemy did not seem to know when they were beaten; the mutineers rarely if ever gained a victory but never seemed to be disheartened by defeat. They retreated, only to collect and fight again so that the British troops seldom felt that a victory would give them an unquestionably permanent advantage. To the private soldiers in the ranks, knowing nothing of their commander's intentions, life seemed to consist of interminable marching on dusty roads under a blazing hot sun, with the occasional all-too-rare stimulus of action, only to be inevitably followed by more marching.

The route from Lucknow to Bareilly went through a region ill-provided with roads. Not only did this mean that the force had to march in the heat of the day because night marches were impossible, but it accentuated the difficulty of dragging the guns, and both cavalry and infantry were irritatingly delayed in frequent halts to allow the ponderous pieces of artillery to catch up.

Walpole, advancing north-westward from Lucknow, clearing the country in front of him as he went, had to rendezvous at Bareilly with Brigadier Jones's column on or about the 24th April. The column marched by day and rested at night under shady groves. On the 14th April, after they had gone about fifty miles, they came up to Fort Ruhya, one of the many fortified strongholds that dotted Oude. Situated in dense jungle which almost completely hid it from view, Ruhya was a small fort or group of houses enclosed by a high mud-wall, loopholed for musketry, provided with irregular bastions at the angles and having two gates. In relation to the largeness of the force about to attack it (nearly 6,000 men) it was a petty place. Walpole had heard that 1,500 insurgents had thrown themselves into the fort, but it later was discovered that the number was much smaller.

General Walpole sent forward four companies of the 42nd Highlanders with the 4th Punjab Infantry, in extended order. Characteristically, Brigadier Adrian Hope, commanding the Highland Brigade, went forward at the head of the attacking party. In the front rank, Hector MacDonald took a firm grip of the musket held out in front of his body and glanced at the reassuring glitter of its bayonet-tip. Under his feet the dry grass and twigs crackled and his bare knees below his kilt were whipped and torn by the thorn bushes and undergrowth through which they were pushing. At first there was nothing to be seen but trees and dense vegetation, then the undergrowth thinned and about 150 yards to their front the drab-coloured mud walls of the fort loomed up. At exactly the same moment as they came in sight of the fort, the dry crackle and rustling of men forcing their way through undergrowth was drowned by the cascading crash of musketry from unseen places. Looking wildly around him, Hector could see the flash of the muskets from the loopholed walls of the fort, from the bushes to their front and sides and from the tree tops that loomed overhead. He saw Brigadier Hope throw up his arms and fall and a few feet to his front, Lieutenant Douglas, his Company Officer, dropped to the ground. Above the din, Hector heard harsh-voiced sergeants crying "Lie down! Lie down!" Thankfully, the Highlanders dropped to the ground, burrowing as deeply as they could into the scrub and vegetation.

For six hours they lay there, so exposed that even an involuntary movement of a limb brought down a well-directed and heavy fire upon them from the fort. In all those long hours, few shots were fired at the enemy—muzzle-loading rifles could not be reloaded in the prone position and no one fancied facing an enemy sally from the fort with an unloaded rifle. Head hunched between his shoulders and body pressed against the ground, bare knees rasped by thorns and twigs, Hector glared in frustration at the walls of the fort. Now and again, he dozed off, to be rudely awakened by the thud of a bullet into the ground near-by, or the scream of a near miss whistling overhead. As time passed, with nothing apparently being done to extricate them from their exposed position, Hector began to seethe with rage. Why had they been sent forward so stupidly without any previous scouting? It had been said that Sir Colin Campbell had laid down strict rules for attacking these forts—why had not General Walpole used his artillery?[68]

The day drew to a close, the fast fading light bringing a degree of protection to the trapped soldiers as the shadows began to lengthen in the jungle area around the fort. Spurning the absolute safety that would come with darkness, General Walpole ordered a retreat whilst there was still daylight. Sudden words of command rent the still air and on all sides men rose stiffly to their feet and made their way back as quickly as they were able. From the fort came irregular volleys of musketry and shouts of triumph; one or two Highlanders dropped to add to the motionless bundles of clothing that remained amid the dense vegetation.

Once out of the jungle, the Regiment formed up and a roll

was called—three officers were missing together with one sergeant and six privates; three sergeants and thirty-four privates were wounded. When they heard that comrades had been left behind, a muttering arose from the ranks. Quarter-Master Sergeant John Simpson stepped forward and respectfully asked for permission to go back and bring out any wounded who had been left behind. Privates Davis, Thompson and Edward Spence stepped forward with him, seeking permission to accompany the Quarter-Master Sergeant. Permission was freely given and, to a round of cheers, the four men went forward. The rest of the column marched off to a camping ground some two miles away, while the 42nd remained behind to wait for the return of Simpson and his party.

After about half an hour they were seen slowly pushing their way through the scrub at the borders of the jungle. Men broke ranks and ran forward to help them. Quarter-Master Sergeant Simpson was carrying the body of Lieutenant Douglas, whilst Private Davis walked slowly behind him bent under the weight of the body of Lieutenant Bramley. Unable to find any of the 42nd casualties, Private Thompson had brought in the body of Lieutenant Willoughby of the 4th Punjab Rifles. Private Spence had been severely wounded whilst placing himself in an exposed position to cover the party bearing away the body of Lieutenant Willoughby. He died on the 17th April from the effects of his wounds.[69] Later, it was ascertained that all four men had gone to within thirty or forty yards of the walls of the fort and had recovered the bodies under very heavy fire. As Simpson laid the body of Lieutenant Douglas tenderly on the ground, it was discovered that the officer was still alive, although gravely wounded.* Believing that there might be other men still in the jungle, wounded and unable to move, Quarter-Master Sergeant Simpson turned and trudged back into the dark and forbidding greenery. He returned some time later carrying a severely wounded private soldier of the 42nd. Simpson, Davis and Thompson were all awarded the Victoria Cross for these acts of gallantry.

That night camp was a gloomy place. Everyone keenly felt the disgrace at being beaten by the Pandies,[70] particularly when such a mess had been made of the whole business. It turned out that the supporting troops were too late and that the reserves had been sent to another part of the jungle from which they were unable to reach the point of attack. The death

*Lieutenant Douglas died later.

of the Brigadier cast everybody into the deepest despair. Adrian Hope was much loved and appreciated as a truly talented and thoughtful commander, and it was strongly rumoured that he had remonstrated against the folly of the order assigning the 42nd and the Punjab Rifles to the attack but had been overruled. Every Highlander felt as if a deep personal injury had been inflicted upon him by the commander of the column and for weeks afterwards the feeling against Walpole was so strong as almost to endanger discipline. During the night, General Walpole had his heavy guns brought up to batter a breach in the wall of the fort, but it was discovered when dawn came that the enemy had stolen silently away during the night.

Walpole's column continued its march, having a successful encounter on the 22nd April with a large body of the enemy at Sirsa. It was a battle won by cavalry and artillery who attacked the rebels so vigorously as to capture their guns and camp, leaving them no time to destroy the bridge of boats over the river. This enabled Walpole, on the 23rd, to transport his heavy guns quickly and safely over the Ramgunga River at Allygunje. Campbell had marched from Cawnpore with a column made slow by an enormous train of ammunition and supplies. Crossing the bridge of boats captured by Walpole, the Commander-in-Chief and his column soon afterwards joined Walpole on the banks of the Ramgunga. The force marched to Kanth on the 29th and on the 30th captured the city of Shahjehanpur, although the rebel leader, the Moulvie of Fyzabad, escaped.

On the 2nd May the Rohilkand Field Force, under the command of Sir Colin Campbell in person, started their march to commence operations against Bareilly. Each day's march was much like that which preceded it—the same early start, and the fatiguing march over a fertile flat country, dotted with *topes*[71] of trees, everything overladen with stifling dust. Each camp was the same and always there was the eternal struggle with the camp-followers who, however closely watched, plundered the villages through which they passed so that they terrified and exasperated the villagers, whether they were friendly or unfriendly to the British. No threats or punishments seemed to deter the ravaging camp-followers whose activities were a great source of trouble to the British force during this part of the campaign.

On the 3rd May, Sir Colin Campbell was joined by the column lately commanded by Brigadier Penny, who had lost his life after allowing his troops to fall into an ambush from which they were saved with difficulty. Another column under Brigadier Jones was simultaneously marching towards Bareilly from the opposite direction. Arriving at the town, Jones's column captured the bridge, hearing at the same time the cannon of Campbell's column signalling their approach from the opposite side of the town. At daybreak on the 5th May they came up with the enemy's outposts in the suburbs of Bareilly. The rebels fired a few shots from a battery, but only half-heartedly defended the stream that crossed the high road and the bridge over the stream. Falling back, the mutineers occupied the old cantonments or Sepoy-lines while their cavalry hovered about in the topes of trees. To winkle them out it was necessary to shell every tope and house before advancing, which made for slow progress under the scorching sun.

At about ten a.m. the enemy made a bold attempt to turn the British left flank and the 42nd were ordered forward in support of the 4th Punjab Rifles, who had been sent to occupy the old cavalry lines. The native infantry regiment suddenly came under a very heavy fire from a large body of men, armed with matchlocks and concealed in the ruined mass of one-storeyed houses. Thrown into confusion, they fell rapidly back in disorder among the advancing Highlanders. The Punjabis were hotly pursued by a large body of Ghazis, Moslem fanatics brandishing tulwars, their heads held low and covered by small circular shields on their left arms. They wore green cummerbunds around dirty white robes. Wildly screaming "Deen, deen!" the fanatics were slashing and stabbing at the retreating backs of the native troops. For a few moments, the Highlanders were undecided whether to fire, because their own troops were mixed up with the enemy. Sir Colin Campbell, close up with the 42nd, cried loud and clear in his familiar voice:

"Fire away, men! Shoot them down! . . . every man jack of them! Bayonet them as they come on!"

Officers and N.C.O.'s added their voices:

"Steady, men, steady! Close up the ranks! Close up! Close up!"

A fierce fight of cold steel took place to the front of the Regiment whilst a party of the Ghazis, running with bodies bent and heads low, waving their tulwars with a circular motion in the air, dashed furiously around the flanks of the Regiment and into the rear. Three of them rushed upon Colonel Cameron, the commanding officer and, before he could unsheath his sword, had dragged him from his horse. Rushing out from the ranks Colour-Sergeant William Gardener bayoneted two of them. A few yards away, Hector MacDonald raised his rifle and shot down the third Ghazi before he could slash at the prostrate officer. Colonel Cameron escaped with small cuts on his wrists and hands.[72]

The slashing and hacking was over as soon as it began, and 133 Ghazis lay dead on the dusty ground. In this affair, the 42nd lost one private killed, two officers, one sergeant and twelve privates being wounded. General Walpole had a similar narrow escape, being pulled from his horse by two or three of the Ghazis, cutting at him all the while with their tulwars. Previous grievances forgotten, the General's life was saved by the quick bayonets of the 42nd.

Not much real fighting took place during the day; the intense heat laid low many of the European soldiers and everyone suffered greatly from thirst and fatigue. Soon after midday, Campbell resolved to bivouac on the plain for that night, postponing until the next day an advance into the city of Bareilly. Before this, however, the enemy's cavalry had succeeded in creating an indescribable amount of alarm among the camp-followers by a dash across the plain towards the baggage in the rear. William Russell was with this part of the column, riding in a litter after having been kicked by a horse. He describes the scene thus:

> "There was a confused clamour of shrieks and shouting in my ear . . . I heard my bearers shouting 'Sowar! Sowar!' and I saw them flying with terror in their faces. All the camp-followers, in a wild confusion, were rushing for the road. It was a veritable stampede of men and animals . . . elephants were trumpeting shrilly as they thundered over the fields, camels slung along at their utmost joggling stride, horses and carts, women and children, were all pouring in a stream, which converged and tossed in heaps of white as it neared the road—an awful panic. The mutineers were quickly among the column, as they came on, camp-followers fell with cleft skulls and bleeding wounds upon the field; the left wing of the wild cavalry was coming straight for the tope in which we lay. The eye takes in at a glance what the tongue cannot tell or hand write in an hour. Here it was, it appeared, an inglorious miserable death swooping down on us in the heart of that yelling crowd."

Russell tells how his faithful *syce* came up with his horse, and clad only in his shirt how he

> "flew across the plain under that awful sun, turning my head to look back I saw a black bearded scoundrel, ahead of three sowars, who were coming right at me. I had neither sword nor pistol . . . I felt my time was come. My naked heels could make no impression on the panting horse. I saw, indeed, a cloud of dust and a body of men advancing from the road . . . but just at that moment a pain so keen shot through my head that my eyes flashed fire!"

A sowar had actually raised his tulwar to strike Russell's head from his shoulders when Sergeant Forbes Mitchell of the 42nd shot down the rebel trooper. Russell lay dangerously ill for some days with sunstroke before returning to Delhi.*

No. 5 Company of the 42nd took possession of the captured buildings and a line of pickets of the 42nd and the 79th Highlanders was posted from the buildings to the extreme right of the Commander-in-Chief's camp. Next morning it was discovered that many of the leaders and a large body of rebel troops had quietly left Bareilly. Throughout that day, the 6th May, guns were brought to bear upon certain buildings in the city, known or suspected to conceal insurgents. On the following day, the 7th, the Commander-in-Chief's column and that of Brigadier Jones advanced into the city and took complete possession of it, without capturing any of the leaders or preventing the escape of the main body of rebels.

***The First War Correspondent*, by Rupert Furneaux (London, 1944), p. 110.

Chapter 20

With the fall of Bareilly, it was no longer deemed necessary to maintain the Rohilkand Field Force, and so the various brigades and formations were broken up and given separate roles. Formed for special service in the country districts, under the command of Brigadier Coke, one of these columns was formed of:

A wing of the 42nd Highlanders.
The 1st Punjab Rifles.
The 1st Sikh Infantry.
A detachment of the 24th Punjab Infantry.
A squadron of Carabiniers.
The Multan Horse.
A detachment of the 17th Irregular Cavalry and a considerable force of artillery.

With three weeks' supplies for the European and four weeks' for the native troops, this column set out from Bareilly on the 12th May. On the 5th June, when the column was at Bedaon, the wing of the 42nd under the command of Lieutenant-Colonel Wilkinson were ordered to march to Muradabad. On this march the men suffered greatly from exhaustion and from the heat,[73] and forty men fell out through sunstroke and had to be borne in doolies.[74] Hector MacDonald and his brother, Alexander, were with this wing and managed to keep going, but both found it very distressing to see their comrades lying back in the doolies gasping for air. In the manner of the time, the surgeon had bled the men, opening a vein in their arms; in some cases leeches were applied to the temples. The greater number of cases did not respond and among those who recovered there were few fit for active service again except after a long interval of rest. The self-pitying feeling aroused in Hector by the 42nd's grotesque head-gear of black feathers with grey cloth ear pieces, was invariably softened when he saw the men of the Rifle Brigade, in their dark-green tunics which absorbed the heat almost as much as if they were made of black cloth.

Little cloth forage-caps perched on their heads, poorly covered with a few folds of dark cotton.

As the heat of the day began to press upon them they would arrive in a camping site after an early morning march, each man anxiously surveying the trees about his tent as the site was marked out, calculating what shelter they would give him and at what time the sun's merciless rays would strike through every crack and crevice like red-hot shot. Producing stark shadows and outlines, wherever the rays fell on the side of a tent seemed to punch out a fervid blazing pattern on the grey ground of the canvas. Each officer had a tent to himself with punkahs and other fan appliances to reduce the temperature; even so, nearly naked, they lay panting on their charpoys, gasping for breath like carp on the banks of a river. If the officers suffered so much from the heat, it is difficult to imagine what the men endured, packed ten or twelve to a tent (in some regiments eighteen or twenty) without adequate fans and lacking changes of light clothing. Although reduced to a minimum, pickets and the other normal duties pressed heavily upon them.

Sir Colin Campbell, the Commander-in-Chief, was fully conscious of the difficulties and hardships undergone by the men in the ranks. In a congratulatory address issued to the troops of the Anglo-Indian Army on the 18th May, he said:

> "By their patient endurance of fatigue, their unfailing obedience, and their steadfast gallantry, the troops have enabled the generals to fulfil their instructions. In no war has it ever happened that troops have been more often engaged than during the campaigns which have now terminated. In no war has it ever happened that troops should always contend against immense numerical odds, as has invariably been the case in every encounter during the struggle of the last year; and in no war has constant success without a check been more conspicuously achieved. It has not occurred that one column here, another there, has won more honour than the other portions of the army; the various corps have done like hard work, have struggled through the difficulties of a hot weather campaign, and have compensated for paucity of numbers in the vast area of operations by continuous and unexampled marching, notwithstanding the season. It is probable that much yet remains for the army to perform; but now that the Commander-in-Chief is able to give the

greater part of it rest for a time, he chooses this moment to congratulate the generals and troops on the great results which have attended their labours. He can fairly say that they have accomplished in a few months what was believed by the illwishers of England to be either beyond her strength, or to be the work of many years."

The veteran commander himself bore heat and fatigue in a manner that astonished his subordinates, getting through an amount of work which nearly finished his aides-de-camp; and he was always ready to advise or command, as if rest and food were contingencies about which he cared nothing. Natives, who were readily able to obtain an interview with him, were invariably surprised to see the commander of the mighty British Army in shirt-sleeves and a pith-hat; but the keen eye and the cool manner of the old soldier showed that he had his wits about him and was none the worse for the absence of glitter and personal adornment.

The troops who were still under canvas now began to suffer very much from sunstroke, fevers, hepatitis and dysentery. It became imperative to get them into temporary barracks, though in many cases this was not possible until the middle of July, just in time to escape the rains. The 42nd were based on Bareilly, but they had companies and detachments serving in different places. During the month of July, Rohilkand was troubled with nothing much beyond trifling disturbances; these came chiefly from Oude when small bands of brigands crossed the frontier and harried some of the neighbouring villages. These groups of unorganised invaders were easily dealt with by small detachments of troops, and the 42nd had their share of the sporadic operations.

The end of the campaign, together with the stupefying effects of the heat, could easily have encouraged a slackness to spread from the top downwards. Sir Colin Campbell was a general who insisted on all the duties of regimental service being properly attended to by the officers so that all worked for the common cause, in camps and barracks, as well as in the field. During August 1858, he issued an order which read as follows:

"The Commander-in-Chief begs that general officers commanding divisions and brigades will urge commanding officers of Her Majesty's regiments, troops and batteries, to give their most particular attention to all points of interior economy; to examine and correct regimental books; to reenlist soldiers of limited service willing to renew their engagements; to complete soldiers' clothing and necessaries, examine soldiers' accounts, soldiers' claims, and small account books; to close, and render to the proper departments, the accounts of deceased officers and soldiers; to examine arms, accoutrements, and ammunition, and repair deficiencies; to continue judging-distance drills and musketry instruction, as far as the climate will permit; to provide occupation for soldiers without harassing them by mere routine drills; to consider their comforts, diet and amusements; to re-establish the regimental school, and encourage by every means the study of the Hindustani language, both by officers and soldiers disposed to study it; to ascertain by inquiry what means exist in the neighbourhood of their quarters, both in materials and workmen, to furnish their regiments with boots and clothing, in the event of failure of the usual supply; finally, to maintain the most exact discipline, the strict performance of all duties, and proper marks of respect to officers; which will be much assisted by a proper example on the part of officers, in dress and deportment, regularity in their duties, and treatment of native servants and followers."

The last clause, dealing with native servants and followers, was aimed at many of the younger officers, whose knowledge of India extended only over a few months and had acquired the habit of speaking and writing of the natives as if they were all murderers deserving only of sabreing and hanging. The atrocities of some were visited on all and the "Pandies" who had begun the mutiny were now mixed up with everyone else in the common designation of "niggers" and "devils". These young officers were very fond of applying sticks or whips to the shoulders of natives simply because they were natives, even when inoffensively employed. Observant newspapermen and correspondents noted this dangerous tendency and severely commented upon it in their reports back to their journals. Letters from officers, made public in the journals published in India, furnished abundant proof of these feelings. Unless the mutiny were to end with general enmity on both sides, it was essential that an improved tone should prevail in this matter; and to this end, many hints were given by the authorities, in England as well as in India.

August was marked by a quiet but significant proof of an

improved attention towards the well-being of the soldiers. An order was issued that a supply of newspapers and periodicals should be forwarded to the different military hospitals in Calcutta at the public expense. Those for the officers' hospital[75] included some magazines of a higher class than were included in the list for the men's hospital, but orders were given that, after they had been read by the officers, they were to be forwarded to hospitals occupied by the men in the ranks.

On the 9th August the commanding officer of the 42nd died of fever and was succeeded by Lieutenant-Colonel Priestley.

After the hot season of 1858, the rebellion became a guerilla war. The great leaders were discomfited, the minor rajahs and chiefs were captured, hanged, blown away from guns, or, submitting, were pardoned. Anything was better than life in camp and, in spite of the known hardships everyone was glad when a detachment was ordered out on some operation or other. On the 14th October, the headquarters and left wing of the 42nd were ordered to Pilibhit, where they remained encamped until the 24th November. On that day, under command of Colonel Smyth of the Bengal Artillery, they went out in a small column to prevent a party of rebels crossing from Oude into Rohilkand. In order to watch the Ghats possible crossing places, a position was taken up on the banks of the Sarda where No. 6 Company commanded by Captain Lawson, and including Hector MacDonald, joined the column. At the same time, Major M'Leod took four companies of the 42nd, two squadrons of Punjab Cavalry, one company of Kumaon levies and two guns to Madho-Tanda, a central position from which support could be sent in any desired direction. On numerous occasions reports came in that the enemy were approaching but nothing ever happened so that when the alarm was given early in the morning of the 15th January, 1859, no one took it very seriously. As it turned out, this was the real thing—pursued into the district by a force under the command of Colonel Dennis, a body of the enemy about 2,000 strong crossed the Sarda River at Mayla Ghat, about three miles above Colonel Smyth's camp, in an attempt to force their way into Rohilkand.

Grumbling at missing their breakfast, the men threw on their equipment and fell in, hastened by sergeants and officers. The almost indecent haste with which they had been aroused and marched out of camp indicated to Hector that there might possibly be some real cause for alarm. They moved quickly along the dusty tracks that bordered the jungle where it ran close to the river. Suddenly, No. 6 Company was halted by Captain Lawson, who detached Ensign Coleridge to take a picket of forty men, together with forty Kumaon levies, into the jungle to cut off a party of rebels. At the same time, Captain Lawson took the remaining thirty-seven men of the Company and moved into the jungle on a parallel course, but cut off from Coleridge's party. The squadron of irregular cavalry who accompanied them was unable to make any headway in the jungle and were forced to remain in support on the dusty track. Captain Lawson gave the order:

"Open out . . . keep the men on either side of you in sight and push on through the jungle."

Hector MacDonald glanced to his right at Private Duncan Millar and Private MacIntosh on his left and then they thrust their way into the dense, clinging undergrowth that closed around them like a green cloak. Nothing moved to their front and apart from the thrashing noise of the men pushing their way through the jungle, the only sounds were the chirruping of the insects and the occasional raucous cry of a disturbed bird. Soon the undergrowth became so dense that it was like being enmeshed in a net, without sharp knives or swords to cut their way through progress was a very slow and exhausting business. Busily engaged in thrusting his way through a thick thorn bush that caught and tore at his kilt, Hector raised his head to catch a sudden movement of black shadows in the undergrowth ahead. Before he could call out, the air was shattered by the report of muskets and a myriad of bright flashes lit up the gloom to their front. This first volley whistled and screamed overhead, indicating that the rebels were on a slope below them and firing upwards. Instinctively and without waiting for orders, the Highlanders opened fire, shooting low—screams and yells and thrashing movements in the bushes indicated that they had caused casualties.

Now began a fight as deadly as one between aggressive armed men locked in a darkened room. Quickly realising that they were faced with numbers far smaller than their own, the rebels made a furious attempt to break through the thin line of Highland skirmishers. On more than one occasion they outflanked the Highlanders, who quickly changed front, first on on one side then on the other so as to be always ready for them. Captain Lawson received a gun-shot wound in his left knee early in the action and sat on the ground with his back against a tree, firing his pistol and calling out encouragement to his men. Next in command, Colour-Sergeant Landles fell to the ground, shot at short range; in the skirmishing that folowed he was cut to pieces by vengeful natives who slashed at his body as they ran past. At first Hector felt that he was fighting on his own, loading and reloading as fast as he could and loosing off fire at the moving black shadows. Then he noticed from the corner of his eye that Duncan Millar on his right was dodging about, standing behind trees for cover, firing all the time. By sheer weight of numbers the Sepoys thrust forward, but the Highlanders refused to give ground so that a fierce hand-to-hand fight took place—the Sepoys using tulwars and the Highlanders their trusty bayonets. Hector lost count of the number of men into whom he rammed his bayonet until the hilt came up against the flesh of their bodies with a sickening thud. He had to throw them off to make room for another, like a farm labourer forking hay.

At one point, the action died down and Private Millar moved across to Hector, hugging trees and bushes as he moved.

"Hold on here, . . . I'm going to see what's happening along the line . . . we may be the only ones left!"

Hector nodded, and as the Highlander melted into the dense brush, he reflected that a lesser man than Millar might be making his escape while the going was good. But a few minutes later Millar returned, again sliding his way unobtrusively through the bush.

"Captain Lawson is down, . . . S'arn't Landles is dead . . . so are Corporal Ritchie and Thompson . . . Walter Cook is running the other end of the line and we'll hold this one!"

There was no more time for talk as another fierce attack developed. It seemed as though they had been fighting for hours when, during a lull, Hector was startled by noises of men moving through the bush in his rear. He swung round, determined to fight to the last, but to his great relief he recognised men from Nos. 7 and 8 Companies!

Major M'Leod's force were at Sangari, twenty-two miles away, that morning, and it was not until noon that he received orders to send Nos. 7 and 8 Companies of the 42nd to the battle area and the remainder of his force to Madho-Tanda to await the result of the battle. Marching at the fastest possible rate, Nos. 7 and 8 Companies reached the battle scene at five p.m. and their arrival turned the tide of the action. Finding that their efforts were gaining them nothing and that reinforcements had arrived, the survivors of the enemy force recrossed the river in the dark. Next morning many dead and dying were found on the field together with two small guns and a number of cattle.

Privates Walter Cook and Duncan Millar were later awarded the Victoria Cross for their part in the action at Mayla Ghat. Brigadier-General Walpole's citation said that

> ". . . these soldiers went to the front, took a prominent part in directing the Company and displayed a Courage, Coolness, and Discipline, which was the admiration of all who witnessed it."

Sir Colin Campbell also complimented the Regiment very highly on this occasion and, in particular, spoke of Captain Lawson's Company as a pattern of valour and discipline.[76]

Chapter 21

The right wing of the 42nd, under the command of Lieutenant-Colonel Priestley, was sent to the Sarda on 14th March as a replacement for the left wing, who returned to Bareilly. On 15th May, 1859, the right wing returned to Bareilly so that the entire regiment were there. The weather was very hot and the district perfectly quiet. During this period the men were remarkably healthy and very few casualties occurred. During the hot and rainy seasons the regiment occupied the temporary barracks at the old Kutchery, the Jail and Barclay's Compound,[77] where four companies were billeted.

Whilst the 42nd were at Bareilly a drummer was court-martialled for stealing a gold ring from Sergeant Munro. He was found guilty and the Commanding Officer was thereby placed in a dilemma. Normally, the sentence of the court would have been a period of confinement in a military prison and, if the culprit had been other than a young soldier the Commanding Officer would have had little hesitation in confirming such a sentence. Lieutenant-Colonel Priestley felt himself bound to consider the physical and mental effects upon a youth, only seventeen years old, of a number of months shut up in a military prison. Above all, he had to judge whether such a sentence would turn the youth into a better or a worse soldier. He would be thrust into close contact with hardened malefactors, regular and habitual citizens of military prisons throughout the world, who would undoubtedly influence the boy's ways of thinking and harden his attitude towards authority. In the event, it was the physical aspects of the situation which decided the Commanding Officer.

In the course of his duties, the Colonel had regularly to inspect the occupants of the military prison. It was a large building, built in four sections so that it enclosed a square of baked earth in its centre. Its flat tin roof attracted the sun's rays and, during daytime, it gave off a shimmering haze that indicated all too vividly the almost unbearable heat below.

Inside, a long narrow corridor ran down the centre of the building with rows of cell doors on either side. Each cell was about three yards long and one yard broad; a very small barred window and an opening over the door were the sole means of ventilation. On the hard clay floor stood a wooden bench, and in the corner a chipped jug and an old tin pail. The prisoners' rations were spartan in their simplicity—just about enough to enable a man to exist.

As he left the prison, the Commanding Officer reasoned to himself that any punishment he inflicted upon the drummer-boy would be better than sticking him in that hell-hole. That day he put his signature to a sentence ordering fifty lashes on the bare back— ". . . to be administered in the usual way".[78]

When the news spread through the Regiment, it was discussed and argued on all sides. It might be thought strange that few men disagreed with the punishment. Thieving from a comrade, even though he might be a superior officer, was a despicable act and the punishment of a man who could stoop so low might be witnessed with indifference or even with approval. Anyway, the drummer-boy was well known throughout the Regiment as a "cheeky little bugger".

At dawn next day, the whole Regiment attended a ceremonial parade, convened for the purpose of witnessing the punishment. They formed up in the three sides of a hollow square, with officers to the front, facing the high brick wall of a barrack building. As soon as the files were halted and turned inwards, every man's eyes swivelled towards the wall, which, save for two iron rings fixed into the stonework about six feet from the ground, made a bare backcloth for the drama to follow. It was not the first flogging that Hector had seen. He recalled the punishment of a deserter back in Perth when the victim was tied to a triangle composed of sergeants' halberds lashed in the form of a tripod. Later, in garrison at Dover, he had seen men punished on the permanent timber triangle fixed on the parade square.

Suddenly, the Regiment was called up to attention as the Commanding Officer appeared, attended by the Adjutant and by a surgeon. For a minute or two that seemed an age, the whole parade remained in rigid immobility, oppressed by a foreboding silence that could be felt. Then came the sound of marching feet grating in the sand and the Regimental Sergeant-Major, claymore in hand, led on to the parade ground an escort of private soldiers bearing muskets. In their midst, dressed in kilt and hose and naked from the waist upwards, marched the drummer, the smallest figure in the party. As they marched past him, Hector studied the boy intently. His eyes, close-set in a face running with sweat (although the heat of the day was yet to come), moved constantly from side to side as though seeking an avenue of escape. He was convulsively chewing his lip. Moving on rubbery legs, the toes of his boots scuffing into the dusty ground, only years of training and discipline kept him in step with his escort.

In the centre of the open space, the escort and prisoner came smartly up to attention. The Commanding Officer nodded to the Adjutant, who stepped forward and, in an unnaturally loud voice, read the sentence of the court-martial. As soon as he had finished, the harsh clipped bellow of the Regimental Sergeant-Major assailed the ears, ordering the party to move forward to the wall. The drummer's wrists were lashed to the iron rings by two of the escort, who then turned and marched back to their former position leaving the boy spreadeagled, his bare back standing out starkly white against the rough stone-work. On the ground by the side of the triangle was a basin of water and a folded towel. The Drum-Major and two drummers, comrades of the prisoner, stepped forward. One of the drummers was holding the many-thonged lash with which he would administer the first twenty-five strokes before handing over to the other drummer.

In deathly silence, the performers in the grim tableau stood poised—then the stillness was broken by a loud and staccato:

"One!"

Like a hissing blast of wind the stroke was delivered—"as hard as could be at the full length of the arm". With a slapping thud, the thongs landed on the drummer's shoulders and echoed back hollowly from the walls of the surrounding buildings. The boy let out an explosive scream, broken only as he gulped in air. Bare, writhing body pressed hard against the rough wall, he cringed from the blow he knew was to follow.

"Two!"

The drummer's shirt-sleeved arm flashed down, again a hiss and spongy slap as the lash bit home. The drummer's thin scream choked in his throat, to be renewed even more loudly. Mercilessly and monotonously, the lash fell in time with the voice that called the strokes. After the first three or four lashes, weals began to score the flesh in an irregular scarlet pattern.

Hector licked dry lips, eyes riveted on a human back that resembled a map of red ridges. The boy's screams turned to cries and pleadings, he called "Mither . . . don't let them do this to me!" Hector tore his eyes away from the scene and stared at the dusty ground at his feet.

"The poor little devil has pissed himself," muttered the man on his left. Hector looked across at the wall, to see a widening pool of water soaking blackly into the disturbed dust around the weakly gyrating feet of the prisoner. The second drummer had now taken over and was laying into his task, knowing that any shrinking would result in a blow from the cane of the Drum-Major or perhaps even a sentence in the black-hole. Suddenly the surgeon stepped forward and threw up his hand. The drummer paused with the lash uplifted over his shoulder. After listening to the boy's heart and fumbling at his bound wrists, seeking his pulse, the surgeon stood back and nodded to the drummer who again brought down the thongs. A voice within him kept saying to Hector "Why doesn't he stop it . . . why doesn't he stop it?", though he was aware that it would not be kind to the drummer if this were done.[79]

A low whispering sound, scarcely audible, arose from the rigid, silent ranks. Even the most hardened man felt a tight feeling in his chest. Some men felt choked as though they could not get the breath from their chests whilst others retched, being instantaneously silenced by nearby N.C.Os. The sight could be shut out by looking away or closing the eyes but there was no escape from the sound of the lash landing on the bare flesh, nor from the sickly, sweet smell of blood that hung on the warm air of the morning. Sensing that a martyr was fast replacing a malefactor, Lieutenant-Colonel Priestley stepped forward on the fortieth stroke and ordered the boy to be taken down. The Drum-Major picked up the bowl of water and flung it over the drummer's gory back and ordered forward one of the escort to cut the boy down whilst another caught him under the armpits to take his dead weight. The Drum-Major stepped forward and picked up the unconscious boy like a baby and strode from the parade ground in the direction of the hospital. The Drum-Major had been in charge of the drummer for three years and knew that he was not all bad.

The hollow square broke up and the Regiment wheeled into a column to march briskly back to their quarters. N.C.Os hurried them through their scanty breakfast and then chased them out for the parade that had been ordered to take the men's minds off the flogging. With the full band at their head and with bagpipes wailing, the Regiment set off on an exhausting march that achieved its object, purging their minds of the early events of the day.

Chapter 22

Bareilly was a popular station and, compared with many other parts of the country, it was relatively healthy. Although the mutiny had ended, there was still an undercurrent of disaffection in the area and minor skirmishes frequently occurred. It was not safe for a man to be out on his own after dark and there were a number of instances of men being beaten up by parties of rebels and brought into the Guard Room in a very sad state. Contemptuous of their ex-enemies who, unable to triumph in the field, resorted to lying in wait in dark alleys, the Highlanders devised a system of straggling about town in twos and threes pretending to be drunk. When the natives attacked the apparently helpless men, hidden parties of soldiers sprang out and gave them a good thrashing.

There were plenty of military duties to be performed—six guards had to be found, involving three sergeants, seven corporals and fifty-four privates every day. This meant that kit and equipment had repeatedly to be cleaned and furbished, because the Commanding Officer believed that it was essential to prevent soldiers becoming slack after the excitement of a campaign had vanished. Sports and games were organised and everyone enjoyed the frequent horse racing that took place around the dusty race course on the outskirts of the town.

On St. Andrew's day, the band played around the barracks for half an hour before reveille, rousing the men with such stirring tunes as '*Hoorah for the Highlands*'; '*Here's a Health Bonnie Scotland to Thee*'; '*Scotland for Ever*'; '*Blue Bonnets*' and '*Auld Lang Syne*'. That afternoon Highland games were held, with all the usual sports like the caber and the stone.

New Year's Day 1860 was a Sunday, so the celebrations were deferred until the next day when Hector's company commander, Lieutenant Cockburn,[80] provided a splendid dinner with plenty to eat and drink. Before dinner, they had Company Games with prizes ranging from five to fifteen rupees and after dinner everyone joined in singing and dancing.

On the 8th January, 1860, Khan Bahadur Khan, a notorious

rebel chief, was captured and brought into Bareilly where he was kept under close guard. The last of the great and powerful Rohilla chiefs, the tall, strong old man made a great impression on Hector during the occasions he performed sentry-duty over him. With long white beard and small sharp piercing eyes, the prisoner had a fine commanding appearance. Hector felt that he would be glad if old age sat as lightly on his shoulders when his time came. Bahadur Khan was allowed his own servant to wait on him, and spent most of his time writing, filling page after page faster than Hector had ever seen a man write. Addicted to opium, the old man was also allowed regular supplies of the drug. In extremely good English he told Hector on more than one occasion that he would not be executed but that he would be transported away from his homeland and he wondered where he would be sent. But, after a trial lasting nine days, he was found guilty of murder and rebellion and sentenced to death.

As Khan Bahadur Khan was a man of great importance in the area, three companies of the 42nd, two troops of cavalry and two batteries of Royal Horse Artillery were laid on as escort in case of trouble on the day of his execution. All other troops were confined to barracks. In a calculated insult to his religion, the Khan was drawn to his place of execution in a dung cart, in which he sat erect and firm, his face a mirror of bitter hatred and defiance. On the platform of the gallows he was allowed to speak. In his own language and then in English, he declared that he was unrepentant and that he would behave in exactly the same way if he had the chance all over again. With the dignity of a sovereign about to receive a crown, Khan Bahadur Khan stepped on to the trap, angrily refusing the hood. The rope was adjusted and, glancing momentarily upwards, the old man nodded his head. The bolt was drawn and the trap fell with a crash, leaving only a taut, twisting rope in place of the dignified human being who had been present a few seconds before.

Chapter 23

With no fighting to be done, the War Office, in their customary manner, could see little point in keeping a large army eating its head off. So, in the early part of 1860, the British regiments serving in India were notified that all men who had ten years' good service could take a free discharge. The 42nd contained many men with sufficient time in to take advantage of this new ruling. Some of them were all for getting out at once, others had to make a difficult decision, weighing up their present life against the nebulous benefits that civilian life had to offer the ex-soldier. Some were swayed by the heady thoughts of personal freedom from restrictions and discipline; others, who had known no home but the Regiment since their mid-teens, were apprehensive at the thought of voluntarily casting away the protection of a red tunic. It was the sole topic of conversation for weeks and, no less than the others, the MacDonald brothers thrashed it out until they were hoarse.

In the end, Alex and Ian decided to remain with the 42nd. Both were non-commissioned officers and were almost certain to secure further promotion as some of the senior N.C.Os were taking advantage of a free discharge, so that there would be vacancies on the establishment. Lacking such inducements and passing through a patch of the doldrums that periodically affected all soldiers in India, Hector decided to take his discharge, after a great amount of heart-searching and agonising deliberation. He reasoned that it would probably be easier now, at thirty-one years of age,[81] to find some sort of civilian employment and settle down back in Britain.

On a Sunday early in February 1860, along with the other time-expired men, Hector MacDonald turned out for his last Regimental Church Parade. It was perhaps the most moving event of his life and there was not a dry eye in the Regiment when the Padre ended his sermon. The Reverend W. Ross had been with the Regiment throughout their time in India and he used the conclusion of his farewell sermon to say the unsaid words that every time-expired man felt:

"If I forget you, oh 42nd, may my tongue cleave to the roof of my mouth. 42nd, farewell and may the God of our fathers bless you all."[82]

The draft paraded at four o'clock in trews,[83] tunics and feathered bonnets, with haversacks, water bottles and great-coats strapped on. The entire Regiment turned out to see them go and, in an atmosphere highly charged with emotion, men shook hands and bade each other goodbye. A soldier knows and understands men with whom he has lived and fought better than even he knows his own wife, and these partings ended friendships, relationships and habits just as surely as though a rifle bullet or a sword had ended the life of the departing men. Brusque and unnaturally formal in their efforts to retain their composure, both Alex and Ian repeatedly instructed Hector to write to them and he, just as often, assured them that he would. Looking at his two brothers, Hector reflected that once upon a time there had seemed to be such a crowd when the MacDonalds got together. Now, there was just the three of them and soon there would be only two, and himself thousands of miles away across the sea. No one mentioned the three brothers who were not there to see him off, but unspoken their names rang as loud and clear in their separate minds as though they had been uttered with clarion clearness. Hector felt a sense of gratitude that he had been spared to say the farewells denied to Jamie, Charlie and Angus.

The band played *Auld Lang Syne* and everybody joined in, clasping hands in the traditional manner. Then the draft was called to order and those who were remaining behind stepped aside. When the order was given to march off, the time-expired men seemed determined to show the Regiment that those who were going were their best soldiers. Heads held high, they stepped smartly and precisely to the time of the band loudly playing *Home Sweet Home*. Try as he might, Hector could not bring himself to turn his head and look back; when he did, the clouds of dust raised by the marching feet obscured his vision.

Picking up drafts from other regiments, the time-expired men marched to Lucknow. A large number of elephants accompanied the column and the men took it in turns to ride. They marched about twelve miles a day, halting at night in tops of trees; discipline was lax and the men marched at ease without haste or urgency.

Hector found Lucknow very much altered to what it was when he last saw it. Roads had been built through the town, and the old buildings around the new palace cleared away and gardens laid out. The greater part of the old palace was knocked down together with most of the buildings alongside the river, so that clear and pleasant views could be obtained in all directions. There were a great number of troops in the town and the Dilkusha Park was completely covered with barracks, those of a regiment extending for as far as a mile so that each unit was very much on its own and seldom paraded together. Hector tried to find the spot amid the ruined houses where his brother Angus had died, but was unable to locate it in an area that had been cleared and built over. In a way he felt relieved, as though the whole horrible incident had never occurred and Angus was back in the 42nd with Alex and Ian.

They spent six days in Lucknow, picking up drafts from other regiments. On the day they left, many of the men were blind drunk and fighting mad so that the few sober men had to do all the packing. It was a difficult business, for the camels kept running away and throwing their loads off their backs so that, in the end, it was necessary to leave a rear party behind to pack the spare baggage. At the end of the first day's march, camp was pitched on a greatly altered plain of Alam Bagh, where fine crops grew over areas once torn with batteries and trenches. Levelled and covered by crops, there was nothing to show the deadly struggles that had taken place such a short time before.

At Cawnpore they went into huts, being warned to have a sentry continuously posted on each hut to look after the kit, as the natives ran away with anything on which they could lay their hands. More than one man in the draft lost everything on the first night of their arrival. During the four days they spent in the town, Hector had a good look around the place, walking over the area on the plain, now covered with barrack buildings, where the 42nd had first seen action against the rebels. The entrenched camp had not altered much, but the area around the building in which the massacre had taken place had been levelled and the well to which the women and children had been thrown was railed round and a monument had been erected to their memory. Just as in Lucknow, the soldiers found that everything had become very much more expensive than when they were last in the towns.

It was at Cawnpore that the draft first began to be importuned to volunteer to serve on in India by transferring to another corps.[84] Some of the men of the 42nd, regretting their decision and apparently fearing what lay before them in civilian life, changed their minds and signed on. Their favourite choices were the Highland regiments and the Rifle Brigade.

Although played off by regimental bands, the column that marched to the railway station at Cawnpore was a sorry sight, many of the men being so drunk they could hardly stand. Some of the discharged soldiers who had been serving in India before the mutiny were going home with their wives, and Hector was disgusted to see that some of these women were just as drunk as their husbands. With much difficulty, the men and women were persuaded to enter the carriages and the train slowly ground out of Cawnpore, considerably delayed en route by a break-down so that the train did not arrive at Allahabad until eleven o'clock at night. Dumped on the railway station and unable to find guides to lead them to their camping site, the draft bedded down uncomfortably under the baggage shed. It was a bitterly cold night and everyone lay shivering until the welcome light of day brought the sun's warmth to thaw them out. Their temporary camp was on the plain just under the fort and, although Allahabad was a fine place with some interesting walks, life was made miserable by the unceasing canvassing of the draft by representatives of regiments seeking volunteers. Although more men succumbed to the temptations of bounties and improved conditions of service, the draft that left Allahabad was still a large and unwieldy column. Crossing the river, they went into bungalows made for the reception of drafts coming up country. They hung about for a few days until a detachment of the 7th Regiment joined them. Then they marched on for two days more and embarked on the river flats—because of the low water, the steamers were unable to run any higher up the river.

It was an interesting journey, at first, but it was soon made monotonous by the flats repeatedly running aground on sand-banks. For hours Hector sat staring at the river, watching the crocodiles basking in the sun and plunging into the water as the steamer disturbed them. At the many ghats they passed, they saw large numbers of bodies of natives being burned on wood fires made up by sorrowing relatives. The fire lit, all would squat down some yards away leaving one with a long bamboo pole who kept stirring the body until it was burnt to ashes. Then, dispersing in a group, the sorrowing relatives would begin the noisy wailing and drum beating that the British soldiers called "Sammying".

Day after day, the journey interminably unrolled with stops on every second day for coal, and halts at night as the river was too dangerous for navigation in the dark. Now and then, things were enlivened by the large towns, such as Benares. Many of the houses on the river bank had tumbled into ruins, their foundations rushed away by the force of the current so that there was a general dilapidated air about most of the towns they passed. At Dinapore, the river was too shallow to allow them to proceed farther, so they left the River Ganges, running into a branch river and passing through the Sunderbunds, a low-lying area at the mouth of the Ganges. This was a most unpleasant part of the journey as the river was hardly wide enough to allow them to pass, with nothing but dense jungle on either side for several hundred miles. At the night halts they were nearly eaten alive by mosquitoes.

Arriving at Calcutta, they landed and marched into Fort William, a large place, mounting a thousand guns that commanded all the shipping on the river. They were accommodated in the bomb-proof barracks in the Fort, splendid buildings capable of holding 8,000 men. Nevertheless, Hector thought his stay at Fort William was one of the worst experiences of his military life. Most of the men were continually drunk and many were raving in delirium tremens, so that there was no peace by day or night. Hector only returned to barracks when he was too fatigued to walk any longer around the watered streets of Calcutta.

On the 5th June, they embarked on the ship *Holmesdale* and moved out into the river, running down as far as Garden Reach on the following day, where they dropped anchor. There seemed to be no sort of hurry to sail and, in spite of the pleasant view up and down the river with plantations and mansions dotted liberally around, everyone was soon bored and chafing at the seemingly needless delays. Betwixt and between a civilian and a military existence, the draft were most upset at being told off in three watches for the purpose of doing ship's duty. On the 10th they were tugged into deep water by a steamer and got clear of the river, making sail under a steady breeze. In sight of land until dark, on the following morning there was nothing to be seen around them but the sea. Next day they sighted land again on the port bow—a sailor told Hector that it was a part of the Kathiawar Peninsula and that they were bound for Bombay. Four days later they arrived at Bombay and trans-shipped into a steamer lying in the roads, from where they had a fine view of Bombay, which seemed to be a very large town lit up at night by gas lamps. There a great many vessels in the harbour and the place had an air of bustling efficiency.

Dressed in Line of March Order and bearing their baggage, the draft were taken over in a small steamer to the large troop-ship on which they were to sail to England. It was the biggest ship that Hector had ever seen, with two decks for troops and two for walking on, besides two others for stores and the troops' baggage. It seemed to be run in a highly efficient fashion and everyone had fresh bread every second day. At half-past two on the 16th June their steamer made for the open sea, and they crowded the rails staring at the land which dropped quickly behind them. Fairly out of sight of India by six o'clock, everyone felt that they were now well on the way to getting home. Perhaps such optimism was tempting fate because, in the nine days between Bombay and Aden, the steamer broke down twice and caught fire once! From Aden they travelled for another six days until they reached Suez, where they disembarked. Expecting the desert to be a glamorous-looking place, Hector was disappointed when it turned out to be a drab and colourless waste. At Suez they boarded small, uncomfortable, dusty little trains for a day and a night to Alexandria. This journey was so tiring that Hector's sole memory of Alexandria in later days was the welcome cup of coffee he was given at the railway station. In yet another steamer, they sailed from Alexandria on the 4th July, spending the night of the 7th in the harbour at Malta, but without landing. It brought back memories of the six MacDonald brothers on the island in June 1854. On the 12th they passed so close to Gibraltar that they could see the soldiers standing on the batteries. On 17th July, after an uneventful and boring journey, everyone crowded the rails and cheered their heads off at the sight of the Isle of Wight. That night they anchored off Portsmouth and next day steamed into the harbour.

Although it was a fine summer's day, everyone was dressed in full marching order as they left the steamer and marched through the harbour behind a band from the garrison, who suitably played *The Glasgow Quickstep*. Once ashore, the transport staff separated the Highlanders from the rest of the draft and marched them off to another part of the harbour where they embarked in a small coastal vessel for Leith, having spent less than an hour ashore. Three days later the steamer arrived in Leith Roads, here they transhipped on to a steam tug which took them over to Burntisland, where they disembarked and marched to the railway station. Although it was a wet and nasty day, Hector felt that it was the best day he had known for years—he was in his own land again and he was happy. But it was a mood that soon evaporated in the face of the memories held for Hector by Stirling Castle, where the draft were to be accommodated until their discharge. As they marched up to the big gates he remembered the day, so many years ago, when he and Jamie had arrived to join the 42nd. Then they had known that inside the Castle, their four brothers were waiting to greet them. But now Hector felt a sense of unutterable loneliness and all the delight at returning to his homeland vanished, to be replaced by a fearful distraction at the thought of the step he had taken and the fear of what lay ahead. Inside the Castle, he was settled down temporarily and uncomfortably in a bare barrack-room. Later, Hector sought out the room in which he had spent his first night in the Army under the wing of his elder brothers. It was occupied by a bunch of scrawny, shaven-headed recruits who leapt to their feet, awed at the sight of this bronzed Mutiny veteran. That night, in the Wet Canteen, Hector got more drunk than he had ever been in his life.

Next day Hector went before the Board of Discharge. He was passed and all his accounts with the Regiment were cleared off. Now, all he awaited was his discharge, which arrived four days later. The certificate testified that Private Hector MacDonald had served for sixteen years, two months and eleven days and he was discharged from the Army with a "Very Good" character.

Clutching an old carpet-bag containing a few personal belongings, Hector MacDonald walked away from Stirling Castle, his own man and free to go wherever he wished. He set out for the railway station. Throughout his army life he had always known that his first action on discharge would be to go to Edinburgh to see his father. After that, he would find a job and set about making a place for himself in the world.

I came home in 60 stopped at home for a month and went to the United States of America. I stoped in the State of Vermont till the Civil War broke out I listed or rather volunteered into the 2. Vermont Regiment. We went for 3 months we thought the War would be over then but it was not I was at the Battle of Bul run when we got a complete thrashing. I went out with 9 monthsmen I was at the second Bul run and Fredericksburg Harpers ferry I came to the State with the regiment, we all rejoyned for 3 years or during the War we got 300 dollars bounty from the government and 16 dollars a month pay also. 7 dollars a month from the State I was in the 2 Vermont regiment 2 Brigade 2 division 6 army core I was all through the eight days fight of the Wilderness Brandy Station Coal Harbour Winchester and the taking of Richmond and at the surrender of General Lee when he surrendered at Appomatox Court House

to General Grant. We had a grand review at
Washington before we went to the States et get
discharged. We were discharged in July 65. I
went to the State of Machacussets. I took charge
of a coal yard in Worcester all that winter
then I shipped on a whaler out of Newbedford for
the Arctic Ocean to catch whales. I was there for
2 years then I took my discharge in the
Sandwich Islands by paying 130 dollars to the
captain. I stopped there 5 months in charge of
a tannery worked by a Chinaman then I
shipped for Callifornia on a Swedish brig. I
then went into the wood to work for a year then
shipped in the Pacific Mail Company running down
to Mexico, Japan and China then I joined the
Mexico war for 9 months. I went then to British
Columbia to the Cassare Mines then I went messenger
for the Hudson Bay Company through the woods to
the different stations. I was also piper for the
Calodonia Society in San Francisco and Victoria
I won prises in each place my father wrote me to

come home as he would like to see me before he would die. I was his favourite child bein the youngest so I shipped at Vancouver Island British Columbia quarter master on the ship Cultivator for England. I was six months on the passage to Birkenhead we were discharged in Liverpool but I had to pay the counsel 2 months pay for being discharged as I was an american citesen. When I went to Edinburgh my ~~fother~~ father was three months dead so I came to Bristol to look for a ship. That was in January 79. I went to work in the docks I joined Mr. Kings flute Band. I played the picolo I teached them all there music. I am one of the Best Highland Pipers in the United Kingdom but I have no pipes. A few Scotsmen of Bristol presented me with a pair But when I got married I took a house in Avonmouth I took a poor Scothman in to give him a nights lodging one night I was working all night when I came home in the morning he was gone and the pipes with him. I am beginning to get a

little old now if I had a pair. I could make a
better living than working in danger of my
life every day. My wife has had 5 children by me.
2 is dead and 3 alive and I feel it very hard
to support them as I have not a constant job
2 days one week, 3 another some 4 some 1 at
4 shillings a day & I have had a hard time of
it to keep my wife and children since I was
hurted. It is five years the 9th of March since
I was hurted and I have suffered a great deal
since then I would be 10 years a yaunge man
than I am if it had not been for the
accident when I went to Edinburgh Infirmary.
The doctors would hardly believe that I was in
my right mind when I left Bristol. Well Sir they
took out my Brains and cleaned them and the
cap that they lie in then they cut a piece
of the side of my head near the brain then
the cut a piece of the fore part of my leg
above the knee about 8 inches long and
4 inches wide and put that over my brain to
stop the pulsation of my Heart or rather the Blood

from my Heart overflowing my Brain. I suffered a great deal there but I stood it. I have a good constatution and my blood is good. Well they tried to put a plate on my head but they could not do it as there is not bone sufficient to fasten it to so I must go on the remainder of my life with half a head ~~watch~~ watching every man that comes near me for fear he strikes me on the head and kill me now Sir As I am not a very good writer I am not able to put everything as it should be for there is a great many things in my life that could be put down. But I do not know how to do it so I will conclude by hoping this will let you know little the kind of man I am.

Yours Truly

Hector John McDonald

No. 3 Whittington Court

Horse Fair. Bristol

EPILOGUE

There is no way of knowing what happened to Hector MacDonald in the days that followed. Whatever it was, it was sufficient, one short month after returning to Scotland, for him to board a ship and cross an ocean.

If, when he left Bareilly, he had believed that the most arduous, the most eventful and the most dangerous events of his life were behind him, then he was sadly mistaken. The letter that Hector MacDonald wrote to Mr Harvey on the 8th October, 1895, reveals that ahead of him lay many years of hardship and peril . . .

Apparently Mr Harvey was neither touched nor impressed by the old Scotsman's appeal, nor by the story of his eventful life because he was still a dock labourer when he died, of acute bronchitis, pneumonia and haemoptysis, five years later, on the 13th February 1901, aged seventy-one.

Queen Victoria came to the throne in 1837, eight years after Hector MacDonald was born. She reigned for sixty-four years and died on the 22nd January, 1901, three weeks before the death of Hector MacDonald. The end of the Victorian era produced a great blank, the passing of her name and her presence was an unparalleled shock to the imagination of her people. Her very name had held a magical ring throughout the world as, in an unprecedented sense, she had mothered not only her own subjects but even those of other nations. By sheer force of character, Queen Victoria endowed the principal of monarchy with a never-before-possessed moral authority.

It is possible that the death of his Queen hastened the end of the old man who had so faithfully served her as a soldier. Wearily working on as a dock labourer, tired and disillusioned, perhaps Hector MacDonald was so affected by the Queen's passing as to have his own powers of resistance diminished.

He must have been saddened by the massacre of the Highland Brigade at Magersfontein in December 1899, when of 943 men of the Black Watch, 301 were killed or wounded, including their Brigade Commander, Major-General Andy Wauchope, a famous Black Watch character. The daily papers told him of the Highlanders lying for most of the day beneath the savage sun without food or water and with the sun cooking great blisters on the backs of their unprotected knees as they burrowed for cover behind scanty mimosa bushes. Undoubtedly it reminded the old man how, forty-one years before, he had similarly lain in front of Fort Ruhya. A black week for everyone in freezing and foggy Britain, it was even blacker for Hector John MacDonald.

It is doubtful whether he heard of the action of the Black Watch at Koodoosberg Drift on February 7th, six days before his death. Under the command of his famous namesake, General Hector MacDonald—called "Fighting Mac" by his men, the Black Watch, together with the Argyll and Sutherlands, the Seaforths and the Highland Light Infantry fought a hard diversionary battle with the Boers while General French's cavalry moved in on another flank.

Hector MacDonald died as he had lived—in harness and working hard. It is certain that he never imagined that his unavailing letter to Mr Harvey would result, seventy-five years later, in a book telling of him and his stirring life.

NOTES

1. To buy a recruit out a responsible person had to appear before a magistrate within a specified period after enlistment (24 hours is mentioned in some books) and pay a sum of money (20 shillings seems to have been the appropriate price) "smart" money.

2. This area had recently been acquired by Lord Hardinge, the General-Commanding-in-Chief at a cost of about £15,000. The Prince Consort was rumoured to be behind this attempt to give all branches of the army badly needed experience of field conditions. The area consisted of some thousands of acres of wild heath land. See p. 17 of *Aldershot Review* by John Walters (1970).

3. One such instruction began as follows:

"Highland Brigade Office, Camp Gevrekler, 28th July.

No. 1.—No wood is to be cut near any of the springs, as the want of shade will dry them up. This order is to be read to the men at the next two parades. No persons are to wash themselves or their clothes in the springs to the rear of the camp; neither are horses to be watered there. There is water suitable for this latter purpose in front, near some large trees. Commanding Officers are requested to take steps to cause these orders to be strictly attended to. The 79th and 93rd Highlanders will furnish a bayonet sentry each during daylight over the two springs in the rear to prevent washing or watering horses there. A bower will be made for these two sentries by the above-mentioned regiments, one near each spring; and a fatigue party from the 42nd Highlanders will clear the troughs early tomorrow morning. This duty will be performed daily by the regiments in rotation. Commanding Officers will order a bower over each of the regimental cooking-places, as well as one near each of their hospital tents, etc., etc."

4. The Minié rifle was a muzzle-loading weapon, first used in the Kaffir War of 1852. With a bore of 7/10", it had three grooves with a spiral twist of one in seventy-two inches to give rotation to a heavy conical bullet possessing great smashing power. Sighted up to 900 yards, it was reasonably accurate at that range and, although a muzzle-loader, it was a great advance upon the old smoothbore musket. Being a long rifle, it had the advantage of being effective with a fixed bayonet. Although in 1854, the army had begun to be re-armed with the Minié rifle, the Crimean War

was fought primarily with the old smoothbore musket. In flight, the *Minié* bullet made a peculiar, easily recognised whistling sound.

5. Other horses were lowered in slings down into boats where they stamped and snorted in terror so that some of the boats overturned at the water's edge, where the horses were tipped out to flounder in the sea "with their heads in the air and the surf driving into their poor mouths" (Page 66 *The Destruction of Lord Raglan* by Christopher Hibbert). Anthony Sterling, Brigade-Major of the Highland Brigade, records that thousands of horses and mules had to be left behind on the hillside at Varna to take their chance. He says ". . . under the pretence of conveying more soldiers".

6 This bitter fragrance is mentioned on page 214 Chapter XIII Volume 2 of *The Invasion of the Crimea* by A. W. Kinglake. It is also mentioned by Christopher Hibbert on page 70 of his book *The Destruction of Lord Raglan* and by W. Baring Pemberton on page 33 of his book *Battles of the Crimean War*. Just as Napier was the chronicler of the Peninsular War so was Kinglake for the Crimea, and much that he wrote has subsequently been repeated in later works.

7. This remark was actually made at the time by a private soldier and is recorded in at least one account of the battle.

8. Noted by A. W. Kinglake on page 258 Chapter XVI Volume 2 *The Invasion of the Crimea*. Repeated by Christopher Hibbert on page 83 *The Destruction of Lord Raglan* and by W. Baring Pemberton on page 37 *Battles of the Crimean War*.

9. It has been recorded that in places the Russians had carefully marked out the ranges by stakes stuck in the ground (page 79 *The Destruction of Lord Raglan*).

10. The British horse artillery at the Alma were armed with 6pdr. (3.6-inch) and 9pdr. guns (4.2-inch)—many of them had been used at Waterloo nearly fifty years earlier. The 6pdr. had a velocity of 470 feet per second firing shrapnel at 1,100 yards; the 9pdr. shrapnel was more powerful but 300 yards to 1,200 yards was the shrapnel range in 1854. Round-shot ranged farther. Case-shot ranged 250 yards and two or three rounds per minute could be fired. A good horse artillery range was 400 yards—200 yards was even better! The horse artillery guns were comparatively useless unless they galloped right into a fight dashing up to within a few hundred yards of a mass of infantry, unlimbering and coming into action without excessive loss. A pitiless storm of case-shot was often more than a match for the musketry fire that could be brought to bear. At the Alma, when Lord Raglan asked why the English artillery had ceased to fire, he was told that their fire had proved to be ineffectual and was therefore discontinued. (Kinglake. Volume 2, Chapter XVI, page 300). Far from being an encumbrance at the Alma, the

British battery of 9pdr. guns brought up at the order of Lord Raglan, when he had astonishingly ridden right into the enemy's position and found himself on a commanding height from which the guns, when they arrived, caused much inconvenience and dismay among the Russian artillery. The majority of the Russian guns in action at the Alma were 18pdrs. and 24pdrs.

11. The left brigade of Sir George Brown's Division consisted of the 19th, the 88th and the 77th Regiments, commanded by General Buller. During the battle the 19th Regiment slipped from his control and joined with the right Brigade in storming the redoubt, leaving Buller with the 88th and 77th Regiments. Seeing how matters stood at the redoubt, Buller sent an order to Colonel Egerton commanding the 77th telling them to move forward while he himself prepared to advance at the same moment with the 88th. Knowing that a successful attack on his regiment at the extreme left of the British Infantry line would have dire results, Colonel Egerton, without any justification, felt such a great sense of danger that he sent a message to Buller saying that he ought not to obey the order. Buller not only acquiesced in Colonel Egerton's decision by allowing the 77th to remain where they were but he also refrained from advancing with the 88th and threw the regiment into square as though it were about to be attacked by cavalry (pages 64/5, Chapter XVI, Volume 2, Kinglake. Also see page 97 *The Destruction of Lord Raglan* and page 47 *Battles of the Crimean War*).

12. This could have been Sir George Brown who scrambled his horse on to the top of the bank to stare short-sightedly about him, his face scarlet with anger.

13. Before the days of smokeless propellants, one reads of battlefields enveloped in a sort of November fog, swirling and eddying clouds of smoke and dust which choked friend and foe alike and causing them to intermingle without being able to distinguish one from the other. Targets are said to have disappeared in a cloud of smoke after each volley a gun fired.

14. Archibald Forbes, in his books *Colin Campbell, Lord Clyde* and *The Black Watch*, gives the same wording for Campbell's injunction. As a footnote on page 475, Chapter XVI, Volume 2 of *The Invasion of the Crimea*, A. W. Kinglake writes:

> "Of course, the memory of those who unexpectedly found themselves hearing Sir Colin's address to his Brigade, can supply but an imperfect record of the words that were uttered; perhaps, if the impressions of any great number of the heroes were compared, few or none would be found to be closely similar. I think, however, that the address given in the text is not grossly wide of the truth: at all events, I can answer for the substantial accuracy of the injunction against quitting the ranks in order to carry off wounded men."

15. Lieutenant-Colonel Anthony Sterling, Colin Campbell's

Brigade Major, wrote in a letter from "The Field of Battle, 21st September, 1854. The 42nd was pushed on at once . . . marching over the 77th Regiment, which was lying down. The soldiers of this regiment called out to us. 'You are madmen and will all be killed!' "

16. Sir Colin Campbell did not choose his Staff to be with him at this time, for he knew that a group of officers would be likely to draw more fire than a single horseman (Footnote to page 476, Chapter XVI, Volume 2, *Invasion of the Crimea*).

17. In a letter to his sister, Campbell wrote "I lost my best horse—a noble animal . . . he was first shot in the hip the ball passing through my sabretache, and the second ball went right through his body passing through to the heart." Kinglake says that Campbell's charger had been twice wounded already before being struck by a shot in the heart, causing it to sink gently to the earth without a stumble or a plunge.

> "Campbell took his aide-de-camp's charger; but he had not long been in Shadwell's saddle when up came Sir Colin's groom with his second horse. The man, perhaps, under some former master, had been used to be charged with the 'second horse' in the hunting field. At all events, here he was; and if Sir Colin was angered by the apparition, he could not deny that it was opportune. The man touched his cap, and excused himself for being where he was. In the dry, terse way of those Englishmen who are much accustomed to horses, he explained that towards the rear the balls had been dropping about very thick, and that, fearing some harm might come to his master's second horse, he had thought it best to bring him up to the front." (Kinglake, Page 483, Chapter XVI, Volume 2).

18. Kinglake, who was present at the Alma, twice mentions ". . . the sorrowful wail that burst from the heart of the brave Russian infantry when they have to suffer defeat . . ." (See pages 348 and 488, Chapter XVI, Volume 2 *The Invasion of the Crimea*). It is also reported on pages 97 and 112 in *The Destruction of Lord Raglan* and on page 52 of *Battles of the Crimean War*.

19. Writing of this, Kinglake says ". . . the hillsides were made to resound with that joyous, assuring cry, which is the natural utterance of a Northern people so long as it is warlike and free." As a footnote he continues "Many of our people who had heard the cheers of the Highlanders were hindered from seeing them by the bend of the ground, and they supposed that the cheers were uttered in charging. It was not so. The Highlanders advanced in silence."

20. He and his comrades might have been even more touched had they known that it was to be another four days before the *Albion*, a British ship anchored off the mouth of the river, took the 300 surviving casualties to Odessa. Very few of the Russians

survived the journey.

21. Kinglake, who never seemed to miss anything, does not mention this but it is noted on page 270, Chapter XIX, Volume 2 of *England's Battles by Sea and Land* by Lieutenant-Colonel Williams (The London Printing and Publishing Company 1855).

22. Aided by half a dozen men of the 42nd, Lieutenant and Adjutant Drysdale of the Regiment was secretly entrusted with the job of making up such a bonnet for the Brigade Commander. There was some difficulty in combining the hackle of the three regiments of the brigade; finally, it was decided to have the upper third red for the 42nd, and the remaining two-thirds white at the bottom for the 79th and 93rd.

23. Once the home of a Russian admiral of Scottish origin who had made a plantation of trees there for the Imperial Russian Navy.

24. This was an army which Menschikoff, the defeated Russian Commander at the Alma, was marching out of Sebastopol in order that it might be free to operate in the field.

25. The Highlanders must have been able to see the swarming figures of men, women and children who worked all day and through the night, by the light of lamps and flares, building redoubts and earthworks under the direction of Lieutenant-Colonel Franz Eduard Ivanovitch Todleben. This talented military engineer, born in the Baltic provinces of Russia, was given the responsibility of making Sebastopol an impregnable fortress overnight—and he almost succeeded by sheer example and inspiration.

26. Vice-Admiral Korniloff, Chief of Staff of the Black Sea Fleet, had taken over command of the garrison of Sebastopol when Prince Menschikoff, the Commander-in-Chief of the Russian Army defeated at the Alma, had marched out from Sebastopol with his field army, leaving General Möller in command of the land forces and Vice-Admiral Nachimoff sharing command of the navy with Korniloff. Both of these officers were greatly relieved when Admiral Korniloff volunteered to take over command of the garrison consisting of 16,000 men, three-quarters of them sailors from the Russian Black Sea Fleet which had been imprisoned in the Sebastopol roadsteads by the sinking of ships to bar the entrance. Along with Todleben, Korniloff was entirely responsible for inspiring the garrison with the will to defend the town so resolutely, although he commanded them for only a fortnight, being killed at the Malakoff on the 18th October.

27. This refers to that "thin red streak tipped with a line of steel" invariably misquoted as "the thin red line". Sir Colin Campbell, a perfect example of the right man in the right place at the right time, sternly checked an inclination of the 93rd to

charge with the bayonet by exclaiming: "93rd! Damn all that eagerness!"

28. In his book *Britain and her Army* (1970) Correlli Barnet writes

> "It is curious that . . . the charge of the Light Brigade at Balaclava should loom so large in British legend. Only 673 men were involved, and they lost 157 men out of 20,000 war dead. Why have the British chosen to make a sentimental legend out of a pointless effort arising from muddled orders? The entirely successful and equally gallant charge of the Heavy Brigade earlier on in the same day is generally forgotten, as is the charge of the Chasseurs d'Afrique on flanking Russian batteries that helped the Light Brigade's eventual retirement."

29. In his letter to Mr Harvey, Hector MacDonald mentioned taking part in the Battle of Balaclava. Apart from the fleeing Turks and Sir Colin Campbell's small force (the 93rd Highlanders plus about 100 invalids) no other infantry took part in this battle, which was almost exclusively a series of cavalry actions. It must be presumed that the passage of time, more than forty years, had somewhat coloured the old Scotsman's memories of the battles of Balaclava and Inkerman. This last battle is also mentioned because there is no logical reason for Hector MacDonald to have been involved at Inkerman on November 5th. The Highland Brigade were some three miles away, guarding Balaclava and unless Hector was on some duty at the English camps in the area, then he would not have taken part in the battle. Nevertheless, it was a confused, sprawling action into which troops were flung piecemeal and, had he been in the vicinity, there is little doubt that Hector MacDonald would have fought.

30. For greater details of this and other incidents concerning the navvies see pages 212 to 220 of *The Railway Navvies* by Terry Coleman (1965).

31. These complaints were made in a letter written by Anthony Sterling on the 14th February, 1855, from Camp Battery No. 4, Balaclava. Cecil Woodham-Smith, in *Florence Nightingale* (1950) treats Sterling as a "hostile witness" (see pages 121; 138 and 158 of her book).

32. Some of the nurses in the Crimea defied Florence Nightingale's authority. One of them, Miss Clough, a lady of Miss Stanley's party, had broken away and gone to join Sir Colin Campbell's hospital above Balaclava, inspired by romantic enthusiasm for the Highland Brigade. "She must be a funny fellow, she of the Highland Heights," commented Miss Nightingale (see pages 173/4 *Florence Nightingale*).

33. Writing of Major-General George Brown when he was Adjutant-General, J. H. Stocqueler in his book *A Personal History of the Horse Guards from 1750 to 1872* (1873) wrote:

". . . General Brown did not understand the importance of good breeding, he was not deficient in the better qualities of our nature; he had a heart that could feel for misfortune and poverty, but he did not allow his sympathies to extend into his military duties. Brusque in his manner to applicants for small favours, almost boorish in his rebukes, and obstinately wedded to Regulation however oppressive and in arrear of the age, he became a terror to young officers, and the instrument of pain and humiliation to the elders. Useful as a deputy Adjutant-General in adhering to routine, General Brown was quite beyond himself in a more responsible position. The atmosphere of the Horse Guards was much clearer after the General had left to command a division of the Crimean Army."

34. Reporting that Sir George Brown had threatened to put him in irons if he set foot ashore, Russell told his editor Delane: "The old brute is quite capable of carrying out his threat, and I would not care a farthing about the escapade, it would expose me to so much ridiculing and chaffing that I could not remain with the army; and it would degrade me and lower me in the eyes of everyone and gratify my enemies. Can you do nothing to put me on a better footing with these angry old generals?" Though not allowed to land, Russell was able to point out that Kertsch was the spot made famous by Julius Caesar's line "Veni, vidi, vici" (see page 89 *The First War Correspondent* by Rupert Furneaux [1944]).

35. In a letter from Balaclava dated the 11th May, 1855, Lieutenant-Colonel Anthony Sterling wrote these complaints of Florence Nightingale's actions during her stay at Balaclava in May 1855. On pages 177-179 of *Florence Nightingale*, Cecil Woodham-Smith states that Miss Nightingale arrived at Balaclava on May 5th and she spent the afternoon of that day visiting the batteries outside Sebastopol. On the following day she visited the hospitals and prepared plans for their improvement. But before anything could be accomplished she collapsed, and a statement was issued saying that she was suffering from Crimean fever For more than two weeks she hovered between life and death before being sent back to Scutari on Lord Ward's steam yacht. It would seem that Florence Nightingale did not have much opportunity whilst in Balaclava to take the actions about which Sterling complains.

36. Sergeant T. Gowing of the 7th Royal Fusiliers took part in this attack and his description of it, together with a copy of a letter he wrote home to his parents on the day following, provide a most graphic account (See *A Soldier's Experience or a Voice from the Ranks* by T. Gowing.) For full details of the errors and omissions that subscribed to this bloody repulse, see pages 202-217 *Battles of the Crimean War* and pages 332-337 *The Destruction of Lord Raglan.*

37. The small mortars called coehorns were invented by the famed Dutch military engineer, Baron Van Menno Coehoorn, and used by him in 1673 to the great discomfort of French garrisons. In the Crimea, the little brass coehorns were 4 2/5th inches in calibre. The coehorn was still in use during the American Civil War when it consisted of a small bronze mortar, light enough (296 lb. with bed) to be carried by four men. It was useful in trench warfare such as at Petersburg, and mobile enough to appear at a battle like Cold Harbour. Some of them may still be seen in the American battlefield parks today.

38. The taking of the Malakoff was a fortunate fluke for the French. Only a handful of Russians were in the position, the old garrison had been marched out without being relieved by the new garrison and the officer commanding was sitting in a dug-out eating his soup. Even so, it was a desperate struggle in which the French were driven back three times and only the Commander Vinoy's strength of character brought success. He planted his sword in the ground near the flag and threatened to shoot anyone who retired beyond that point. Later it was revealed that the Russians had a mine requiring only two more days work, the completion of which would have blown up the entire French advanced trenches.

39. The troops whose assault failed on the 18th June were worn out. After suffering heavily at the Alma they had been kept for months in the trenches, consistently losing many of their best and bravest officers and men; also they had made one previous assault which had failed. They were a set of raw recruits, undisciplined and unacquainted with each other and their officers, and the column was composed of many different regiments thrown together.

40. *The Red Hackle*, the chronicler of the Black Watch (the Royal Highland Regiment) and of the Black Watch Association, published in its issues for April, July and October 1955, the diary of No. 255 Private Archibald Watt MacIntosh. This soldier enlisted in the 42nd in January 1858. These words are extracted from his diary entry of the 19th April.

41. Towards the close of 1857, the Suez route was adopted for a few regiments and the rapidity of passage was such as to lead to much expression of regret that the route had not been adopted earlier. However, an opinion continued to prevail on the part of the Government and the Company that it would not have been practicable to send the bulk of the Army by that means.

42. Up to the 10th July, out of thirty-one vessels chartered by the Government and the Company for conveying troops to India, nearly all were sailing ships. Between the 10th July and 1st December, fifty-nine ships were chartered, of which twenty-nine were screw-steamers. The average duration of all the voyages was 120 days by sailing vessels and eighty-three days

by steamers. Of the eighty-two ships that carried 30,378 troops from the United Kingdom to India, fifty-three sailing ships carried 16,234 men, averaging 299 each; twenty-seven steamers carried 14,144 men, averaging 522 men each. It was calculated that 14,000 of these British soldiers arrived in India five weeks earlier by the adoption of steamers instead of sailing vessels.

43. They must have looked very much like the group in Plate number one. Writing about this historic photograph in the Journal of the Society for Army Historical Research (Vol. XXXVI No. 146 of June 1958), Major A. McK. Annand says:

> "The uniforms worn by the men are of interest inasmuch as they are of the pattern taken into use in 1855, when the old coatee was discarded.
>
> According to Dress Regulations for 1855, which of course refer only to officers, the jacket was scarlet, double-breasted, with collar and cuffs of regimental facings which, in the case of the 42nd, would be blue, and with two rows of nine gilt diamond-shaped buttons bearing the number of the regiment surmounted by a crown. In the main essentials, the jackets of other ranks would have been much the same. Dress Regulations for 1857 give the jacket as being single-breasted and thus the double-breasted vogue was very short-lived.
>
> At the time of its adoptions the jacket must have seemed a revolutionary change from the coatee, marking as it did, the disappearance of epaulettes, wings and bars of lace across the breast, introducing, instead, plain shoulder-straps, a rounded collar and, in the case of Highland regiments, the clumsy, meaningless skirt flaps.
>
> In the photograph, the new jacket is the most noticeable feature. The jacket of Piper Muir differs from those of the other three in that it has tufts on the shoulders and is of tartan, cut on the cross, with tartan shoulder-straps. The other most marked change from the old style of dress, as far as the regiment is concerned, lies in the turned down red and black diced hose which had hitherto been red and white with scarlet garters worn outside the top of the hose in the correct Highland manner.
>
> The number '42' can be seen plainly on Glen's right shoulder-strap and is also discernible on the buckle of McKenzie's waist-belt. The bonnets, with the famous red hackle or vulture plume in each, have short foxtails. The piper's sword scabbard is of black leather with steel mountings, without rings, indicating that the sword was worn on the belt in the old style and not on slings.
>
> It will be noticed that Colour-Sergeant Gardiner's sash is over the left shoulder. In 1947 the writer received a letter from the late Rev. Percy Sumner (who contributed so many fine articles to the Journal) in which he wrote: 'In 1902 I had some

conversation with the Chief Warder of the Tower of London who was Thos Middleton. He joined the 79th in 1856 and among other information about the uniform he said "Sergeants then wore their sashes over the left shoulder, and not as now".'

All the men in the photograph are wearing the Crimean medal, but it is not possible to see how many clasps are worn by Muir and Gardiner. Glen and McKenzie have three each. According to 'The Royal Highland Regiment, The Black Watch, Medal Roll, 1801-1911', published in Edinburgh in 1913, Piper David Muir was awarded the clasps for Alma, Balaclava and Sebastopol, whilst Gardiner was awarded that for Sebastopol only. No mention is made of either Glen or McKenzie. In addition to the Crimean Medal, McKenzie is shown as wearing the French order 'Valeur et Discipline' presented by Napoleon III to certain non-commissioned officers and men of the British forces for distinguished gallantry. This is recorded in the Medal Roll against the name of Private Donald M'Kenzie, presumably the same man. Gardiner is also wearing what looks as if it might be the Long Service and Good Conduct Medal, but there is no record of this in the Medal Roll."

44. A return had been prepared by order of Parliament, of the odds and ends composing what was called the "sea-kit" of English soldiers going out to India, the cost at which they were estimated, and the mode of paying for them:

Articles	*Price* £	s.	d.
Two canvas frocks at 3s. 3d. (jackets substituted for frocks in the case of sergeants)		6	6
One pair of canvas trousers		3	4
One neck handkerchief			8
One pair of shoes		6	0
Three pounds of marine soap, at 7d.		1	9
Two pounds of yellow soap, at 7d.		1	2
Nine balls of pipeclay			9
One quart tin-pot, with hook		1	0
One scrubbing-brush			8
Three tins of blacking		1	0
One clasp-knife		1	0
One bag in lieu of haversack			10
Needles and thread		1	0
Three pounds of tobacco, at 2s. 8d.		8	0
Two flannel-belts		2	0
Two check shirts, at 2s. 6d.		5	0
	£2	0	8

The return reported:

"The prices are unavoidably liable to variation, but those in the above list will serve as a general standard for guidance. Tobacco is issued to such men only as are in the habit of using it; and if any man be provided already with any of the above articles, and such are in a serviceable condition, a duplicate supply is not given."

45. Fire at sea was the great dread of the troopship and, remembering the loss of the *Kent* in 1825 (see page 114 *Red Coat* by E. W. Sheppard [1952] and *A Gallant Company* by Sir John Fortesque [1927]) the War Office laid down strict rules for smoking on board troopships. Notwithstanding this, in August 1857 the *Sarah Sands* carrying the 54th Regiment was only saved by the manful efforts of its crew and the soldiers.

46. It was rumoured that it was the grease used for lubrication that had caused the original outbreaks of mutiny in India. For a Hindu to bite or even touch beef fat, or a Muslim pig's fat, would cause either to be shorn of his caste, because cattle are sacred to the former and pigs unclean to the latter; such a man could be punished by death or mutilation for having intercourse with his wife. It was the refusal of the native troops to handle these cartridges that had kindled the first flames of the mutiny.

47. A larger number of Europeans resided in Calcutta than in any other city in India and Calcutta itself was not materially affected by the mutiny. It was in the interest of the native townspeople to prefer peace to war. Only a few native soldiers still remained in arms and they were kept in awe by the frequent landings of British troops whilst the Naval Squadron, anchored in the Hoogly, had sufficient power of metal to batter the city to ruins should danger arise.

48. Major-General the Honourable George Anson, Commander-in-Chief in India, died of cholera at the end of May, 1857; the news of his death reached London on the 11th July. Sixty-five years old, Sir Colin Campbell an experienced fighting soldier of nearly fifty years service, was immediately offered the post of Commander-in-Chief in India. At once he accepted and, on being asked how soon he could make his departure replied "Tomorrow".

49. These words were actually written about the 79th Regiment (the Cameron Highlanders) by Russell of *The Times* in May, 1858, when Campbell's Army was sweltering in the Rohilkand Campaign.

50. A contemporary War Department statement reads as follows: ". . . according to existing regulations of some years standing, every soldier on his arrival in India is provided with the following articles of clothing in addition to those which compose his kit in this country:

4 white jackets
1 pair English summer trousers
5 pairs white trousers
5 white shirts
2 check shirts
1 pair white braces.

These articles are not supplied in this country but form a part of the soldier's necessaries on his arrival in India and are composed of materials made on the spot best suited to the climate. During his stay in India he is provided with the tunic and shell-jacket in alternate years; and in the year in which the tunic is not issued the difference in the value of the two articles is paid by the soldier, to be expended by his officer commanding for his benefit in any articles suited to the climate of the station. The force recently sent out to India (in 1857) has been provided with white cotton helmets and forage-cap covers. Any quantity of light clothing for troops can be procured on the spot in India at the shortest notice."

After the Mutiny had been suppressed, the distress experienced by the British troops from the intense heat of the Indian sun, and the severe strictures passed by the Press and by Members of the Legislature on those regimental officers who permitted or compelled their soldiers to swelter in red cloth, led to the issuing of orders concerning light summer clothing. It was found that a kind of grey or dusty coloured linen called khakee or carkey was better suited than anything else—even white—as the material for clothing in the hot season. On the 21st May, 1858, the Adjutant-General issued the following order:

"With the concurrence of the Government, the commander-in-chief is pleased to direct that white clothing shall be discontinued in the European regiments of the Honourable Company's army; and that for the future the summer-clothing of the European soldiers shall consist of two suits of 'khakee', corresponding in pattern and material with the clothing recently sanctioned for the Royal Army of England. Corps are to be permitted to wear out serviceable summer-clothing of the old pattern now in use; but in regiments in which this clothing requires to be renewed, the new pattern now established is to be introduced without delay. Commanding officers will take steps to obtain patterns from regiments of Her Majesty's service. A complete suit, including cap-cover, should not exceed in cost four-twelve rupees. The summer-clothing now authorised will be supplied from the clothing agency of the presidency to all recruits of the Company's service arriving at Calcutta between 1st February and 1st October, to be issued with the least possible delay after arrival of the recruits."

51. Colonel Windham commanded the stormers of the 2nd

Division at the Redan on 8th September, 1855. Although the attempt failed, Windham showed great courage in exposing himself recklessly in his efforts to encourage his men to go forward.

When Sir Colin Campbell marched out to relieve Lucknow, he left behind at Cawnpore a force under General Windham, whose task was to protect the bridge of boats over the Ganges, the only line of communications with Campbell's force. Without orders, Windham decided to take offensive action against the enemy, believed to be about 25,000 strong with forty guns, in order to prevent them concentrating against him. He marched out with about 1,200 men, largely recruits and inexperienced soldiers belonging to a variety of regiments, and drove the enemy back, capturing four of their guns. Lacking cavalry, he was unable to seal his success and had no alternative but to fall back on his forward camp. On the following day the small British force was attacked by vastly superior numbers of Sepoys and was soon in danger of being surrounded and annihilated. Windham had no alternative but to order a general retreat to the main encampment north of Cawnpore, abandoning his forward camp with all the baggage and equipment. It was largely due to the 2nd and 3rd Battalions of the Rifle Brigade that the somewhat precipitate retreat was covered and the enemy held off. Windham lost over 300 killed and wounded, all his baggage and camp equipment and most of his transport; the mutineers destroyed vast amounts of stores and also the clothing that had been collected for the Lucknow refugees. Windham was left hanging on by the skin of his teeth after a defeat that could become a disaster if the bridge of boats over the Ganges were destroyed, thus preventing Sir Colin Campbell getting his twelve mile-long column of women, children and refugees from Lucknow to safety.

52. A Naval Brigade more than 500 strong, under the command of Captain William Peel, V.C., with ten 68pdr. guns and smaller weapons was landed from H.M.S. *Shannon* at Calcutta in August 1857. Their many engagements, including the battle for Cawnpore and first relief and then the capture of Lucknow, are immortalised in *The Devil's Wind* by G. L. Verney (Hutchinson 1956).

53. Every sentence here, put into the mouths of the soldiers, was actually spoken or written by officers and soldiers who entered Cawnpore on the 17th July, 1857.

54. Sir Colin said:

"It appeared to me that if the enemy's right were vigorously attacked, it would be driven from its position without assistance being able to come from other parts of the line; the wall of the town, which gave cover to our attacking columns on the right, being an effective obstacle to the movement of any portion of the enemy's troops from their left to their right."

55. It was said at the time that Mansfield was short-sighted and did not care to trust to the sight of others so that he allowed the rebels to defile close to him, unpunished and unpursued.

56. In the various operations he conducted from the 3rd to the 8th December, Sir Colin Campbell lost thirteen men killed and eighty-six wounded, a trifling figure compared with the strength of his force and the superior numbers of the enemy opposing him.

57. It was during this chase that Lieutenant Frederick Roberts, later to become a Field-Marshal, won the Victoria Cross conferred upon him not only for the specific actions mentioned in the citation but for gallantry throughout the campaign. The citation reads:

"On following up the retreating enemy . . . Lieutenant Roberts saw in the distance two Sepoys going away with a standard. He put spurs to his horse and overtook them just as they were about to enter a village. They immediately turned around and presented their muskets at him and one of the men pulled the trigger, but fortunately the cap snapped and the standard bearers cut down by this gallant young officer, and the standard taken possession of by him. He also on the same day cut down another Sepoy who was standing at bay with musket and bayonet keeping off a trooper. Lieutenant Roberts rode to the assistance of the horseman, and rushing at the Sepoy, with one blow of his sword cut him across the face, killing him on the spot."

58. Captain Peel had been forced to leave his great 8-inch guns, which he had brought from the *Shannon*, at Allahabad where they were abandoned because of lack of carriages big enough to carry them. Manufacturing or adapting from materials found at the gun-carriage factory at Fatehgarh, all these guns (weighing sixty-five hundredweight) were mounted on field-carriages and took their place with Sir Colin Campbell's siege-train.

59. "Whatever may be thought in England in regards to this mode of punishment, it is known by those well acquainted with the Asiatic character to be quite necessary in a crisis like the present in India. Horrible this punishment certainly is, but let us not forget the horror of the occasions that have made it the duty to administer it; and let us not forget, also, what is certainly true, that the administration of this punishment is controlled by humane and just men—not the less humane, be it remembered, because sternness must now be mingled with their justice." *Illustrated London News*, 28th November, 1857.

60. Among the wounded was the gallant Hodson, whose name was a byword among the troops for his dashing feats.

61. See page 359 *The Military Engineer in India* by Lieutenant-Colonel E. W. C. Sandes, RE (1933).
62. Reported by William Russell in a despatch written before Lucknow, 2nd March, 1858.
63. The value of the electric telegraph was said to be quite beyond all estimate during the Mutiny and was worth a large army in itself; this is probably the first recorded instance of its use in war.
64. The reason for the 42nd being forbidden to fire might be because experience had inclined Sir Colin Campbell to believe that the morale effect of the sight of the bayonet upon the enemy might cause them to withdraw earlier than otherwise. There is also the point that, had the advancing men fired during the course of their charge, they would be into the enemy with unloaded rifles, lacking the time to halt and reload.
65. The almost-legendary Major Hodson accompanied as a volunteer the force that stormed the Martinière; wounded in the stomach by a grapeshot, he died on the 12th. His death was mourned by the whole army.
66. According to contemporary pictures and prints, certain dress concessions had been made, such as a peaked cap covered by a loose type of white pugri material with a havelock hanging down to protect the neck. In some cases a white linen shirt or a white hot-climate jacket was worn.
67. It had been reasonably anticipated that if the main force of rebels could be crushed at Lucknow, the smaller bodies of insurgents might be dealt with at leisure. But the escape of the greater portion of the rebel troops from that place into Rohilkand opened a new field for exertion and materially interfered with the realisation of the original design.

There was severe criticism and discontent over Campbell's strategy, increased when it was learned that Sir Colin had lingered at Lucknow until the hot season, in all its fury, fell upon the plains of India. It was disappointing not to detect any prompt and energetic action, no bold or enterprising undertakings following the conquest of Lucknow. It was claimed that earlier flight of the mutineers than could be expected, according to the rules of war, left Campbell unprepared for pursuit. This criticism is not entirely valid as it is quite likely that Campbell did not have enough troops to assault Lucknow with reasonable hope of all success and also block all escape routes.
68. On the 24th March, just when the Army of Oude was about to be broken up, Sir Colin Campbell had issued a general order concerning the arrangements to be made for attacking the forts that so liberally dotted the province. Knowing that his officers would dash at them as at other obstacles, Sir Colin forbade enterprises likely to be followed by losses which good guns might obviate. His orders read as follows:

"The Commander-in-Chief prohibits columns from moving to the attack of forts, whether large or small, without at least two heavy guns, or a heavy gun and a heavy howitzer. If possible, such columns should always have mortars also; namely, two 8-inch and two 5½-inch. Arrangements are to be made by the inspector-general of ordnance to insure the presence of a proportion of heavy guns, howitzers, mortars and coehorns, all at stations where British regiments are quartered. Wherever there is a possiblity of movable columns being organised, the necessary elephant and bullock draught should be maintained. When an expedition against a fort is deemed absolutely necessary, and heavy ordnance cannot be obtained, a special reference is to be made to the chief of staff by telegraph. If, however, the station be removed from the wire, the general officer commanding the division or station must, of course, exercise a discretionary power; but the Commander-in-Chief begs that it may be recollected, as a principle, that, except in cases of the most absolute necessity, forts are not to be attacked with light guns only."

69. Private Spence would have been recommended to Her Majesty for the decoration of the Victoria Cross had he survived. The decoration earned by Private Spence was awarded to his relatives by His Majesty King Edward, the notification appearing in the Gazette dated 15th January, 1907. It was not until 1902 that posthumous awards were authorised to be made.

70. Mangal Pande, a Sepoy of the 34th Native Infantry at Barrackpore, was egged on by his fellows to defy authority. Four hundred men watched Pande, berserk with drugs, cut down two white officers before he was ridden down by General Hearsey. Tried by courtmartial, Mangal Pande was hanged for mutiny on 8th April, 1857. From then on, all mutineers were known to the British soldiers as 'Pandies'.

71. Groves of trees, sometimes mango and tamarind, near villages, each with a masonry-enclosed well. Pious men who had been successful in business often planted the groves and dug the attendant well for the benefit of travellers.

72. Colour-Sergeant Gardner was later awarded the Victoria Cross for his prompt act of rescue.

73. The heat was always a great problem to the Europeans—during the fighting at Bareilly ten men died of sunstroke. A morbid theory, strongly believed by men in the ranks, held that every march after ten o'clock in the morning must be attended with loss of life.

74. Long cots slung from bamboo poles, borne on the shoulders of four men, two in front and two behind, shuffling along the road at the rate of four miles an hour with two spare men following as relief. The bottom of the doolie hung close to the ground so that the occupant had more than his share of the

dust because, with the curtains let down, the heat became insufferable.

75. Journals sent to the officer's hospitals were *The Calcutta Englishman, The Bengal Hurkaru, The Phoenix, The Illustrated London News, Punch, Blackwood's Magazine, Fraser's Magazine, New Monthly Magazine, Monthly Army List*, 4 copies of *Chamber's Journal*, 4 copies of *Family Herald*. To the men's hospital went 2 copies of *The Calcutta Englishman*, 2 copies *The Bengal Hurkaru*, 2 copies *The Phoenix*, 2 copies *The Illustrated London News*, 2 copies *Punch*, 2 copies *Household Words*, 12 copies *Chamber's Journal*, 12 copies *Family Herald*.

76. The pipe tune '*Lawson's Men*' commemorates the gallant day long action of the small party.

77. Barclay was an old soldier who had settled in the country after buying his discharge and made a fortune as an indigo-planter. Murdoch McLeod, one of the 42nd officers, married one of Barclay's daughters, which caused the men drily to remark that he had been set on his feet, as he was very poor.

78. After a long reign the lash had fallen into comparative disuse throughout the British Army, but, as the Regiment was on active service, the Commanding Officer was justified in confirming such a punishment.

Earlier in the century, James Anton, a quarter-master-sergeant of the 42nd wrote:

> "Philanthropists, who decry the lash ought to consider in what manner the good men—the deserving, exemplary soldiers—are to be protected; if no coercive measures are to be resorted to in purpose to prevent ruthless ruffians from insulting with immunity the temperate, the well-inclined, and the orderly-disposed, the good must be left to the mercy of the worthless. . . ."
>
> *Peninsular Preparation: The Reform of the British Army 1795-1809* by Richard Glover (1963) page 178.

79. When a prisoner showed signs of collapse he would be examined by the surgeon and brought to with restoratives, after which the punishment might or might not be resumed, according to the surgeon's view. But in fairness to the surgeons it must be said that they acted thus rather than expose the wretched prisoner to be brought out a second time for the rest of his punishment when his back had partially healed.

80. George Cockburn joined the regiment in 1855 and lived on to become a very old man, dying in March 1924.

81. Hector MacDonald's "army" age was thirty-five because when he had enlisted in 1843 at the age of fourteen years and six months he had been accepted as being eighteen years of age.

82. On the 19th October, 1867, the 42nd left Cherat to march down country on its way home, having been ten years in India. On Sunday, 10th November the Regiment took leave of their

faithful Padre, the Reverend W. Ross who had been with them throughout their time in India. These words concluded his farewell sermon to the Regiment.

83. Private Archibald Watt MacIntosh records in his diary that the 42nd paraded to return to Britain wearing trews. It is considered not unreasonable to assume that Hector MacDonald might have been similarly garbed on his return home.

84. To provide replacements to bring regiments in India up to strength it was the usual custom, when a unit was leaving India, that those men who did not wish to leave were permitted to volunteer to other corps, and every effort was made by the authorities to induce soldiers to remain in India. All discipline was suspended, and the most disgraceful scenes of drunkenness were not only connived at but even encouraged during the weeks immediately before embarkation. Many men were inveigled by these discreditable means into volunteering to other regiments and to extend their Indian service without realising what they were doing.